Russia's International Rel in the Twentieth Century

Russia has long been a major player in the international relations arena, but only by examining the whole century can Russian foreign policy be properly understood, and the key questions as to the impact of war, of revolution, of collapse, the emergence of the Cold War and Russia's post-Soviet development be addressed.

Surveying the whole of the twentieth century in an accessible and clear manner *Russia's International Relations in the Twentieth Century* provides an overview and narrative, with analysis, that will serve as an introduction and resource for students of Russian foreign policy in the period and for those who seek to understand the development of modern Russia in an international context.

The volume includes:

- an analysis of the major themes which surrounded Russia's position in world affairs as one of the European Great Powers before the First World War
- the impact of Revolution and the emergence of Soviet foreign policy, with its dual aims of normalization and world revolution
- the changes wrought to the international order by the rise of Nazi Germany and by the Second World War
- the origins and development of the Cold War
- the end of the Cold War and the Soviet collapse
- how Russia has rebuilt itself as an international power in the post-Soviet era.

An essential resource for students of Russian history and international policy.

Alastair Kocho-Williams is a Senior Lecturer in Modern European History at Aberystwyth University. He is the editor of *The Twentieth Century Russia Reader* (Routledge, 2011) and author of *Russian and Soviet Diplomacy, 1900–1939* (2011).

Russia's International Relations in the Twentieth Century

Alastair Kocho-Williams

Routledge
Taylor & Francis Group

LONDON AND NEW YORK

First published 2013
by Routledge
2 Park Square, Milton Park, Abingdon, Oxon OX14 4RN

Simultaneously published in the USA and Canada
by Routledge
711 Third Avenue, New York, NY 10017

Routledge is an imprint of the Taylor & Francis Group, an informa business

British Library Cataloguing in Publication Data
A catalogue record for this book is available from the British Library

Library of Congress Cataloging in Publication Data
Kocho-Williams, Alastair.
Russia's international relations in the twentieth century /
Aalastair Kocho-Williams.
pages; cm
Includes bibliographical references.
1. Russia–Foreign relations–History–20th century. 2. Soviet Union–Foreign
relations–History. 3. Russia (Federation)–Foreign relations–History–20th century.
I. Title.
DK66.K56 2012
327.47009'04–dc23

ISBN: 978-0-415-60637-0 (hbk)
ISBN: 978-0-415-61919-6 (pbk)
ISBN: 978-0-203-07887-7 (ebk)

Typeset in Garamond
by Taylor & Francis Books

Printed and bound in Great Britain by the MPG Books Group

For Sasha, Max and Zoya

Contents

    policy, 1957–64   112

    Discord within the socialist world: Yugoslavia and China 1957–64   113
    From peaceful coexistence with the West to crisis, 1957–62   118
    Fallout: the implications of the Cuban missile crisis and
        the end of Khrushchev   125
    Conclusion   126
    Further reading   126

9   The Brezhnev era   128

    Reaction, retreat, restalinization   129
    Czechoslovakia 1968: the Prague Spring and the Brezhnev Doctrine   132
    Healing the wounds of the Cold War: détente with the
        United States and attempted rapprochement with China   134
    The Soviet invasion of Afghanistan, 1979   138
    The Cold War re-ignited   140
    Conclusion   141
    Further reading   141

10 Gorbachev and the end of the Soviet Union   143

    Gorbachev's new thinking   143
    Reform and foreign policy   144
    The challenge of Eastern Europe   145
    'A man to do business with': working with the West   147
    The end of the Soviet Union   150
    Conclusion   151
    Further reading   152

11 Russian foreign policy in the last decade of the
    twentieth century   153

    The Soviet Union after collapse   153
    A new direction in foreign policy?   157
    Russia and Europe   158
    Russia and the United States   160
    A resurgent super-power?   160
    Conclusion   161
    Further reading   162

    Select bibliography   163
    Index   186

Abbreviations

ABM	Anti-Ballistic Missile treaty (1972)
ARCOS	All-Russian Co-operative Society
ASSR	Autonomous Soviet Socialist Republic
CC	Central Committee
CFE	Conventional Forces in Europe treaty (1990)
CPC	Communist Party of China
Cheka	Chrezvychainaya Komissiya, Soviet Political Police, 1918–22
CIS	Commonwealth of Independent States
COMECON	Council for Mutual Economic Assistance
Cominform	Communist Information Bureau
Comintern	Communist International (also Third International)
CPD	Congress of People's Deputies
CPSU	Communist Party of the Soviet Union
ECCI	Executive Committee of Comintern
FSB	Federal'naya sluzhba bezopasnosti, Federal Security Service
GKChP	Gosudarstvennyi komitet cherezvychainoi polozhenie, State Committee of the State of Emergency
INF	Intermediate Nuclear Forces Treaty (1987)
KGB	Komitet gosudarstvennogo bezopasnosti, Committee of State
KMT	Kuomintang
MID	Ministerstvo inostrannykh del, Ministry of Foreign Affairs
MVD	Ministerstvo vnutrennykh del, Ministry of Internal Affairs
Narkomindel	People's Commissariat for Foreign Affairs (see also NKID)
NATO	North Atlantic Treaty Organisation
NEP	New Economic Policy
NIC	Non-Intervention Committee
NKID	People's Commissariat for Foreign Affairs (see also Narkomindel)
NKVD	People's Commissariat of Internal Affairs
NPT	Non-proliferation Treaty (1968)
OGPU	Unified State Political Administration, Soviet political police
OS	Old Style
OSCE	Organisation for Security and Cooperation in Europe

Politburo	Political Bureau of the Central Committee
RF	Russian Federation
RSFSR	Russian Soviet Federated Socialist Republic
SALT	Strategic Arms Limitation Talks
Security.	
Sovnarkom	Council of People's Commissars
SR	Socialist Revolutionary
SSR	Soviet Socialist Republic
START	Strategic Arms Reduction Talks
UN	United Nations
USSR	Union of Soviet Socialist Republics
WTO	Warsaw Treaty Organisation, Warsaw Pact

Preface

This book stems from the author's research and teaching in twentieth-century Russian foreign policy over the course of his academic career. It offers a view of the conduct and content of Russian foreign relations during the twentieth century. The idea to write it stemmed from a desire to produce a textbook that spanned the entirety of the century rather than dealing with one of the sub-periodizations that are prevalent in much of the existing literature (often with good reason). I am grateful for having had the opportunity to work on the volume.

The purpose of this book is to inform university students and the general reader. As a result, clarity and concision have been the main concern over providing a deeply scholarly text that addresses what can be, at times, a deeply complex subject. Further reading is indicated at the end of each chapter in order to aid in the pursuit of additional reading beyond the scope of the material presented here, and a periodized bibliography will be found at the end of the book.

AKW, 2012

Introduction

Russia, in all three of its twentieth-century incarnations – the Russian Empire, the Soviet Union and post-Soviet Russia – had a challenging relationship with the rest of the world, dogged by confrontation with other powers but also able to find scope to cooperate with some. Its domestic history during the century was tumultuous, but so too were its international relations. It is the latter that is the subject of this book, and while foreign affairs cannot be entirely divorced from domestic concerns it is not the intention to present an all-encompassing history of twentieth-century Russia within these pages.

This volume examines Russian international relations in the twentieth century as a whole. While the use of the name 'Russia' to label the state throughout the century is not unproblematic in its precision, it is used as a common identifier for a geopolitical entity which shifted several times in the course of a hundred years but nonetheless can be seen to have addressed a great deal of continuity in the challenges presented to it, and to some extent in the way they were dealt with. It is this continuity which is the rationale behind the structure of this book – the contention that in order to understand any element of Russian foreign policy in the present and during the preceding century there is a very real need to address all of it. While far from homogenous, it will be seen that Russia's foreign relations in the twentieth century cannot be properly understood by examining only select periods.

As has been noted above, there is a linkage between Russia's domestic affairs and the formulation and conduct of foreign policy. The one informed the other, and vice versa, in a number of ways. Significantly, the impact of the Russian Revolution, economics, war and systemic collapse in 1991 all resonated strongly in Russia's relations with the outside world. The connections are made here where relevant, as they provide the context for Russian foreign policy in the twentieth century, although they are not always dealt with in full detail, for the sake of practicality.

It is important to understand Russia as a global power, and also as both a European and an Asiatic power, and with that to appreciate that others viewed it as problematic as a result. Some saw Russia as a power outside of Europe that attempted to integrate with Europe, while others saw it as a

European power that attempted to encroach on the Asian world. The reality is that Russia was both, and thereby lies a great challenge in attempting to understand a large and powerful state. Accordingly, Russia's foreign policy with regard to both Europe and Asia bears consideration.

Additionally, Russian foreign affairs need examining both at the micro-level of various phases and challenges and also from the standpoint of a long-term study that allows for an unpicking of the continuities and changes across the century. Russia, as its differing political entities, occupied a similar (although shifting) geographical space. Its enemies and partners, although they at times changed places, had some degree of consistency. Issues surrounding certain problems or areas arose for Russia again and again during the twentieth century, despite (or sometime as a result of) the regime at the time. The relationships with Germany, Poland, China and the United States were all repetitive battlegrounds. Importantly, Russia seems to have stood mostly as state to be opposed, contained and limited by other powers during the twentieth century. And with this went the sense that Russia was somehow different to the other major powers of the globe during that century – it was the 'other', to be dealt with using great caution and circumspection.

At the beginning of the twentieth century Russia was an empire, and one of the great powers of Europe. Russia was different, however, to its imperial rivals, even though Tsar Nicholas II was related to the European dynasties in Germany and Britain. The Russian Empire was a contiguous landmass, rather than an empire with far-flung colonial holdings, with long borders and physical contact with numerous other powers. Russia was also reviled in the eyes of outsiders at the dawn of the twentieth century as backward, autocratic and aggressively expansionist. Rather than an abundance of friends, it had numerous enemies, although alliances in the face of common enemies were achieved in the second half of the nineteenth century.

As the First World War neared, the Russian Empire deepened some of its animosity with other powers, while establishing enough of a relationship with Britain and France that it could fight against the Central Powers alongside them. Still, Russia's relations with the rest of the world remained fraught with tensions, as Russia dealt with a series of problems in the early twentieth century that included war with Japan, confrontation with Austria-Hungary in the Balkans, rapprochement with Britain, revolution in 1905, and the coming of the First World War. That Russia was in a continuum of crisis in the last years of the Russian Empire is clear, and the autocracy did not always handle the situation well in domestic and foreign policy. Secret diplomacy and Russian actions contributed to the tensions in the Balkans that led to the outbreak of the First World War; Russia failed on the military front in both the Russo-Japanese War of 1904–5 and the First World War, before collapsing into revolution in 1917.

While the Russian Empire's relationship with other powers had been difficult, not least as other powers viewed it with intense suspicion as to its intentions, the rise of a new regime after 1917 far from remedied the perception of Russia on the international stage. While foreign powers welcomed the short-lived Provisional Government that replaced tsarist autocracy in the February Revolution of 1917, when the October Revolution brought the Bolsheviks to power later in the year the view of foreign powers was distinctly negative. Indeed, with the rise of a new revolutionary regime, the fledgling Soviet Russia was ostracized from the international community as a pariah. Part of this stemmed from a lack of Bolshevik desire to engage with the rest of the world in the immediate aftermath of the Revolution, instead preaching propaganda of world revolution and holding an expectation that the Russian Revolution would be the spark that would ignite the powder keg of revolution across Europe at the end of the First World War.

The Soviets did, however, turn to a desire to deal with the world. They found in the early 1920s that they could enter into foreign relations with other governments, although the situation was rarely cordial. A two-pronged approach to foreign policy developed in the early Soviet state, on the one hand a traditional diplomacy pursued by capable individuals that aimed at securing a 'normal' relationship with the outside world, and on the other a drive to foment socialist revolution outside of Russia. The twists and turns of the relationship with other powers were shaped by both of these strands in a world that was recovering from the First World War. Still, though, the Soviets became the inheritors of the Russian Empire's space in diplomacy, encountering the attendant caution exercised by foreign governments. For the rest of the world, the Soviet Union was still Russia and retained its expansionist intent.

During the 1930s, the Soviet Union existed in a troubled world in which threats to peace from both Europe and the Far East prevailed. Managing these threats became a major priority, both for the Soviet Union and for other powers, with the key desire being the avoidance of war. With fear of a common aggressor in the form of Germany or Japan, the Soviets were able to attempt to forge a relationship with foreign governments, but their efforts were largely unsuccessful. Even in the face of a burgeoning global conflict, other powers were not keen to enter into an alliance with the Soviets. Concerns about intentions, capabilities and the nature of the Soviet regime abounded, and still the problems of perceptions could not be overcome.

The Second World War, however, brought the Soviet Union into an alliance against the Axis powers. With the German invasion of the Soviet Union in June 1941 the Soviets became partners with Great Britain and the United States in fighting the Second World War. Suspicions remained, but in the face of a common enemy other powers were able to work with the Soviets. The wartime alliance shows an important point, however – that there were circumstances in which the Soviet Union and other powers could enjoy favourable relations with other powers; but, as in the First World War, alliances were built much more on the basis of resistance to a common foe than on a relationship of friendship.

With the end of the Second World War, the Soviet relationship with foreign governments sharply deteriorated. As the Soviets pushed to exert their dominion over Eastern Europe, effectively creating a Soviet Empire in the way in which they created and maintained the Eastern bloc, and with the Soviet Union emerging from the Second World War as a developing superpower, a deep rift between the Soviet Union and the West, in particular the United States, opened up. The onset of the Cold War is often dated to the 'declarations' of 1946 and 1947 from both sides, but there is sufficient ground to argue that in fact the Cold War had been extant in the way that foreign governments had approached the Soviet state since 1917. In the late 1940s, though, a clear division developed on the global stage between the Soviet Union and the United States.

This division made the world apparently bipolar, although the reality was that the situation was somewhat more nuanced. Nonetheless, the view that the Soviet Union was an enemy, and something to be opposed, became firmly entrenched in the post-war world. Despite being a victor of the Second World War, Russia remained the 'other' in world politics. For those in the Western world, the Soviet Union and what it represented would shape world-views for the rest of the twentieth century. Within the Soviet Union the opposition to the West was keenly felt. Between the two, the Cold War tussles developed.

While the Cold War was a situation of deep global division between the Soviet Union and the United States, the relationship ebbed and flowed. The major contention remained what the Soviets represented – namely Communism and a perceived desire for global domination – and a notable propensity of the Soviets to alienate others in the pursuit of their aims. The Cold War era was one of a conflict of ideologies and systems, and a competition for influence. This led to a great deal of Soviet conflict within the socialist world as well as with the capitalists. One of the key concerns of the Cold War, though, was nuclear arms, and the Cold War was conducted with a desire to avoid their deployment. This shaped the conduct of relations during the period and ensured that global concerns would be dealt with using a degree of care.

While the Soviet Union would be drawn into conflict during the Cold War, it avoided direct armed struggle with the United States. This is not, however, to say that the Soviet Union did not resort to the use of force as a strategy for dealing with challenges to authority. Just as the Russian Empire had been, the Soviets became involved in a series of conflicts where military engagement was used as a means to maintain control, once again confirming the aggressive approach of Russia to the world in the minds of observers and making it a pariah in international society, particularly with the repression of uprisings within Eastern Europe.

Just as there was conflict, there was cooperation between the Soviet Union and other powers during the period, particularly as the Soviets became more open to the West in the 1980s. Reform, and a relaxation of ideology, led to a progressive opening and growth of friendship with the outside world for the Soviet Union, and increasingly Russia was rehabilitated into international society. One of the results of this, however, was that in ceasing to be defined in opposition to a hostile world, Soviet power lost legitimacy and crumbled. In the late 1980s the Soviets lost control of their Eastern European satellites before the Soviet Union itself collapsed in 1991. Without being in opposition, Russia could not maintain its global position.

With the Soviet Union ended, post-Soviet Russia emerged. Here a major difference was that for the first time in the twentieth century Russia stood as a political entity that did not encompass the other states of the former Russian Empire or Soviet Union. New challenges arose as to the relationship of Russia with the other member states of the Commonwealth of Independent States (CIS), and it began on an uneasy path towards building a new state and finding its place in the world. While Russia had entered a transition, though, it was still Russia in the eyes of outsiders, and the imperial and Soviet legacies could not be ignored. The desire to maintain control and to maintain dominance in its sphere of interest appeared to persist. Crucially, though, for the first time in the twentieth century Russia was relatively open to the West. This last shift has been of great significance in the trajectory of foreign relations between post-Soviet Russia and the world, in an environment where the United States remained the dominant power in the world.

Throughout the twentieth century, therefore, Russia exhibited a great deal of continuity as well as change in its international relations. In the eyes of outsiders, to a large extent, it remained Russia throughout the century – different, dangerous, bent on expansion and global dominance, wracked by a tumultuous internal situation, and a state that was more one to be in opposition to than to be in league with.

With this in mind, one could be seduced into seeing twentieth-century Russian international relations in an entirely negative light, and indeed there are numerous accounts that do just that. As will be seen within this book, that view does not always hold true. The history of Russian foreign relations in the twentieth century is complex, nuanced and bears a thorough examination. It is the intention of the current book to offer an account that will allow the reader to examine the direction of Russia's relations with the rest of the world during a challenging century and, by covering the entirety of the century, to show the continuities and changes in Russia's approach to global affairs.

1   Russian foreign policy under the last Tsar

As Russia entered the twentieth century, it was faced with foreign policy challenges on a number of fronts. Expansion towards the Far East, not least via the construction of the Trans-Siberian Railway in the late nineteenth century, had brought it into competition with other great powers in vying for trade and influence, and into confrontation with Japan. At the same time, Russian interests in the Balkans were sustained, and unrest within the Empire was spreading.

The late Russian Empire was faced, therefore, with a diverse set of challenges. On the one hand there was a need to protect old interests and to remain strong in the interplay with the Great Powers. On the other hand there was a desire to expand its influence, and increasingly to maintain domestic stability as the tide of revolution built within Russia.

The situation of the Russian Empire in the early years of the twentieth century needs some contextualization. In the 1870s the Russian Empire had entered into an alliance system with Germany and Austria-Hungary. The brainchild of Count Otto von Bismarck, the alliance was designed to bring Russia and Austria-Hungary into an alliance system that would prevent their coming to blows as a result of a clash of interests in the Balkans, while at the same time reassuring Russia that Germany did not pose a threat to Russia and keeping Russia from forging an alliance with the French or British. Bismarck's alliance system was complicated, ridden with contradictions, and proved ultimately unworkable with Russia as a partner.

In 1890 the alliance between Russia and Germany ceased. Isolated, the Russian Empire sought for a new partnership to counter a potential threat from Germany or Austria. It was as a result of this that the Russian Empire was to forge an alliance with France in 1893–94. The Franco-Russian Alliance was not only an important step in finding a new international partner, it led to an influx of capital which the Russian Empire was able to use to equip its army and develop its industrial and rail capacity.

Tsar Alexander III saw the Franco-Russian alliance as a basis for dealing with a German threat. Officials in the Ministry of Foreign Affairs were concerned about this, not least as the Tsar appeared to have an intention to use the alliance as a basis for launching an assault on Germany. While he never took his plan to fruition, the fact that France could be counted on to support Russia in conflict with Germany and Austria nonetheless stood as a factor in late imperial Russian foreign policy considerations.

In 1893 construction on the Trans-Siberian Railway commenced. This brought Russia to a point where it was able to open up trade with the Far East, which brought the Russian Empire into a relatively strong position in the Far East and led to its having an increasing involvement in the region. Russia played an active role in the settlement of the 1894–95 Sino-Japanese War. While Japan had been victorious, Russia stripped the Japanese of most of their gains, seizing territory for itself and gaining control of the Chinese and Korean economies as a result of extending Russian financing. Japan was snubbed, but sought to ensure that Russia did not encroach further on its interests.

The maintenance of Russian pressure on British interests in Central Asia and the Far East led to a somewhat fraught relationship with Great Britain. Russia challenged the security of British India by impinging on British influence in Persia, Afghanistan and the Far East, while also competing for trade. The opening of the Trans-Siberian Railway had given Russia an edge in the Chinese market, and Russian gains after the Sino-Japanese War of 1894–95 made it a major player in the region. When the Great Powers joined to suppress the Boxer Rebellion in China in 1901, Russia became the steward of the settlement, thus gaining more sway in the Far East. As Russia gained dominance and began on a collision course with Japan, Britain took steps to forge alliances with the Japanese in 1902 and to send an expedition to Tibet in 1903. Conflict in Afghanistan remained, but had been largely settled by border agreements in the 1890s, but as Britain fought a war in South Africa at the turn of the century, the Tsar was keen to point out that Russian pressure on routes to India could well determine the outcome of the British military campaign against the Boers. The closest-fought area, though, was Persia, where in 1900 both Russia and Britain had opened embassies. While the British had given assurances to support the Shah, the Russian Empire secured dominance in road and rail building. The British were concerned that they were not only losing important ground to Russia in Persia, but also to keep Russia from gaining access to a warm-water port on the Persian Gulf, and to limit Russian agitation amongst indigenous tribes in Khorana that could lead to the Shah's power being challenged. Many of the British concerns about the Russians centred on the security of India. While there was no outright conflict in the early twentieth century between Britain and Russia, the relationship was shaky and the British were clearly wary of the Russian Empire and what they saw as its expansionist tendencies.

All of these aspects of Russia's situation in the world at the beginning of the twentieth century would come to bear on the challenges and events that faced the Russian Empire in its last years. While some would be resolved without resort to war, others saw Russia embroiled in conflict, not least in the First World War.

It is rather simplistic to see the Russian Empire as on a path to war in 1914. Nonetheless, it is difficult to escape 1914 as a product of Russian foreign policy in the early years of the twentieth century. Sustained Russian involvement in the Balkans, particularly the support for Serbia, led to Russian interests colliding with those of both the Ottoman and Austro-Hungarian Empires. Even so, it was not with Russia's most likely imperial rivals that the Russian Empire first found itself at war in the early years of the twentieth century. It was with Japan that Russia was to fight its first conflict of the twentieth century.

The Russo-Japanese War, 1904–5

Russian aspirations in the Far East led to conflict with Japan. Having snubbed the Japanese in the aftermath of the Sino-Japanese War, Russia failed to respond adequately to repeated Japanese demands to respect spheres of influence, and Japan ultimately waged war on the Russian Empire. In part this line was pushed by the Minister of the Interior V. K. Pleve, who argued that matters in the Far East should be settled by force rather than diplomacy, and that a brief victorious war with Japan would serve to stem the tide of revolution in Russia. Officials in the Ministry for Foreign Affairs disagreed, as did Sergei Witte, who, believing that war with Japan had become inevitable, resigned as Minister of Finance in 1903.

With support for adventurism in the Far East, the tide of war with Japan was almost impossible to hold back. Following Russian rebuttal of a proposal over the recognition of a Russian sphere of influence in Manchuria and a Japanese sphere in Korea in 1901, Japan had turned to Britain and concluded a defensive alliance against Russia in 1902. In the summer of 1903 the Japanese again attempted to conclude an agreement with the Russians along the same lines as in 1901. Again, the Tsar refused to agree, as he did again in December 1903. General Kuropatkin suggested the restoration of Port Arthur, Kwantung Province to Japan and selling it the Chinese Eastern Railway in return for a guarantee on rights in Manchuria. The Japanese gave their final warning in January 1904 that if an agreement could not be reached, then war would break out. Tsar Nicholas II arrogantly refused to believe that Japan would start a war with Russia and gave no response to the Japanese demands. In doing so he was to find that his faith both in Japan's willingness to go to war with Russia and in the superiority of Russian military and naval power was misplaced. Without warning or any formal declaration of war, Japan launched an attack on Port Arthur and Chemulpo in February 1904.

Just as indecision, arrogance and adventurism had led to the outbreak of the Russo-Japanese War, they also led to an ineffectiveness and confusion in fighting it that was compounded by serious military and naval defeats.

The surprise attacks that had begun the war at Port Arthur and Chemulpo had neutralized Russia's far eastern naval squadron by sinking ships and blockading ports. Following this, the Japanese sent troops to Korea, who outnumbered and defeated Russian forces at the Yalu River, which served as the natural border between Manchuria and Korea, before moving to cut the South Manchuria Railway north of Port Arthur. By May 1904, both the port of Dalny and Port Arthur were besieged.

Russian forces did not receive significant reinforcement until August 1904, at which point a Russian campaign began in Manchuria. Russia continued to fare badly, being defeated at Liaoyang and the Shaho River, before being forced to retreat from the Battle of Mukden in February 1905. Kuropatkin was able to establish a front south of Harbin and the Chinese Eastern Railway, which he held until the end of the war.

The Russian navy also suffered serious defeat and humiliation. After being blockaded in Port Arthur, the Port Arthur Squadron attempted to break out and reach Vladivostok in August 1904. The Japanese Admiral Togo destroyed it in the attempt. In October the Baltic Fleet was sent from St Petersburg. While in the North Sea, crossing the Dogger Bank, the fleet fired upon British fishing vessels in the belief that they were Japanese torpedo boats. This caused an outcry from Britain, with British public opinion calling for war with Russia. The embarrassed fleet was escorted by the Royal Navy to Africa and continued on its journey to the Far East. On arriving, in May 1905 the fleet attempted to sail through the straits between Korea and Japan, where it was destroyed at the Battle of Tsushima. This embarrassing defeat was the catalyst for Nicholas II to admit that peace with Japan should be sought.

Despite the extent of Russian military and naval defeat, Japan was eager for peace too. Japan approached the United States President, Theodore Roosevelt, to act as mediator of the peace, and in August 1905, Russia and Japan met at Portsmouth, New Hampshire to discuss terms. The Russian delegate was Sergei Witte, who had been instructed by the Tsar not to concede any territory, agree to reparations or give up the Chinese Eastern Railway. Witte was unable to work entirely within these constraints, but nonetheless salvaged a reasonable settlement for Russia.

Under the Treaty of Portsmouth Russia ceded to Japan the Liaotung Peninsula, Port Arthur, the South Manchuria Railway and the southern half of Sakhalin Island. Both parties agreed to a withdrawal of troops from Manchuria, with the exception of those stationed as railway guards. Japan's sphere of interest over Korea was enforced and Manchuria was divided into two spheres of interest – Russian in the north and Japanese in the south. Witte was able to ensure that Russia did not have to pay reparations to Japan.

On the face of it, the Russo-Japanese War appears to have been a disaster for Russia, and in many senses it was, particularly in the short term. The war had been very costly, both financially and with respect to loss of life, and Russia lost a significant amount of prestige as the first of the European

Great Powers to be defeated by an Asian power. The Franco-Russian Alliance was weakened by the conflict and the defeat was viewed in a negative light by the Russian population, contributing significantly to the outbreak of revolution in 1905.

In the longer term, however, Russia was able to make some gains. The loss of the Russian fleet at the Battle of Tsushima brought an end to British concerns about the Russian navy and contributed to the easing of Anglo-Russian tension that led to the conclusion of the Anglo-Russian Convention in 1907. Additionally, the Treaty of Portsmouth paved the way for Russo-Japanese cooperation and further agreements, which took on particular significance as the Chinese Manchu Empire declined. In July 1907 Japan and Russia drew up a convention which reaffirmed the Treaty of Portsmouth and gave Japan a free hand within its sphere of Korea, South Manchuria and Inner Mongolia, and Russia the same in North Manchuria and Outer Mongolia. A further Russo-Japanese treaty was concluded along the same lines in July 1910, in part as a response to the United States' desire to place the Manchurian railways under joint American and Japanese control. When Sun Yat-Sen was overthrown in 1911, leading to the collapse of the Chinese Manchu Empire, Russia and Japan worked together to mutually respect each other's interests, while dismembering China and profiting from its demise. A secret treaty between Russia and Japan in July 1912 confirmed Russia's and Japan's dominance over their respective spheres. Russia, by 1912 had become entangled in dealing with its interests in the Balkans and the secure and stable relationship with Japan allowed for the concentration of efforts away from the Far East.

1905: revolution and reform

As mentioned above, one of the hopes of the Minister of the Interior, Pleve, was that a brief, victorious war with Japan would stem the tide of revolution in Russia. Defeat at the hands of the Japanese in a costly and disastrous war had quite the opposite effect. While not the root cause of the 1905 Revolution – the cause is generally viewed as being the result of Nicholas II's unwillingness to respond to calls for liberal reform – the Russo-Japanese War certainly acted as something of a catalyst for it. It was shortly after the loss of Port Arthur at the end of 1904 that Bloody Sunday took place on 9 January 1905 in the Russian capital. Mutiny broke out in pockets across the Russian army and navy, most notoriously aboard the battleship *Potemkin*, which was unable to leave the Black Sea.

The 1905 Revolution took hold in the cities and countryside as strikes broke out and peasants took up the revolt against landlords. The Tsar was ultimately persuaded that some degree of reform should be agreed to, and issued the October Manifesto, which, while it safeguarded his autocratic rule over Russia, made provision for a parliament, or Duma and granted limited civil liberties. The Tsar then followed this by the issuing of the

Fundamental Laws of 1906, which gave rise to limited reforms and con-sultative government. While reform was significant in bringing Russia back from the brink of revolution in 1905–6, it also had an impact on Russia's position in international politics.

The defeat at the hands of the Japanese and its connection to the outbreak of revolution in Russia highlighted that Russian foreign policy needed to undergo change. While this was one of the things that Russian newspapers had called for in the years immediately preceding 1905, there had been no real reform. A new Foreign Minister was appointed, Alexander Izvolsky, who set about attempting to reform the Ministerstvo Inostrannykh Del (MID) or Foreign Ministry. While his reforms were never fully carried through, they serve to highlight an adjustment in the conduct of foreign affairs that was deemed necessary by the failure of diplomacy to prevent war with Japan, and a sense that Russia could not continue to behave in such a manner on the world stage, not least because it was plain that Russia needed the maintenance of peace in order to be able to develop economically and to maintain of the regime's political control.

While there was not so much a Russian 'diplomatic revolution' after 1905, Russian foreign affairs did change in the aftermath. The granting of constitutional concessions by the Tsar was viewed in a favourable light by other powers, and Russia's ability to engage in military or naval conflict had waned. It was clear that Russia was not in a position either politically or financially to throw its weight around on the international stage, which led to new opportunities for the improvement of relations. Those gains came from a number of directions. The Franco-Russian Alliance was reinvigorated by new loans, but it was with Great Britain that perhaps the most sig-nificant gain was made in the immediate aftermath of 1905.

Rapprochement with Britain: the Anglo-Russian Convention, 1907

While Russia had been in conflict with the British Empire for the best part of a century, and the Dogger Bank incident in 1904 had brought relations to a low point, the two powers were able to settle matters between them-selves in 1907. The rapprochement of the two powers was in part facilitated by a mutual link with France, the British and French having concluded their *Entente Cordiale* in 1904. The relationship with Russia was also improving as a result of the evaporation of British fears about Russian naval power, but it was in Russian support for the British and French against the Central Powers of Germany and Austro-Hungary at the Algeciras Conference in January 1906, in the aftermath of the First Moroccan Crisis, that the two powers began to see eye to eye. So impressed by the support were the British that Sir Edward Grey, Foreign Secretary, went to St Petersburg immediately after the conclusion of the treaty to seek an accommodation with the Russians.

What emerged was the Anglo-Russian Convention, signed on 31 August 1907, which covered territorial influence in Persia, Afghanistan and Tibet. The agreement effectively partitioned these states into spheres of British and Russian influence, with neutral zones that created buffers between them. The British safeguarded India and kept the Russians away from a warm-water port, while the Russians gained an opportunity to relax with respect to foreign policy in Asia and to concentrate on policy towards Europe and domestic matters. The Convention was, however, limited to the delineation of spheres of influence – there was no aspect of it that dealt with an alliance against Germany. While it would provide the basis for an alliance against Germany, that came about as the result of German actions.

Russia had hoped, though, that the Anglo-Russian Convention might allow for a revision of the prohibition on Russian warships passing through the Turkish Straits, and when the Russian Foreign Minister, Izvolsky, had raised the matter, Sir Edward Grey had indicated that this might become a possibility. It was to become apparent, however, that this was not the reality of the situation, not least as Russia turned its attention to the Balkans.

Russia and the Balkans 1908–14

With matters with Britain seemingly settled, and matters in the Far East concluded, Russia shifted its foreign policy attention to the Balkans. Here it faced both the Ottoman and Austro-Hungarian Empires in vying for influence. This situation was nothing new; indeed Bismarck's nineteenth-century alliance system had in part been formed in response to these tensions. For Russia, the key state in the region was Serbia, with whom it had strong ties of friendship that were reinforced by the ideological concerns of pan-laicism.

Russian foreign policy towards the Balkans became more prominent after 1906, although the 1903 Serbian coup had ushered in a more pro-Russian regime under King Peter Karadjordevic. Russia's renewed interest in the Balkans stemmed from the alignment of Serbia as an ally, but was also partly due to a geographical shift in focus once Far Eastern and Central Asian affairs had been settled, or were about to be settled, with Japan and Great Britain. More significant, though, was the role played by the new Foreign Minister, Alexander Izvolsky, who believed that he could score a major coup in securing an agreement that Russian warships could pass through the Turkish Straits, and thus make his mark. Izvolsky's policy moves in the Balkans, while at times misguided in their haste, remained tempered by the importance of avoiding war with Germany, which was allied with Austria-Hungary. With Austria-Hungary as the major rival for influence in the Balkans, particularly in Serbia, Russian policy became a series of moves and counter-moves aimed at avoiding conflict with the Austrians, but also at maintaining influence and prestige in the region.

While Russian policy had become more focused on the Balkans, matters began to come to a head with a change in the Austro-Hungarian approach to Serbia. In 1906, Colonel Conrad von Hotzendorf, newly appointed as Chief of the General Staff, called for war against Serbia in order to assert Austrian dominance in the region. Later that year, a new Austro-Hungarian Foreign Minister, Alois von Aerenthal, was appointed. Like his military colleague, he was also concerned to show Austrian strength and to limit Serbian power. Instead, however, of waging war, Aerenthal argued for the annexation of Bosnia and Herzegovina, which had been under Austrian occupation since the Treaty of Berlin in 1878 but remained nominally Ottoman possessions. The logic of Aerenthal's desire was that the Serbs viewed the territories of Bosnia and Herzegovina as a necessary part of a unified, more powerful, Serbia, but it also stemmed from the fact that, under the terms of the Treaty of Berlin, Austria-Hungary was permitted to annexe the territory, should it deem this necessary for its security. The only thing that seemed to stand in the way of Austria-Hungary's carrying out the annexation of the territories was Russia.

Aerenthal was able to find a way around this last issue, not least because, when Izvolsky met with him in Vienna in September 1907, the Russian made known his desire to achieve an opening of the Turkish Straits to Russian warships, revealing rather too much of the Russian hand. This then led – after Izvolsky had discussed military action against the Ottomans in order to take control of the Straits only to be rebuffed by the Russian Prime Minister, Peter Stolypin, on the grounds that Russia lacked the military and naval strength – to a further meeting between Aerenthal and Izvolsky in September 1908 in order to strike a deal over their respective Balkan policy aims. At their meeting in Buchlau, Aerenthal was plain about the Austro-Hungarian intention to annexe Bosnia and Herzegovina and, with Izvolsky believing that the Austrian move was inevitable, an agreement was made that Russia would support the annexation of the Sonja of Novi Pazar, where the Austro-Hungarians were keen to develop a railway, in return for Austro-Hungarian support of Russian aims with respect to the Straits. Izvolsky believed that he had scored a great coup for Russia, even if it was at the expense of Russia's Serbian allies.

It transpired, however, that Izvolsky had been dazzled by the prospect of achieving a historic aim of Russian foreign policy in gaining the opening of the Straits to Russian naval vessels, and had failed to grasp some of the ways in which Aerenthal intended to go about the annexation. Izvolsky expected that, with Russian approval for the move, the Austro-Hungarians would now seek the agreement of the other signatory powers to the Treaty of Berlin for the territorial revision that Austria-Hungary intended to make. This was not how Aerenthal handled the matter, and Izvolsky discovered that the annexation was to be announced on 7 October 1908, much faster than had been expected. Izvolsky was outmanoeuvred by Aerenthal's pace in proceeding with the annexation, and in fact gained nothing for Russia. The Russian Prime Minister, Stolypin, and Kokovstov, the Russian Finance Minister, were indignant at Izvolsky's unauthorized and irresponsible move, not least because he had given up Slavic territory to the Austro-Hungarians without authorization from St Petersburg without gaining anything for the Russian Empire. Russia was left embarrassed by Izvolsky's rash policy moves and Izvolsky was given a sharp lesson in realism when neither Britain nor the Ottoman Empire gave their support to a Russian revision of restrictions on the Straits.

While this situation led to a loss of face for Russia and showed a failed policy line over the Straits, the annexation of Bosnian territory blew up into a crisis that had the potential to explode into a pan-European war. The Serbian government, challenged by Austro-Hungarian moves, called for Bosnia-Herzegovina to be granted autonomous status and for compensation to be given to Bosnia for the annexation of the Sanjak of Novi Pazar. With Germany offering support to Austria-Hungary and indicating to Russia that Russian support of Serbia would likely trigger a wider conflict, the Russian Empire chose not to support Serbia's claims to the Austrians, and instead advised the Serbs to agree to the Austrian annexation. An Imperial Conference (a meeting of the leaders of Britain and its dominions and colonies) had concluded that Russia was in no way able to wage war against Austria-Hungary and Germany, as it lacked the military and economic might to do so, and, as Stolypin had outlined, needed peace to develop its economy. The crisis ended with Serbia being forced to accept the Austrian terms and with Izvolsky publicly humiliated. Anti-German and Austrian sentiment was inflamed in Russia, and the crisis fuelled an already growing Serbian nationalism.

The marked failure of 1908–9 was Izvolsky's, and it was not long before he was dismissed from office, his policies and reforms having faltered. In later years, he would reflect upon the outbreak of First World War as having been in part a result of his Balkan policy failure. His replacement as Foreign Minister, Sergei Sazonov, did not abandon Russian involvement in the Balkans when he was appointed in 1910. Sazonov lacked a certain degree of control over the Russian diplomatic corps, and Russian foreign policy towards the Balkans continued to be focused upon securing the Straits and, increasingly, on working with Balkan nationalists to force Austria-Hungary and the Ottoman Empire out of the region.

The major players in the pursuit of these goals were Anatoly Nekluidov and Nikolai Hartvig, who were the ambassadors to Sofia and Belgrade, respectively. Both men had pan-Slavic tendencies. While Sazonov was convalescing in Switzerland, Hartvig convinced the Deputy Foreign Minister Neratov to espouse a policy whereby Russia would render assistance to Slavic states in the Balkans to achieve independence. The prospect that Russian access to the Straits might also be achieved was dangled in front of Neratov, who encouraged the pursuit of this line. Accordingly, Serbia and Bulgaria concluded a military alliance in March 1912, in which Nekluidov's and

Hartvig's hands were clearly visible as the Russian Empire became the arbiter of outstanding disputes between Bulgaria and Serbia, particularly with regard to Macedonia. Building on this, Bulgaria then made a similar agreement with Greece; and with Macedonia also joining the alliance, the Balkan League was born.

The strong anti-Ottoman thread of the Balkan League caused some concern to Sazonov, who had hoped that it might serve more as a bulwark against Austro-Hungarian encroachments into the Balkans, and also feared that the Balkan League could quickly become a bloc that would wage war on the Ottomans. Simonov's lack of control over his diplomats, however, meant that Nekluidov and Hartvig urged the newly formed Balkan League to wage war on the Ottoman Empire, with the intent of forcing it out of the Balkan Peninsula for good. When the League attacked the Ottomans on 8 October 1912, despite warnings from Austria-Hungary and Russia that they would not support seizure of Ottoman territory, the Balkan states achieved a quick and decisive victory that achieved the goal of forcing the Ottomans out of Europe. The Great Powers intervened to act as arbiters of the peace settlement of the first Balkan War, meeting in London in December 1912, although it was not until 30 May 1913 that the Treaty of London was concluded. The outcome of the settlement was the creation of an independent Albania and the ceding of Ottoman territory in the Balkans to the Balkan League. The weakness of the settlement was that it failed to handle issues regarding the division of territory gained between the members of the Balkan League, and disputes arose, notably over Macedonia. While Serbia and Greece were able to overcome their differences, with Sazonov's assistance as arbiter, Bulgaria remained intractable. On 1 May 1913, before the Treaty of London was concluded, Greece and Serbia concluded an alliance against Bulgaria.

When Bulgaria turned on its former allies in June 1913, a Second Balkan War broke out in which Bulgaria was swiftly defeated by its former allies and the Ottomans. The subsequent Treaty of Bucharest, concluded on 10 August 1913, partitioned Macedonia between Serbia and Greece and left Bulgaria stripped of most of its gains. The Second Balkan War also brought about the collapse of the Balkan League, much to the disappointment of Russia. Not only had the hoped-for unity of Balkan states been lost, but the Russian Empire had once again bowed to Austrian pressure over Serbia in the process of the peace settlements. Russian prestige was damaged and, seemingly, any change of Russian dominance in the Balkans slipped away.

After a series of policy moves with respect to the Balkans on the eve of the First World War, the Russian Empire had failed either to achieve Russian access to the Turkish Straits or to develop a unified Slavic bloc that would resist Austro-Hungarian dominance in the region. While the Ottomans had been forced out and the Ottoman Empire looked increasingly weak after war with Italy in 1911–12, revolution, and defeat at the hands of the

Balkan League, Russia remained suspicious of the Ottomans, not least because they developed increasingly strong ties with Germany. Despite failures and the appearance that Russia would never achieve Balkan dominance, Russia retained an interest in the region. The main thrust of Russian policy towards the Balkans after 1912 was security against Ottoman moves in the Black Sea and the continued support of Serbia against Austria-Hungary. It was this last thread of Russia's Balkan policy that would lead the Russian Empire to confrontation with Austria in 1914 and to the outbreak of the First World War.

Russia and the eve of the First World War

Russian attention was brought sharply to the Balkans in 1914, following the assassination of the Austrian Archduke Franz Ferdinand and his wife in Sarajevo, the capital of Bosnia-Herzegovina, on 28 June. The assassination by Gavrilo Princip – a member of the Serbian nationalist group the Black Hand – of the heir to the Austrian throne, in territory that had been annexed by Austria-Hungary in 1908, prompted fierce reprisals from Austria-Hungary against Serbia, and was the spark that began the First World War.

It is important, though, to understand that the events in Sarajevo in June 1914 were the final spark that ignited the First World War, rather than a direct cause of it. When Franz Ferdinand was assassinated, Europe was already riven by a series of secret alliances, unresolved conflicts and tensions, and the Great Powers were locked in an arms race as military forces grew in size and technology was developed in the pursuit of security. With nationalist sentiment, defined partly in opposition to other states and fuelled by old grievances, riding high in the summer of 1914, Europe stood on the brink of war. The assassination of the heir to the Austrian throne, and the events which immediately followed, merely served to tip the balance.

Austria immediately sought to deal with the situation, not just in response to the assassination of Franz Ferdinand, but also to curb what was seen as a dangerous current of Serb nationalism which called for a unified Greater Serbia. Austria turned to Germany to gain support in dealing with the perceived threat, and on 5 July 1914 the Germans promised their full support for Austria in taking forceful action against Serbia. The so-called 'Blank Cheque' gave confidence to Austria-Hungary, while also tying Germany into whatever action was pursued. The Austrians deliberated over precisely what course of action they should take, and produced an ultimatum to be handed to the Serbian government, in which the threat of war was clear, should Serbia fail to comply.

Despite the Austrian threat of reprisals, the Russians did not see the danger of war as being particularly grave in early July 1914. The situation changed markedly when the Austrians delivered their ultimatum to Serbia on 23 July 1914 and it became immediately clear that the ultimatum had been concocted in such a way that Serbia could not agree to its terms and remain independent of Austria-Hungary. The ultimatum demanded that the Serbian government remove all anti-Austrian civil and military officials from their posts, that nationalist newspapers and organizations be suppressed and that Austrian officials should be allowed to operate within Serbia in order to ensure that all traces of anti-Austrian activity in Serbia were wiped out. Serbia was given twenty-four hours to respond to the ultimatum. Sazonov opined that while the ultimatum meant that war was inevitable in Europe, Serbia should exercise caution in its response, and not offer military resistance, but appeal to other powers for support and ask for an extension of the time limit of the ultimatum. Serbia's response was to agree to meet those demands made by Austria that were permissible under Serbian law, and request that all other matters be discussed at the International Court of Justice in The Hague. Austria-Hungary interpreted the Serbian response as a refusal to meet the terms of the ultimatum and mobilized against Serbia. On 28 July 1914 Austria-Hungary declared war on Serbia and commenced bombardment of Belgrade.

During the few days between the issuing of the ultimatum and the Austro-Hungarian declaration of war on Serbia, the Russian Empire had been preparing to render support to the Serbs. It was clear to officials in St Petersburg that Russia could not desert its Serbian ally as it had done in 1908, nor give way to Austrian and German pressure as it had done in 1913, without a disastrous loss of prestige. Indeed, even before the July crisis, the Russians had already indicated to Serbia that they would support it against Austrian invasion in January 1914, and they had reiterated that promise on 27 July 1914. Even before the Austrian attack on Serbia, though, with war in Europe looming on the horizon, Russia's Council of Ministers had agreed on 24 July 1914, the day after the Austrian ultimatum was handed to Serbia, that the Russian army and navy should be partially mobilized in order to render support to Serbia against Austria-Hungary if necessary. On 28 July, following the Austrian declaration of war on Serbia, Sazonov announced to European powers the partial mobilization of Russian forces in support of Serbia. When Sazonov was warned that Russia had no plans for partial mobilization and that the move could delay further mobilization of Russian troops, he successfully persuaded the Tsar to fully mobilize Russia's armed forces on 30 July.

Sazonov's view was that Russia could not abandon Serbia to Austria-Hungary, that it had become clear that Germany would not prevent Austrian aggression and that only full-scale Russian mobilization could be relied upon to counter German militarism. With Russia fully mobilizing on 30 July 1914, however, there could be no diplomatic solution to the situation, and pan-European war broke out as the series of secret alliances came into play. With Russia mobilized against Austria-Hungary, France was obliged to render support to Russia, as was Germany obliged to support Austria-Hungary. Germany accordingly declared war on Russia and France, hoping to strike swiftly at France, but in doing so brought Great Britain into the conflict by violating Belgian neutrality. The First World War had begun, and Russian actions were in part to blame for its outbreak.

Russia and the First World War

While Russian actions certainly contributed to the outbreak of the First World War, not least through the support of Serbia against Austria-Hungary and the support of Balkan nationalism during the years preceding 1914, the Russian Empire had neither concrete plans for the conflict nor any articulated war aims when it became involved. The main reasons why the Russian Empire had become involved in the conflict appear to have lain in its supporting Serbia and opposing Austria, with lesser considerations of countering German militarism and, to some extent, stemming a building tide of domestic unrest. Even so, none of this was part of a grand plan and the Russian Empire blundered into war seemingly for the sole purpose of defending Serbian and Russian interests.

Several weeks into the war, Sazonov first began to articulate Russian war aims, although it was not until September that a clear set of aims materialized. The first calls came on 16 August 1914, when Sazonov persuaded the Tsar that the Russian Empire should seek to reintegrate a unified Poland into the Russian Empire and to annexe Ukrainian territory from Austria-Hungary. The French Ambassador to Russia, Maurice Paleologue, indicated that these aims would be approved of by Paris and urged Sazonov to announce further Russian war aims. Accordingly, in September 1914 Sazonov issued a further, more clearly articulated and broader-ranging set of Russian war aims to the French and British ambassadors in Russia.

Sazonov's war aims followed early Russian successes against Austria-Hungary, and he announced the general intention of the Russian Empire to liberate the people of the Austro-Hungarian Empire. Key in this was the creation of a new Czech state, although Sazonov remained deliberately vague about its boundaries. Even so, Sazonov announced the aim of the reduction of Austria-Hungary to a triple monarchy of Austria, Hungary and a new Czech component as the third part. The Russian war aims also included the destruction of German militarism, the territorial acquisition of East Prussia, Posen and Silesia from Germany and Galicia and Western Bukovina from Austria-Hungary, the expulsion of the Ottomans from Europe and the placing of Constantinople under a neutral international regime which would allow for Russian access to the Straits. Serbia was to gain Bosnia, Herzegovina, Dalmatia and Northern Albania. Greece would receive Southern Albania, with Valona being passed to Italy, and Bulgaria might be granted concessions in Macedonia. Clearly, the programme rested upon the destruction of the German, Austro-Hungarian and Ottoman Empires, with the victors able to carve up the spoils between them.

These were fairly grand war aims, and in the end would prove to be somewhat unrealistic. Witte, now retired, did not share the grandiose ideals of the espoused aims, seeing in them the seed for the proclamation of independent states across Eastern and Central Europe as the old empires crumbled away, rather than an extension of the Russian Empire. In recognizing this, Witte foresaw one major aspect of the Versailles settlement of the First World War in 1919.

Russian war aims were to shift, however, after the Ottoman Empire joined the conflict in 1915. The Straits remained a major focus of Russian attention, but with Turkey involved in the war, Russian aims became even grander. Nicholas II issued a manifesto in which he declared that Russia should aim to achieve its historic mission in the Black Sea, which included the liberation of Constantinople for the Russian Orthodox Church. The liberal Grigorii Trubetskoi, and Pavel Miliukov, the leader of the Kadets, followed this line, arguing that Russia should control both Constantinople and the Straits, leading to this becoming a central Russian war aim. On 4 March 1915 a memorandum from Sazonov stated Russian intentions to annexe the western shores of the Bosphorus, the Dardanelles, Southern Thrace and the southern coast of the Black Sea. Keen to keep Russia fighting, Britain and France approved of these revised Russian war aims, although Britain agreed only on the condition that the neutral zone in Persia should become British, and France only after the Russians had told the French that they would not oppose French territorial gains from Germany.

Russian aims were further modified with the conclusion of the secret Treaty of London in April 1915, which brought Italy into the war on the side of the allies. The treaty promised Italy much of Dalmatia, which Russia allowed to be granted to the Italians against the interests of Serbia. Further, Anglo-French agreements on the partition of the Ottoman Empire granted Russia Eastern Anatolia. In September 1916, Ottoman portions of Armenia and Kurdistan were granted to Russia, with the Russian Empire as protector of the Armenian population. These, connected to earlier agreed annexations, represented significant gains for the Russian Empire and would have made Russia the dominant power in both Eastern Europe and the Near East. They were predicated, however, on the ability of the Russian Empire to achieve the aims militarily and were agreed in no small part because both Britain and France needed Russia to continue fighting on the Eastern Front, lest they themselves suffer defeat.

The problem for the Russian Empire was that it was unable to achieve its war aims. While it had grandiose plans, it was unable to achieve these, as its military efforts faltered. With the loss of most of Poland to Germany during the summer of 1915, Sazonov called for the creation of an independent Poland, based on the declaration he had made in 1914. This move did not square with the views of the Tsarina, Alexandra, nor of her close confidant, Grigorii Rasputin, and Sazonov was forced from office in July 1916, to be replaced by Boris Stürmer. Stürmer was unversed in international politics and woefully incompetent as Foreign Minister. As a result both of Russia's failure to press its aims militarily and of the change of personnel at the head of Russia's Foreign Ministry, Russia was on the wane as a Great Power.

The decline of Russia: military defeat and the road to revolution

While the Russian Empire failed to achieve its war aims, grand as they were, some assessment needs to be made as to why, not least because Russia would ultimately be a defeated power in the First World War and collapse into revolution in 1917. As has been mentioned above, Russia stumbled into the war with no plan for fighting the Central Powers of Germany and Austria-Hungary. On top of this, Russia's unpreparedness for war and flawed military tactics proved to be disastrous. While it was more numerous, the Russian army was consistently defeated by a better trained and equipped German army under more effective leadership. The 'steamroller' of numbers on which Russia had relied proved to be ineffective and outdated. Despite this, the Russians did prove successful against Austria-Hungary, whose forces were weaker still.

The Russian leadership initially viewed the war as a process of fighting by sheer weight of numbers. The Tsar's uncle, Grand Duke Nicholas Nikolaevich, was appointed Commander in Chief of the Russian army in 1914, although he was largely unprepared for the task. Initially, Russian tactics called for a defensive war against Germany, which was recognized as being militarily superior, and an offensive war against Austria-Hungary in Galicia. France, desperate for the lifting of German pressure, persuaded the Russians to launch an early offensive into Eastern Prussia. The Germans surrounded the Russians at Dannenberg, which resulted in the surrender and loss of two Russian divisions at the end of August 1914. At the same time, the Russian offensive in Galicia was successful.

By the summer of 1915, German offensives had taken Poland, parts of the Baltic and Galicia. The strain of war was starting to take its toll on Russia, not just in terms of territorial loss, but also in the failure of Russia's diplomats, unaccustomed to diplomacy in a time of total war, to negotiate suitable supply arrangements with their allies. Morale began to collapse on the Eastern Front as equipment and food supply problems became acute. In London and Paris, serious doubts as to Russia's ability to survive the war began to surface.

The Tsar concluded that Russian failures were due to ineffective leadership, and replaced his uncle as Commander in Chief of the Russian army with himself. In removing himself from Petrograd and leaving the Tsarina in charge, he lost control of his capital. Some even questioned whether the Tsar was not in fact guilty of treason, as he no longer seemed to have Russia's interests as his main focus.

The successful Russian Brusilov offensive in June 1916, a major offensive that marked the high point of Russian military efforts in the First World War and crippled Austria-Hungary, brought some respite from the crisis, with Russian victory in Galicia and the effective destruction of Austro-Hungarian militarism, and led Sazonov to declare that the war had been won, even though it would drag on for some time. Morale was buoyed up and the Russians were able to continue fighting, despite being unable to defeat Germany. Even so, by early 1917 morale was once again collapsing on the Eastern Front.

The Russian Empire proved to be unable to achieve its aims in the First World War. The Russian army was not up to the task, despite superior numbers. The economy was underdeveloped and the transportation network had not been sufficiently developed to support the strain of supplying the army in the field. Additionally, as Germany advanced into Russian territory an additional strain was put on the Russian rail network by the displacement of the population in the western Russian Empire. The war was costly, costing nearly ten times what the Russo-Japanese War had called for, and the Russian treasury relied heavily on borrowing from its own population and on loans from Britain and France, which were increasingly begrudgingly granted as Russian efforts faltered. With a prohibition on alcohol, tax revenues dropped and the treasury lost almost a third of its revenue. Inflation ran out of control and by 1917 the economy was near to collapse.

The architecture of state also proved to be poorly suited to total war. Diplomats were ineffective in a time of total war, although the creation of the Military Supply Committee to some extent absorbed certain aspects of their failings, but was unable to overcome some of the practicalities of moving materials to the front that were imposed by the war and the inadequate Russian rail network. In Petrograd, particularly after Nicholas II deserted his capital to take up command at the front, signs of decay were evident during 1916. The Tsarina, Alexandra, along with Rasputin, took charge, and removed most of the more competent ministers, among them the Foreign Minister, Sazonov. Within the rest of the government a struggle was waged between liberal Duma representatives and a bureaucracy that was proving to be increasingly ineffective in dealing with Russia in a time of total war. Despite Rasputin's murder by Prince Felix Yusupov in December 1916, orchestrated by members of the Royal Family, by 1917 Russia was in a state of crisis on both the home and the military fronts.

At the beginning of 1917 Petrograd was wracked by a series of crises. Food was in short supply, leading to strikes and demonstrations. Morale had all but collapsed on the Eastern Front, and it was clear that the regime was losing control. On 22 February (OS), when workers struck and demonstrated over a lack of bread the Tsarist regime began to lose control of Russia and spontaneous revolution took hold. A week later, on 2 March (OS) the Tsar was forced to abdicate the Imperial throne.

Conclusion

The Russian Empire faced many foreign policy challenges in the early twentieth century. Some were resolved, but others led to disastrous failure and even to the collapse of the Tsarist regime. The biggest challenges lay in Russia's inability to successfully defeat its enemies in the early twentieth century, both in the Far East and in Europe. Russian imperial aims were grandiose, and proved to outstrip the capability of the Russian armed forces, and even of Russian diplomacy.

One of the major facets of the last years of Tsarism was the secret diplomacy endemic on the international stage that led inexorably towards conflict. While the Russian Empire was not the only state involved in such machinations, it was nonetheless involved in the system and hence complicit. The contradictions, alliances and counter-alliances became increasingly complex and unworkable. Having emerged from one alliance system in the late nineteenth century, Russia entered into another in order to counter the Triple Alliance. Europe thus became divided into the two camps that would fight the First World War. Even early warnings as to the hazards of war inherent in this system were largely ignored by the Russians.

Despite a crushing military defeat at the hands of Japan in 1905, and the concurrent Revolution in Russia, the Russian Empire clung to traditional foreign policy goals to some extent. While there was some decrease in tension, and even cooperation, with other powers in the immediate aftermath of the 1905 Revolution, Russia's interests in the Balkans and in controlling the Straits brought it into conflict with other powers and led to its making diplomatic blunders that were harmful to Russian prestige and credibility. The agenda for reform that was apparent in the wake of the 1905 Revolution was abandoned as apparent opportunities to achieve long-standing foreign policy goals appeared on the horizon, only to turn into larger problems.

By 1914, the Russian Empire had occupied a position whereby it stumbled into the First World War with no plan for fighting it, nor aims to achieve beyond the support of Serbia against Austro-Hungarian aggression. Unable to match German militarism, although capable of dealing with Austria-Hungary, the Russian war effort resulted in defeat and Revolution and the eclipse of Russia as a Great Power.

While much of Russia's international relations in the last years of the Empire can be viewed in a negative light, particularly when the regime's demise is related to the topic, there were positive aspects as well. French financing, stemming from the Franco-Russian Alliance of the 1890s, was vital in developing the Russian railway network and the industrial economy, even if it did fall short of bringing Russia to the level of other European economies. The alliance with France also gave Russia a degree of security, even if the limitations of the arrangement were not always well understood by the Russians, and paved the way for a better relationship with Britain. When Russia showed herself to be willing to work with Britain and bury the hatchet of long-standing rivalries, the Russian Empire again benefited politically and economically. So too, the relationship with Japan forged after the Russo-Japanese War yielded benefits for Russia. By the time of the February Revolution of 1917, the Russian Empire had gained allies that were beneficial to it, and who relied upon Russian involvement in the war against the Central Powers. Military failure, ineffective wartime diplomacy and the Tsar's abandonment of his capital, however, meant that the building crisis could not be averted, and the Russian Empire collapsed.

Further reading

Asakawa, K., *The Russo-Japanese Conflict. Its causes and issues* (Boston, MA: Houghton Mifflin, 1904).

Bobroff, Ronald, 'Behind the Balkan Wars: Russian Policy toward Bulgaria and the Turkish Straits, 1912–13', *Russian Review* vol. 59 no. 1 (2000).

Collins, D. N., 'The Franco-Russian Alliance and Russian Railways 1891–1914', *Historical Journal* vol. 16 no. 4 (1973).

Connaughton, R., *The War of the Rising Sun and Tumbling Bear* (London: Routledge, 1988).

Craig, A., 'The Russo-Japanese War', *Eastern World* vol. 18 no. 9 (1964).

Ding, M., and Zhaowu, H., 'A Decade of Japan's Aggressive Tactics toward China Oriented by its "National Policy" of Waging a Final War with Russia (1895–1904)', *Chinese Studies in History* vol. 19 no. 4 (1986).

Dyulgerova, Nina, 'Count Kapnist: Imperial Plans for the Balkans', *Etudes Balkaniques* vol. 31 nos 3–4 (1995).

Esthus, R. A., *Double Eagle and Rising Sun: The Russians and Japanese at Portsmouth in 1905* (Durham, NC: Duke University Press, 1988).

Gatrell, P., *Government, Industry and Rearmament in Russia, 1900–1914: the Last Argument of Tsarism* (Cambridge: Cambridge University Press, 1994).

Gatrell, P., *Russia's First World War* (Harlow: Pearson Longman, 2005).

Geiss, I (ed.), *July 1914: the Outbreak of the First World War* (New York: Scribner, 1967).

Geyer, Dietrich, *Russian Imperialism: The Interaction of Domestic and Foreign Policy, 1860–1914* (New Haven: Yale University Press, 1987).

Gillard, D. R., *Anglo-Russian Rivalry in Asia 1828–1914* (London: Cass, 1984).

Hughes, M., 'British Diplomats in Russia on the Eve of War and Revolution', *European History Quarterly* vol. 24 no. 3 (1994).

Hunczak, T., *Russian Imperialism from Ivan the Great to the Revolution* (New Brunswick, NJ: Rutgers University Press, 1974).

Jelavich, B., 'Tsarist Russia and the Balkan Slavic Connection', *Canadian Review of Studies in Nationalism* vol. 16 nos 1–2 (1989).

Jelavich, B., *Russia's Balkan Entanglements, 1806–1914* (Cambridge: Cambridge University Press, 1991).

Joll, J. and Martell, G., *The Origins of the First World War* (3rd edn, Harlow: Pearson Longman, 2007).

Katkov, G., et al., *Russia Enters the Twentieth Century* (London: Methuen, 1983).

Kazemzadeh, F., *Russia and Britain in Persia, 1864–1914* (New Haven: Yale University Press, 1968).

Klein, I., 'The Anglo-Russian Convention and the Problem of Central Asia, 1907–14', *Journal of British Studies* vol. 11 no. 1 (1971).

Kowner, R., 'Nicholas II and the Japanese Body: Images and Decision-Making on the Eve of the Russo-Japanese War', *Psychohistory Review* vol. 26 no. 3 (1998).

Lensen, G. A., 'Japan and Tsarist Russia – the Changing Relationships, 1875–1917', *Jahrbücher fur Geschichte Osteuropas* vol. 10 no. 3 (1962).

Lieven, D. C. B., 'Dilemmas of Empire 1850–1918. Power, Territory, Identity', *Journal of Contemporary History* vol. 34 (1999).

Lieven, D. C. B., 'Pro-Germans and Russian foreign policy 1890–1914', *International History Review* vol. 2 (1980).

Lieven, D. C. B., *Russia and the Origins of the First World War* (New York: Macmillan, 1983).

Long, J., 'Franco-Russian Relations during the Russo-Japanese War', *Slavonic and East European Review* vol. 52 (1974).

Martin, Vanessa, 'Hartwig and Russian Policy in Iran, 1906–8', *Middle Eastern Studies* vol. 29 no. 1 (1993).

Matsui, M., 'The Russo-Japanese Agreement of 1907: Its Causes and the Progress of Negotiations', *Modern Asian Studies* vol. 6 no. 1 (1972).

McDonald, D. M., 'A lever without a fulcrum: domestic factors and Russian foreign policy, 1905–14' in H. Ragsdale (ed.), *Imperial Russian Foreign Policy* (Cambridge: Cambridge University Press, 1993).

Menning, B. W., 'Miscalculating One's Enemies: Russian Military Intelligence before the Russo-Japanese War', *War in History* vol. 13 no. 2 (2006).

Neilson, K., 'Russia' in K. Wilson (ed.), *Decisions for War, 1914* (London: UCL Press, 1995).

Neilson, K., *Britain and the Last Tsar: British Policy and Russia, 1894–1917* (Oxford: Clarendon Press, 1995.

Nish, I., *The Origins of the Russo-Japanese War* (London: Longman, 1985).

Rogger, H., 'Russia in 1914', *Journal of Contemporary History* vol. 1 no. 4 (1966).

Rossos, A., *Russia and the Balkans: Inter-Balkan Rivalries and Russian Foreign Policy, 1908–1914* (Toronto: University of Toronto Press, 1981).

Schimmelpenninck van der Oye, D., *Toward the Rising Sun: Russian Ideologies of Empire and the Path to War with Japan* (Dekalb, IL: Northern Illinois University Press, 2006).

Schmitt, B. E., *The Coming of the War, 1914* (New York: H Fertig, 1966).

Seton Watson, H., *The Russian Empire, 1801–1917* (Oxford: Clarendon Press, 1967).

Siegel, J., *Endgame: Britain Russia and the Final Struggle for Central Asia* (London: I.B. Tauris, 2002).

Spring, D. W., 'Russia and the Coming of War', in R. J. W. Evans and H. Pogge von Strandmann (eds), *The Coming of the First World War* (Oxford: Clarendon Press, 1990).

Steiner, Z., *Britain and the Origins of the First World War* (2nd edn, Basingstoke: Palgrave Macmillan, 2003).

Strachan, H., *The Outbreak of the First World War* (Oxford, Oxford University Press, 2004).

Sumner, B., *Tsardom and Imperialism in the Far East and Middle East, 1880–1914* (London: H. Milford, 1942).

Sweet, D., and Langhorne, R., 'Great Britain and Russia, 1907–14', in F. Hinsley (ed.), *British Foreign Policy under Sir Edward Grey* (Cambridge: Cambridge University Press, 1977).

Taylor, A. J. P., *The Struggle for Mastery in Europe, 1848–1918* (Oxford: Clarendon Press, 1954).

Tomaszewski, F., *A Great Russia: Russia and the Triple Entente, 1905–1914* (London: Praeger, 2002).

Walder, D., *The Short Victorious War* (London: Hutchinson, 1973).

Warner, D., and Warner, P., *The Tide at Sunrise: A History of the Russo-Japanese War* (London: Angus and Robertson, 1975).

Westwood, J. N., *Russia against Japan, 1904–05: A New Look at the Russo-Japanese War* (Basingstoke: Macmillan, 1986).

White, J. A., *The Diplomacy of the Russo-Japanese War* (Princeton, NJ: Princeton University Press, 1964).

Williams, B. J., 'Great Britain and Russia, 1905 to the 1907 Convention', in F. Hinsley (ed.), *British Foreign Policy under Sir Edward Grey* (Cambridge: Cambridge University Press, 1977).

Williams, B. J., 'The Revolution of 1905 and Russian Foreign Policy', in C. Abramsky (ed.), *Essays in Honour of E. H. Carr* (London: Macmillan, 1974).

Williams, B. J., 'The Strategic Background to the Anglo-Russian Entente of August 1907', *Historical Journal* 9 (1966).

Zeman, Z., *A Diplomatic History of the First World War* (London: Weidenfeld and Nicolson, 1971).

Zotiades, G., 'Russia and the Question of Constantinople and the Turkish Straits during the Balkan Wars', *Balkan Studies* vol. 11 no. 2 (1970).

2 The Russian revolutions of 1917 and the Russian Civil War in international context

In February 1917 (OS) Russia underwent the first of two revolutions that year. The Tsar had lost control of his capital, and with military failure and supply shortages on the home front, Petrograd erupted into revolution. The Tsar abdicated, to be replaced by a Provisional Government, which was in turn swept aside in October 1917 in a Bolshevik-led coup. Both revolutions resonated internationally, and provoked responses from foreign governments.

The two revolutions had different characteristics, both domestically and in terms of how they affected Russia's relations with foreign powers. While the Provisional Government showed a commitment to the continuance of Russian involvement in the First World War, the Bolsheviks did not. While the February Revolution put Russia onto a democratic path in the eyes if its international partners, the Bolshevik Revolution led to a new, revolutionary regime that rejected diplomacy as a bourgeois practice and believed that a new era of revolutions would sweep over the globe.

Beyond the revolutions, it is important to consider the international reactions to them. The new Soviet regime threw down a challenge on the global stage. Initial reactions were to hope that it would collapse, but when this failed to occur and Russia entered a period of civil war, the Russian Empire's former allies intervened against the Bolsheviks in the Russian Civil War. This chapter will consider the international context of the Russian revolutions of 1917 and the Russian Civil War, and the development of the Soviets as an international power in the revolutionary period.

The February Revolution and the world

The February Revolution began with the outbreak of unrest in Petrograd on 23 February 1917 (OS). Women workers protesting at food shortages directly challenged the regime, and protests grew. By the following day, Petrograd had been flooded with protestors, and when orders were given to the army to use force against the crowds on 26 February, it mutinied and began to go over to the side of the revolution. This was decisive, and the regime lost control of the capital of the Russian Empire. On 27 February, the bulk of the Tsar's ministers were arrested, while Nicholas II set out to return to Petrograd from the front. On his arrival, the Tsar was advised to abdicate the throne. Following this advice, he abdicated on 2 March 1917, also abdicating for his son, the Tsarevich Alexei, who, as a haemophiliac, was not considered well enough to occupy the throne. Instead the imperial crown was offered to the Tsar's brother, Grand Duke Mikhail, who duly refused to accept it and commanded the Russian people to obey the newly established Provisional Government. Nicholas II, now known as Nicholas Romanov, was placed under house arrest with his family at Tsarskoe Selo. With little resistance, the Russian Empire came to an end.

With the Tsar deposed, a new Provisional Government was formed. Its membership was largely drawn from liberal Duma representatives and it was constituted with a view to a democratically elected government being formed in due course. The Provisional Government was initially headed by Prince Georgii Lvov, with Pavel Miliukov as Foreign Minister. While the Provisional Government was the successor to the Tsar and his ministers, it did not hold a monopoly on the ruling power in Petrograd, nor indeed in Russia, but shared 'dual power' with the Petrograd Soviet of Workers' and Soldiers' Deputies. The Petrograd Soviet took charge of much of Petrograd and functioned as the coordinator of other soviets across Russia. The Soviet and the Provisional Government clashed on numerous issues, among them the direction of Russia's armed forces and Russian foreign policy.

Despite this state of 'dual power' and the tension between the Provisional Government and the Petrograd Soviet, the Provisional Government occupied the space vacated by Tsarism and was highly visible to the outside world as the new ruling body of the Russian Empire. Allied governments, while seemingly surprised by the collapse of the Tsarist regime, welcomed the more democratic Provisional Government. For the United States, the end of Tsarism was particularly relevant in the decision to enter the First World War on the side of the allies in April 1917, as it no longer meant siding with an autocratic power. Russia's other allies had much the same opinion of the transition to a democratic government, but more important for them was that the Provisional Government confirmed their intention to keep Russia fighting in the First World War and to pursue its war aims.

Accordingly, diplomatic recognition was extended to the Provisional Government almost immediately it took power, with the United States the first power to recognize the new Russia on 22 March, and Britain, France and Italy following two days later. The trappings of the Russian Empire, the imperial eagle and portraits of the royal family, were removed from Russian embassies, but for the conduct of Russia's foreign affairs the situation remained largely as it had been prior to the February Revolution. There was some reshuffling of ambassadors, and the Ambassador to the United States resigned his post, but Russia's diplomatic corps continued to serve Russia under the Provisional Government. In this, it can be seen that the continued commitment to Russia's war aims was of importance to Russia's foreign relations for both its diplomats and foreign governments.

Despite remaining in the war after the February Revolution, the decision was contentious, not least as the matter of Russia's ability to sustain the war effort was in part to blame for the end of the Tsarist regime. Within the Provisional Government, members of the Kadet and Octoberist parties held to the line that Russia should continue to honour the secret treaties made with other powers by the Russian Empire and to pursue the war aims that had been agreed among the allies. The most vociferous proponent of this was Pavel Miliukov, the Foreign Minister, who argued that Russia's foreign relations could not undergo a rapid reorientation, as had been the case with its domestic affairs, and that the entry of the United States into the war had strengthened the allied war effort and hence Russia's determination to fight on, and who, in a note to Russia's allies on 18 April 1917, dismissed rumours that Russia would conclude a separate peace with the Central Powers. This view, however, was not held by members of the Petrograd Soviet, who argued that while Russia should continue to fight in the war, it should do so not in the pursuit of territorial gains, but rather, adopt a defensive character. Under the influence of the Soviet, and with discipline and morale faltering within the army at the front, Miliukov's assurance to the allies that Russia would fight to the bitter end prompted large-scale demonstrations in Petrograd on 20 and 21 April. Miliukov, along with the War Minister, Gorchakov, was forced to resign.

A new Provisional Government was formed on 5 May 1917, following a proposal that a coalition of the Provisional Government and the Petrograd Soviet be formed. The new Foreign Minister, Mikhail Tereschenko, largely adhered to Miliukov's line, although the newly formed Provisional Government was now heavily influence by the more left-leaning members who had joined from the Soviet, and called for the conclusion of a peace that involved neither territorial annexation nor political indemnity.

While Tereschenko clung to his position, the dominant figure that emerged within the Provisional Government was the new leader of the government and Minister for War, Alexander Kerensky. Kerensky walked the tightrope of attempting to provide assurances to Russia's allies that it remained committed to remaining in the war and would not conclude a separate peace with the Central Powers, while also working to satisfy the demands of the Petrograd Soviet. His argument was that Russia should remain in the war – not to secure territory, but with the destruction of German militarism as the aim. Here, his line was that if Russia were to leave the war early or not allow the allies to pursue their war aims, then it would be difficult for the new Russian regime to maintain political and financial support of its wartime allies, both of which Kerensky was acutely aware would be necessary for Russia's post-war recovery.

Keen to show the allies that Russia remained an active belligerent in the war, to answer French calls for action on the Eastern Front in order to prevent the transfer of German troops to the Western Front, and to raise the morale of the Russian army, Kerensky planned the last Russian offensive of the war. The Kerensky Offensive, launched against Austria-Hungary in Galicia on 18 June 1917, was initially successful, but quickly faltered and collapsed into mutiny and retreat. The collapse on the Eastern Front triggered unrest in Petrograd between 3 and 7 July, the period that became known as the 'July Days'. At this point, the Bolsheviks' agitation against continued Russian involvement in the war gained a great deal of traction and Lenin's slogans of 'Land, Peace and Bread' and 'All Power to the Soviets' were taken up by the crowds. The Provisional Government called for the armed suppression of protest on 4 July, with orders for Lenin and other leading Bolsheviks to be arrested on charges of complicity with Germany. Lenin escaped to Finland, but Lev Trotsky and Anatolii Lunacharsky were both arrested and imprisoned. Despite attempts to defuse the protests, it was becoming clear, both in domestic eyes and in those of foreign powers, that the Provisional Government's power over Russia was seriously challenged and that Russia had become exhausted militarily.

Beset by such severe challenges, the Provisional Government found that its situation worsened as a new conflict emerged between moderates following Kerensky and conservatives who backed the new Commander in Chief of the Russian Army, General Laver Kornilov. Kornilov was vocal about the need for continued Russian military involvement in the war, despite the collapsing morale at the Front, and gained backing from Russia's allies as a result. Kornilov, though, did not believe that Kerensky shared the same commitment and, in a belief that the Bolsheviks had kidnapped him and were forcing withdrawal from the war, launched an abortive military coup, advancing on Petrograd in late August 1917. When this failed, Kornilov was removed from his post and morale all but collapsed within the Russian army. One of the consequences of the Kornilov Affair was that Kerensky released political prisoners, among them key Bolshevik figures, and, with the Bolsheviks prominent in the defence of Petrograd against Kornilov and gaining strong support in both Petrograd and Moscow, the Provisional Government's days were numbered.

With Russia in chaos on both the home and military fronts and with nationalities seeking to secede from the Russian Empire, it was apparent to Lenin that the time was ripe for the Bolsheviks to take power. He returned to Petrograd in October 1917, in disguise, and persuaded the Central Committee of the Bolshevik Party that action should be taken. In a near-bloodless coup, the Provisional Government having next to no loyal forces, the Bolsheviks took the Winter Palace and arrested the ministers of the Provisional Government on the night of 25 October 1917.

The October Revolution and the world

With the Bolshevik seizure of power, a series of declarations were made by Lenin on 26 October. These followed on from the slogans of Land, Peace and Bread, which had brought the Bolsheviks much support amongst a population tired of a failed and unpopular war. The Bolsheviks, better organized and more militant than other political parties, had pressed their edge and sought to consolidate their new position of power.

The Bolshevik coup was carried out under the cover of the Second Congress of Soviets, which was subsequently used to create the early architecture of the Bolshevik regime. While some within the Congress, notably the Socialist Revolutionaries, believed that the Bolsheviks had seized power illegally and without legitimacy, the Congress elected a Council of People's Commissars (Sovnarkom) on 26 October 1917, pending the formation of a Constituent Assembly, with Lenin as its Chairman. On 26 October, Lenin issued a series of decrees, among them the Decree on Peace, announcing Russian intentions to immediately withdraw from the war, and a series of decrees repudiating foreign debts and nationalizing all businesses, including those that were foreign owned. While this was a popular move within Russia, with the announcement of Russia's departure from the war, allied governments were enraged.

Aside from its domestic aspects, the Bolshevik Revolution had dramatically different characteristics from the February Revolution in terms of foreign policy and the reactions of the international community. While the Provisional Government had been quickly recognized by the allies, the same recognition was not forthcoming for the Bolsheviks. Bolshevik intentions to withdraw from the war ran counter to allied war aims, the repudiation of debts meant that the allied investment in the Russian war effort was lost and capital from loans and the establishment of foreign-owned business was subsumed by the new regime. There was also the intangible aspect of a new, radical regime, which caused consternation amongst other powers, not least as Bolshevik ideology spoke in international terms and held the spread of world revolution as an aim. While the Provisional Government and the February Revolution had been well received by Russia's allies, the October Revolution presented starkly different prospects for cooperation.

Indeed, cooperation with other powers was not a part of the Bolshevik agenda. Although Bolshevik ideology spoke in terms of internationalism, it viewed international relations as an aspect of the old order that had been overthrown, considered the secret diplomacy of the Great Powers to have been a cause of the First World War and saw the practice of diplomacy as distinctly bourgeois. When they came to power the Bolsheviks had no expectation that they would need to be involved in diplomacy, or to conduct relations with other governments.

They were shortly to find that the reality of the situation differed from their ideological standpoint. While Russia had undergone regime change, the rest of the world had not and Russia was still involved in the First World War, despite Lenin's decrees concerning Russian exit from the conflict. So it was that the Bolsheviks embarked on the diplomatic path, despite their distaste for it and their earlier beliefs that they would not need to be involved in foreign relations.

The beginnings of Bolshevik diplomacy were in Sovnarkom's appointment of Trotsky as People's Commissar for Foreign Affairs in early November 1917, two weeks after the Bolshevik coup. While Trotsky publicly stated his intent to issue revolutionary proclamations and then shut up shop, the reality of the situation was somewhat different. On 7 November 1917 he issued a call to the staff of the MID in which he requested that they continue to serve the new regime, or leave their posts and forfeit all benefits. The hope was that those who possessed technical expertise in the conduct of Russian diplomacy would continue to serve the Bolshevik regime, just as they had continued to serve the Provisional Government. To a man, the MID staff refused to serve Russia's new government and walked out, passing the keys to the Ministry and its Archives to Ivan Talking. Trotsky issued a similar request to the diplomatic corps serving abroad. Like their colleagues in Petrograd, they too refused to serve the Bolsheviks, but, rather than relinquish their embassies, they instead chose to continue to occupy their positions. Beyond the reach of Bolshevik power, and with established relations with foreign governments, Russia's foreign missions were harder to dislodge.

This led to a peculiar situation in which Russia's former diplomats continued to enjoy some status as representatives of a regime that no longer existed. This arose not only because they refused to leave their posts, but also because foreign governments showed themselves less than willing to deal with the Bolsheviks. In their limbo, Russia's former diplomats created a new body, the Council of Ambassadors, to act on the behalf of a now non-existent Russia and with the aim of blocking recognition of the Bolshevik government by foreign powers. While never a particularly effective body, the Council of Ambassadors and its members continued to enjoy diplomatic status with some governments, was allowed to attend as an unofficial delegation to the Paris Peace Conference in 1919 and continued to represent Russian émigrés long after it had become clear to foreign powers that the Bolsheviks were Russia's new rulers.

With a Bolshevik takeover of the MID, and a battle for Russia's foreign missions on-going, the Soviets began their first forays into diplomacy. The first wave of Soviet diplomats were, in many cases, drawn from those who had experience of other countries and spoke foreign languages, not least because many of them had been in exile before the Revolution. For overseas posts, the initial appointees as diplomatic representatives were individuals who were already abroad when the Revolution happened, and hence situated to take up their posts immediately. None had any experience of diplomacy before the Revolution. While the task for many of these new Bolshevik diplomats was to dislodge Russia's old diplomats and take control of embassies and archives, they set about establishing themselves as Russia's new representatives and demanded the concessions due to those who held diplomatic status, namely immunity from prosecution, and the right to the use of ciphers, diplomatic couriers and the diplomatic pouch.

Host governments, despite refusing to recognize the Bolsheviks, permitted these concessions to some extent but were adamant that the Bolsheviks should refrain from revolutionary activity via their diplomatic missions.

The issue of revolutionary activity's being conducted through the constructs of diplomacy was part of the Bolsheviks' intentions in the immediate aftermath of the Revolution. While they had a distaste for diplomacy, particularly secret diplomacy, they realized that it did afford them certain opportunities for pursuing the spread of revolution outside of Russia. Publicly, the Bolsheviks displayed their contempt for the secret diplomacy of the Great Powers in their publication of Imperial Russia's secret treaties and a number of secret diplomatic communications in early 1918 in the form of a 'Blue Book'. While not particularly damaging to the Russian Empire, nor particularly revelatory, this was nonetheless a fierce propaganda move aimed at discrediting the Great Power system in the last days of the First World War.

The Bolsheviks, though, had another agenda that they were keen to pursue through their new diplomatic service, which was to use the privileges granted to diplomatic missions as a means to spread propaganda and conduct agitation outside of Russia. Subverting the norms of diplomacy, which called for an absence of such activity, Soviet embassies became bases for furthering the revolution. Printing presses were set up, propaganda material, money and, on occasion, arms were sent in diplomatic baggage, more couriers were sent abroad than ever returned to Russia and diplomats were instructed to focus on revolutionary work. The Bolsheviks were, however, well aware that what they were doing was unacceptable and took measures to hide their activities, not always with great success. In November 1918, German railway workers dropped a crate, which broke open to reveal large volumes of propaganda material, leading to the expulsion of the Soviet missions to Germany and Switzerland, both of which had been heavily used as bases for attempting to spread the worldwide revolution. Despite this setback, it was clear that in the immediate aftermath of the October Revolution the Bolsheviks saw diplomacy as a tool of the Revolution, rather than as a necessary aspect of state management.

The Treaty of Brest-Litovsk

While the Bolsheviks did not believe that their involvement in diplomacy would last long, they found a need for it in negotiating a peace settlement with the Central Powers in order to withdraw Russia from the war. Having issued the Decree on Peace, this was a logical next step. The first move had been a call for an armistice and the opening of peace negotiations, sent by Trotsky to allied powers in mid-November 1917. While Russia's allies delayed in their response, it was clear that Russia desperately needed peace, and by the end of November 1917 the Central Powers concluded a ceasefire with Russia. The allies, still refusing to recognize the Bolshevik regime, failed to respond, and in early December the Soviets concluded an armistice with Germany, which allowed for the opening of peace negotiations between the Soviets and the Central Powers at Brest-Litovsk. The first session convened on 22 December 1917, with the Soviet delegation led by Adolf Ioffe, accompanied by Grigorii Sokolnikov and Lev Kamenev. The Soviets had selected these men because they spoke German, and also to limit the reactionary moves that were anticipated by Trotsky. Even so, the Soviets were keen to use the negotiations as a propaganda platform, requesting that there be no secret sessions and announcing their intentions to publish immediately the content of the negotiations.

Ioffe laid out a series of points in the initial negotiations which did not allow for territorial annexations or indemnities, called for the restoration of the independence of states that had been occupied, and allowed for the self-determination of states and the protection of the rights of minority peoples. These aims, while they repudiated the Tsarist ambition of territorial aggrandizement, also put forward an agenda for nationalism in certain areas, rather than an extension of revolution beyond Russia's borders. Even so, Ioffe was keen to point out that revolution might take hold in Germany and Austria-Hungary. The German General Hoffman, who led the Central Powers in the negotiations, refused to agree to these points, making plain that Germany intended to establish satellites in Poland, Ukraine and the Baltics and, noting that many of the borderlands of the former Russian Empire that Germany occupied were not ethnically Russian, argued that this reflected self-determination. The Soviet delegation, shocked by this, broke off negotiations and departed.

The Soviets returned to negotiations at Brest-Litovsk in January 1918, this time with Trotsky leading the delegation. Trotsky played a delaying game and used the negotiations as a platform for a series of propaganda speeches. While he blustered, on 8 February 1918 the Central Powers concluded a settlement with the Ukrainian Rada which separated Ukraine from Russia. With this matter settled, the Germans pressured the Soviet delegation for a swift settlement of peace between Russia and the Central Powers. At this point, Trotsky broke off relations, touting the slogan 'neither peace not war', through which he intended to convey that Russia would neither fight an imperialist war nor consent to an imperialist peace settlement. Trotsky's views were not shared by others within the Bolshevik Central Committee – Lenin argued that peace must be concluded, even if the terms were harsh, while the Left Bolsheviks, spearheaded by Nikolai Bukharin, called for a revolutionary war. The discussion was brought to an abrupt end when, on 18 February, German forces launched a new offensive that threatened to push through to Petrograd and enable the Germans to dictate peace on the basis of territory that they had conquered. At this point, Lenin was permitted to sue for peace with Germany. Negotiations were reopened, with a three-day time window.

On 3 March 1918 a peace treaty was concluded between the Soviets and Germany at Brest-Litovsk. The Soviets portrayed it as a forced peace settlement, which they did not expect to last. The terms were extremely harsh, harsher indeed than those imposed on Germany at the end of the First World War. Russia was forced to cede to Germany almost the entirety of its western borderlands, including Ukraine, Poland, the Baltics and Finland, which included approximately a third of its population. In August 1918 a further addendum was concluded which forced Russia to pay heavy reparations to Germany. The Treaty of Brest-Litovsk was, for Russia, a brutal peace settlement, but a vital one. Viewed as temporary in a world that remained at war and was, or so the Bolsheviks believed, on the brink of revolution, the Treaty achieved the Soviet aim of withdrawing Russia from the First World War.

The Russian Civil War and foreign intervention

Although the Bolsheviks concluded peace with Germany in 1918, the situation within Russia was far from peaceful. The Bolsheviks faced severe challenges to their authority, and by 1918 Russia had become embroiled in a civil war between Bolshevik forces and counter-revolutionary groups that found support from foreign powers. The Russian Civil War did not, however, erupt immediately after the Bolsheviks swept to power in October 1917, but in connection with the events of early 1918. Foreign intervention became the product of Soviet negotiation with Germany and a desire to avoid the Germans capturing allied war material, but quickly saw foreign powers join the forces of those who opposed the Bolshevik regime.

Why was there such a challenge to the Bolsheviks? While one might accept the notion that counter-revolution was an inevitability to some extent, the reality was that the Bolsheviks inherited a state in turmoil. They gained power in 1917 with little difficulty, but quickly found that the challenges they faced were significant. The first issue was that the Bolsheviks, although having captured power, were but a fairly small entity in a vast sea of political unrest, economic collapse and imminent military defeat. The Bolsheviks moved swiftly to consolidate their power across Russia, and force became a key aspect of the extension of Bolshevik rule in the face of opposition from within. Within a few weeks of taking power they had control of Petrograd and Moscow, and by the end of 1917 were in command of most of the major cities west of the Urals. While significant, the Bolsheviks' power was largely confined to the cities, and they lacked control over the vast swathes of countryside and in the non-Russian fringe of the former Russian Empire. The Bolsheviks, despite their desires, were not entirely masters of Russia in late 1917.

This situation was reflected in the reactions of other political parties to the Bolsheviks. The key battleground in this regard was the issues of the regime that should rule over Russia in the longer term, beyond the revolutionary upheaval, what shape it should take, and that the Bolsheviks had promised to establish a Constituent Assembly that would make this decision.

The Bolsheviks had not, by the end of 1917, succeeded in convening the Constituent Assembly. In no small part this stemmed from the fact that other difficulties had seemingly prevented them doing so, but other parties believed that the Bolsheviks had not wanted the Constituent Assembly to be set up, lest they should lose their hold on power in Russia. At the end of 1917, however, the Bolsheviks lacked the power to prevent the convocation of the body.

Elections to the Constituent Assembly were duly organized and representatives were elected. The Bolsheviks secured only about a quarter of the total votes, while the Socialist Revolutionaries (SRs) gained more than twice that number and secured the majority position. The elections brought into serious question the popular legitimacy of Bolshevik power, which was furthered when the Assembly met on 18 January 1918 and a slew of anti-Bolshevik resolutions were passed, before Lenin had the Assembly dissolved. It was never reconvened, not least because Bolshevik forces were used to stop the Constituent Assembly from meeting again.

While this inflamed an already tense political situation, Lenin moved quickly to the establishment of Russia as a one-party state with the Bolsheviks as the party of government. He split the SR majority by briefly including Left SRs in the new government, declared the Constitutional Democrats (Kadets) to be bourgeois and put pressure on other socialists groups to disband during the spring and summer of 1918. While this put the Bolsheviks into a position of greater power, it also served to alienate other revolutionary and progressive groups, which would have consequences later in 1918. So too the Bolsheviks found that their adoption of centralized planning and requisitioning, labelled War Communism, would alienate sectors of the Russian population, particularly the peasantry. While the disastrous situation caused by War Communism would not really be felt until famine and peasant unrest in 1920 and 1921, Russia was on the brink of civil war by summer 1918.

Against the backdrop of a political climate that showed that the Bolsheviks were not universally perceived to be legitimate in the first half of 1918, the forces of counter-revolution crystallized. The White movement, in opposition to the Bolshevik Reds, was multifaceted and disparate in terms of political background, desire and geographical location. The one thing that the Whites had, though, was a common goal – the destruction of Bolshevik power. With the organization of military units under Generals Alexander Kornilov, Anton Denikin and Peter Wrangel in the Caucasus and under Baron Roman Ungern-Sternberg and Admiral Alexander Kolchak in Siberia, the Whites and the Reds became locked in civil war. There was no clear aim beyond the removal of the Bolsheviks, although Denikin and Kolchak had notions of forming some kind of government, the latter having more success in the establishment of the 'Directorate' at Omsk. The lack of a single purpose meant that the Whites were somewhat disorganized and ineffective against the more coordinated Red forces that the Bolsheviks commanded. Even so, a bitter and fierce Civil War raged in the period 1918–20.

White forces, despite their deficiencies of unified purpose beyond the destruction of Bolshevism, pushed towards the Russian core, which the Bolsheviks had successfully gained in late 1917 and early 1918, in European Russia. The assault came from three main directions: Siberia, the South and via the Baltic States. There was some degree of success of the part of the Whites into 1919, but in the end it was the Bolsheviks who were the victors of the Civil War and repelled the forces of counter-revolution.

Those who fought against the Bolsheviks were not only anti-Bolshevik elements from the former Russian Empire. Foreign powers intervened on the side of the Whites in the Russian Civil War, making the conflict one with an international dimension. Forces from Great Britain, France, the United States and Japan joined the fray in the summer of 1918, initially stating their aim as being the prevention of allied war materials from falling into German hands, and in order to potentially reignite the Eastern Front and defeat Germany. However, foreign forces remained in Russia after the German defeat and joined in the fight against the Reds.

Allied intervention in the Russian Civil War began from the north with a combined American, British and French expedition to Archangel and Murmansk. Further British and French forces were sent to Ukraine and Southern Russia, and American and Japanese to Siberia. Supplies and funds were supplied by Britain to Kolchak in Siberia, Denikin in the South and General Nikolai Iudenich in Estonia during 1919. The motivation of the allies, Britain in particular, began to shift somewhat as the Reds steadily pushed the Whites back in late 1919 and early 1920 to one of defence of their global interests. The British were particularly concerned at the spread of Bolshevik control towards Siberia and Central Asia, fearful of a potential Bolshevik threat to the British Empire, with Persia and India being the key areas of concern. By 1920, though, allied intervention was over and forces were withdrawn. In the face of Red victory, foreign powers were no longer committed to supporting the Whites.

Allied intervention in the Russian Civil War was far from decisive, nor particularly effective, as a result of the relatively small scale of the troops dispatched to Russia by the allies. The Bolsheviks emerged victorious, even if Russia had been brought to its knees economically by the policies of War Communism. What allied intervention in the Russian Civil War did achieve, however, was to cement in the Soviet political consciousness the notion that the capitalist and imperialist powers were opposed to the Soviets, to the extent that they had been prepared to be involved in military action against the Bolsheviks immediately after the Russian Revolution, and to foster the notion that the Soviets were under an almost pervasive threat from them of capitalist encirclement. The Russian Civil War was formative for the Soviet state in many ways, not least in the way in which allied involvement informed Soviet perceptions of other states' opinions of post-Revolutionary Russia as the Bolsheviks consolidated their power in the early 1920s.

Beyond Russia: the spread of revolution

While the Soviets were victorious in the Russian Civil War by 1921, the chain of revolutions that they hoped would be sparked across Europe in the wake of October 1917 failed to materialize successfully. This is not to say that there were no revolutions outside of Russia during the period – there were – but they were short lived, or quickly put down. These revolutions erupted in late 1918 and early 1919 in Germany and Hungary. The first of these was the revolutionary upheaval in November 1918 in Germany, which had largely reformist character and was typified by the Bolsheviks as bearing similarities to the Russian February Revolution of the previous year. After the German November, a Communist Party (KPD) was established in Germany, drawn from the left of the Social Democratic Party, which had played a major role in the reforms of November 1918. In January 1919 a radical faction of the KPD, calling themselves the Spartacists, launched a revolt against German power but was swiftly crushed by the Freikorps, which was tasked with keeping order. The ostensible leadership of the Spartacists, Rosa Luxemburg and Karl Liebknecht, who were both killed as the Freikorps put the uprising down, had urged caution and that Germany was unprepared for such action to be successful in early 1919. However, it seems that the mass of the Spartacist group had been buoyed up by Bolshevik propaganda which suggested that Europe was teetering on the brink of a revolutionary cataclysm.

Beyond the Spartacist uprising, there was some revolutionary success in early 1919 for the communist movement. In March 1919 a Socialist Communist regime was established in Hungary under Bela Kun. It was short lived, as Kun could not resist the forces that sought to oust him, and although Lenin had wanted to send Bolshevik forces to support the Hungarians, he was unable to do so. In April a Bavarian Soviet Socialist Republic was set up by two Russian émigrés, but survived only a few weeks before being destroyed. The initial revolutionary upsurge outside of Russia had an inauspicious beginning, but the Bolsheviks remained convinced that it would still materialize, even as it looked increasingly unlikely.

An opportunity for the extension of revolution into Europe seemed to present itself in April 1920 when the Soviets came into conflict with Poland under Marshall Josef Pilsudski. Pilsudski advanced on Ukraine, having made an agreement with White forces that he would do so. In May 1920 the Poles occupied Kiev and the Red Army launched a counter-offensive under Marshall Tukhashevksii. At the beginning of July Red Army forces had pushed Pilsudski back to Warsaw, and the Bolsheviks set about forging Soviets behind their lines in Poland and pushing for renewed revolution in Hungary and Germany. The Poles appealed for assistance from Britain and

France against the spread of communism and threat of a Soviet conquest of Poland. Little more than advice was forthcoming, but Pilsudski was strongly encouraged to exploit military errors by the Red Army and the resistance to the forced extension of communism, and pushed back against the Bolsheviks. Territory was quickly regained, with the entirety of ethnic Poland being restored by the end of August 1920. Treaty negotiations were opened between the Soviets and Poland, resulting in the Treaty of Riga, drafted in October 1920, which gave Poland more territory than the British had suggested in the discussion of Poland's post-war settlement, which had been entirely based on a line drawn on Polish ethnicity. The Treaty was formally concluded in March 1921, granting Poland territory that included a sizeable number of Belorussians and Ukrainians and left Poland as a somewhat larger state than it had been before the First World War. The Soviets, though, had been resoundingly defeated and the forces of revolution seemed to be ebbing away.

Despite the failure to extend revolution outside of Russia, either by force or by its erupting of its own accord, the Bolsheviks maintained a commitment to the ideology of the World Revolution and remained of the belief that revolution would eventually take hold outside of Russia. To that end, and having discovered that traditional diplomacy was ill suited to the propagation of international revolution, the Soviets set about the creation of a body to direct and foment communist revolution around the globe. This new body was the Communist International (Comintern, also known as the Third International), established in Moscow in March 1919.

The Comintern embodied the Bolshevik ideal of the export of revolution. With the brief success of revolution in Hungary and Germany and the rise of Communist parties outside Russia, the Bolsheviks were of the belief that a coordinated communist body would ensure the success of global revolution. While, as will be seen in subsequent chapters, world revolution did not take hold in 1919–20, the Bolsheviks clearly still had some belief that it would. The decision to found the Comintern in 1919 was made in some haste, and the First Congress in March 1919 was attended by a diverse group of representatives from socialist and communist groups. The rush to found the Comintern stemmed in part from the Soviet belief that the world stood on the brink of revolution in early 1919, and also from the fact that the Bolsheviks were keen to stamp their authority on the nature of possible revolution outside of Russia at a time when they were concerned that other factions might challenge them. The Comintern was established by general agreement of the delegates to the First Congress, with necessarily little in the manner of formal structure. In many ways it represented a federation of the international Communist movement at this stage, although not all groups had yet coalesced under the banner of Communism. Even so, from the outset the Soviets dominated the Comintern, with Grigorii Zinoviev appointed as its head but with Lenin effectively in charge until his death.

Soviet domination of the Comintern and the desire to inflict rigid Bolshevik discipline on it were furthered at the Second Congress, at much the same time that the Soviets were moving towards victory in the Russian Civil War. Believing that they had pushed back the tide of counter-revolution, the Second Congress included Trotsky's elaboration of the twenty-one conditions for membership of the Comintern, and the articulation of its programme was made. Significantly, the issue of empire and colonialism was discussed, with the intent of posing a threat to the stability of the imperial powers on a global scale.

The Comintern, in its beginnings, embodied Soviet desires for World Revolution and the notion that the Soviet route to successful revolution needed to be emulated lest it fail to take hold. The push for this was born out of the short-term failure of revolutionary movements outside Russia in 1919, but would become more entrenched as revolution failed to spread in the 1920s and as the Soviet regime moved towards consolidation at home and attempted to engage in foreign relations with other powers by a means other than direct conflict.

Conclusion

The Russian Revolution threw Russia into turmoil, but it resonated internationally. Not only had one of the Great Powers of Europe collapsed into revolution, but a new, reactionary regime had risen with an ideology that preached the development of revolution around the world. In 1917 Russia's allies in the First World War could ignore neither Russia's exit from the war nor the challenging new regime.

While the Russian Revolution prompted a strong international reaction, this moved in several phases. The first was one of acceptance that a beleaguered autocratic regime had been replaced by a Provisional Government that promised to keep Russia fighting in the war. The next was almost one of denial, not that it the Bolshevik Revolution had occurred, but of the legitimacy of Russia's new leadership. The matter of continued involvement in the war was clearly a key issue here, but so too was the extent to which Bolshevism was seen as something to be stamped out by foreign governments. So it was, in the context of the aftermath of the October Revolution and a developing Civil War, that foreign powers intervened against the Bolsheviks in Russia during the period 1918–20. Foreign hostility to the Bolsheviks was apparent, and led to the development of a siege mentality of capitalist encirclement within the newly forged Soviet state.

At the same time, the Bolsheviks made moves to be recognized as Russia's new masters on the international stage. While foreign powers were keen to deal with them, the fact that the Soviets made efforts was significant. So too, the fact that Russia's former diplomats were allowed to have a continued existence is important. Revolutionary Russia occupied an unusual and challenging situation in world affairs as both its new and former masters fought for recognition from other powers, and during the revolutionary period nothing was resolved.

Even so, the Bolsheviks had gained power in the Revolution and, having achieved victory in the Russian Civil War, moved to consolidate their power over Russia. As the 1920s dawned the Soviets had definitely become Russia's new rulers and foreign powers would begin increasingly to engage with them on the diplomatic stage, even if on both sides scepticism as to true intentions prevailed.

Further reading

Armstrong, D., *Revolution and World Order: The Revolutionary State in International Society* (Oxford: Clarendon Press, 1993).

Bradley, J., *Allied Intervention in Russia, 1917–1920* (London: Weidenfeld and Nicolson, 1968).

Carrol, E. M., *Soviet Communism and Western Opinion, 1919–1921* (Chapel Hill: University of North Carolina Press, 1965).

Claudin, F., *The Communist Movement: From Comintern to Cominform* (Harmondsworth: Penguin, 1975).

Debo, R. K., *Revolution and Survival: The Foreign Policy of Soviet Russia, 1917–1918* (Liverpool: Liverpool University Press, 1979).

Debo, R. K., *Survival and Consolidation: The Foreign Policy of Soviet Russia, 1918–1921* (Montreal: McGill Queen's University Press, 1992).

Fiddick, T. C., *Russia's Retreat from Poland, 1920: From Permanent Revolution to Peaceful Co-existence* (London: Macmillan, 1990).

Fry, M. G., 'Britain, the Allies, and the Problem of Russia 1918–19', *Canadian Journal of History* vol. 2 no. 2 (1967).

Hughes, M., *Diplomacy before the Russian Revolution* (Basingstoke: Palgrave Macmillan, 1999).

Kocho-Williams, A., *Russian and Soviet Diplomacy, 1900–1939* (Basingstoke: Palgrave, 2012).

Lazic, B. M., *Lenin and the Comintern* (Stanford, CA: Hoover Institution Press, 1972).

Lazitch, B., 'The Founding of the Comintern: Letters from Souvarine to Zinoviev', *Survey* vol. 30 no. 4 (1989).

McDermott, K., and Agnew, J., *The Comintern: A History of International Communism from Lenin to Stalin* (Basingstoke: Macmillan, 1996).

Melgrani, P., *Lenin and the Myth of World Revolution* (Atlantic Highlands, NJ: Humanities Press International, 1989).

Miliukov, P. N., *Political Memoirs* (Ann Arbor: University of Michigan Press, 1967).

Morris, L. P., 'The Russians, the Allies and the War, February–July 1917', *Slavonic and East European Review* vol. 50 no. 1 (1972).

Narinsky, Mikhail and Rojahn, Jürgen (eds), *Centre and Periphery: The History of the Comintern in the Light of New Documents* (Amsterdam: International Institute of Social History, 1996).

O'Connor, T. *Diplomacy and Revolution: G. V. Chicherin and Soviet Foreign Affairs, 1918–1930* (Ames: Iowa State University Press, 1988).

Occleshaw, M., *Dances in Deep Shadows* (London: Constable, 2006).

Rees, Tim, and Andrew Thorpe, *International Communism and the Communist International 1919–1943* (Manchester: Manchester University Press, 1998).

Senn, A., *Diplomacy and Revolution: The Soviet Mission to Switzerland, 1918* (Notre Dame, IN: University of Notre Dame Press, 1974).

Uldricks, T., *Diplomacy and Ideology* (London: Sage, 1979).

Wade, R. A., *The Russian Search for Peace: February–October 1917* (Stanford, CA: Stanford University Press, 1969).

White, S., *Britain and the Bolshevik Revolution* (London: Macmillan, 1979).

Worth, R. D., *The Allies and the Russian Revolution* (Durham, NC: Duke University Press, 1954).

3   Soviet foreign policy in the 1920s

Soviet foreign policy in the 1920s was complex and at times paradoxical. As the Bolsheviks emerged victorious from the Russian Civil War they still appeared to have an unclear agenda in foreign policy, but would find greater clarity of their objectives as the decade wore on. In part, the Bolsheviks were trying to consolidate the Soviet state, but they also clung to their revolutionary ideology, which led to the conflicts and, at times, confusion over where the policy line may have lain. What is apparent, then, is that during the 1920s a dualistic aspect to Soviet foreign policy emerged, with the pursuit of world revolution on the one hand and the extension of a normalization of relations with other powers on the other. These two policies were at loggerheads with one another, sometimes to the point of the one seriously jeopardizing the pursuit of the other.

In order to understand the dualism it is important to consider Soviet foreign policy during the 1920s, and the priorities of the Soviets and how they changed during the decade. As the 1920s began, the hope for worldwide revolution still existed in Soviet quarters, but it would gradually wane before being reignited by the financial crash at the end of the decade. This serves to highlight that Soviet foreign policy was the product of a mix of Marxist ideology and pragmatism in the face of what could realistically be brought about.

In unpicking Soviet foreign affairs in the 1920s, therefore, it is helpful to have some sense of where the two threads lay, both in their ideological underpinnings and in terms of their practicalities. Following the Russian Civil War, the Bolsheviks needed breathing space for Russia to develop. The Bolsheviks were acutely aware of the fact that they had a very real need to shore up the fledgling state, lest it collapse. In their minds, if Soviet Russia were to fall, then the revolution had little hope of spreading elsewhere. As a result, the pushing of the line of world revolution became somewhat downplayed, and the notion of peaceful coexistence with the capitalist powers came to the fore. While the revolutionary line never disappeared, it became secondary to the other more important aspect of state building. That this was not supposed to be a permanent state of affairs is telling, even if the realities were to prove to be different.

In order to pursue two different strands of foreign policy, the Soviets had multiple foreign policy agencies on which to bear. While at times the lines would be blurred, the People's Commissariat for Foreign Affairs, or Narkomindel was charged with diplomatic relations, while the Communist International or Comintern was concerned with the export of revolution to the world. While the latter was not officially a Soviet institution, nor technically subject to the Soviet government, the reality of the situation was that it was used, and acted, as such.

With two threads of foreign policy to contend with, with multiple foreign policy institutions and with the Soviet need to respond to both European and Asian challenges, the foreign policy of the Soviets in the 1920s perhaps seems overly complex. It need not be so, and although it was rife with contradiction and clashes, an analysis of the policies and their conduct, as well as the response of other powers, can be made. Important here is to gain a clear understanding of where Soviet priorities lay and where the Soviets recognized that their limitations were, as well as an appreciation that the Soviet state faced challenges from within and without, some of which were real and some of which were imagined.

The NEP and international trade as a beginning

The first major challenge to Soviet Russia was apparent at the end of the Civil War. Domestically, Soviet Russia faced severe economic problems in 1921. The ravages of the First World War and the Russian Civil War left the economy in much the same position as it had been in 1913. The harsh requisitioning policies of War Communism that the Bolsheviks had administered during the Civil War had depleted food stocks to the point of famine, and reduced popular support for the Bolsheviks. Facing the threat, and in some areas the reality, of revolt, what the Bolsheviks needed was a new policy. Their response was the New Economic Policy (NEP), which Lenin announced at the 10th Party Congress in 1921. NEP, an acknowledged ideological step backwards, allowed for the flourishing of limited capitalism. The production of surplus was encouraged and the population were told to enrich themselves. Productivity rose, and the Russian economy slowly began to grow.

With the growth and the production of surplus, Russia had a very real need to establish trade with other powers. A surplus requires a market in which it can be sold, and Russia had a need for goods that it could not produce itself. At the same time, other powers desired a trading relationship with Russia. So it was that the flourishing of domestic policy in the form of the NEP led to the pursuit of relations with other powers on the basis of trade. While there was hope that these might develop into better-established diplomatic and political relationships, in the first instance they were based solely on economics.

The first realization of Soviet Russian international trade relations came in the form of the Anglo-Russian Trade Agreement of February 1921.

The British, in need of foreign trading partners to reinvigorate their own post-war economy, were keen to trade with the Soviets. They also had another agenda in concluding an agreement with Soviet Russia, and that was to push the Soviets into ceasing anti-British agitation and propaganda in the British Empire, particularly in India. To put this clearly to the Soviets, the preamble to the Agreement made explicit reference to the Agreement being conditional on an adherence to a complete absence of propaganda and revolutionary activity against either party.

The Soviets saw the Anglo-Russian Trade Agreement as a step towards achieving diplomatic recognition and further concessions. The British were not so convinced, particularly when they uncovered what they believed to be continued Soviet activity directed against the British Empire. In September 1921 the British presented a letter to the Soviet government which made accusations of systematic violation of the Anglo-Soviet Trade Agreement by the Soviets, and which the Soviets refuted. The British were not entirely convinced by this line, particularly as they viewed the Comintern as a Soviet agency, regardless of Soviet protests that there were no links to the Soviet government. The British remained suspicious, but took no action against Soviet Russia at this point – Great Britain needed trade with Russia, just as the reverse was true, and without concrete proof it would have been hard to justify a rupture of relations.

The Anglo-Russian Trade Agreement did serve to give the Soviet state a certain degree of legitimacy on the international stage. While full *de jure* recognition from other powers would come later, the conclusion of a trade agreement between Britain and Russia was of importance to early Soviet foreign policy. Firstly, it pointed to the acceptance by other powers that the Bolsheviks had emerged from the Civil War as the masters of Russia, and that the Soviet regime did not look as though its collapse was imminent. Secondly, it gave Soviet Russia a benchmark of acceptability as a partner in international affairs and paved the way for the opening of trade relations with other powers and for the Soviets to eventually become more accepted in international relations. Thirdly, and perhaps most importantly, it signalled to the world that the Soviets wanted to join the international system as full and equal partners, abiding by its rules rather than being bent on the pursuit of world revolution.

As a result of this, the Soviets were invited to the World Economic Conference in Genoa in 1922. Part of the reason for the invitation's being extended to them was that other powers wished to discuss the issue of the repayment of Tsarist debts, which the Soviets had repudiated. There was some hope that the Soviets might be persuaded to repay Russia's old debts in return for political concessions from other powers. The Soviets, however, were keen to use the Genoa Conference as a platform to show the world that they were able to conform to the rules of international society and wished to be accepted into it. So it was that the Soviets brought Russia back onto the international stage.

The Genoa Conference had significance for Soviet foreign affairs for a number of reasons. It showed the world a public face of Soviet diplomacy – of conformity with the rules and expectations of diplomatic conduct – and indicated that the Soviets were on the road to full acceptance as diplomatic partners on the world stage. It also, however, gave rise to the conclusion of a treaty with Weimar Germany, in secret negotiations at the nearby town of Rapallo.

The Treaty of Rapallo, concluded between Soviet Russia and Weimar Germany in 1922, took the world by surprise and effectively brought the Genoa Conference to an end. The two pariah states of post-war Europe entered into a treaty which was mutually beneficial and brought them both out of diplomatic isolation. The agreement allowed for trade and the extension of diplomatic and consular agencies within each other's territory. A secret addendum to the treaty also allowed for the use of Soviet territory by the German army for training. For the Soviets, the Treaty of Rapallo also served to prevent the formation of an anti-Soviet bloc in Europe – something that the Soviets constantly feared, with their memory of intervention in the Russian Civil War by Britain and France.

By 1922, then, the Soviets had made significant ground in international affairs. They had emerged from the Civil War as victors and had opened trade relations with Great Britain that led to the opening of trade with other powers. They had gained acceptance as partners on the international stage and had even managed to conclude a significant treaty with another power. The path towards the normalization of relations with other powers appeared to be proceeding fairly smoothly.

1923–27: challenges and responses

At the end of 1922, the Soviet Union was created and the Bolsheviks had cemented their rule over most of the former Russian Empire. This gave further weight to the Soviet position in foreign affairs, but there were troubles ahead. In 1923 the Soviets faced major challenges and disappointment on the world stage. The first of these came in the form of an ultimatum from the British government. Written by the British Foreign Secretary, Lord Curzon, the note issued on 8 May 1923, which became known as the Curzon Ultimatum, gave the Soviets ten days in which to respond satisfactorily to British demands or face the prospect of a rupture in relations. Gambling on the notion that the Soviets could not afford to lose trade with Great Britain, Curzon raised four points: the issue of the persecution of priests in Russia; the protection of fishing rights; a request for recompense for Soviet repression of British spies; and finally, a demand that the Soviets cease and desist from activity against the British Empire in India and recall their ambassadors from Iran and Afghanistan. It was the last point that was the most important.

Curzon had evidence of Soviet-sponsored activity against British rule in India, which he cited in the note, but which the Soviets refuted, again claiming that the activities of the Comintern were not under the control of the Soviet government and that the spread of Bolshevik ideology was not something that proved Soviet involvement. The Soviets, despite their denials, were involved in the activities of which Curzon accused them. The Comintern, under the direction of the Soviet government, although with agents acting partly on their own initiative, was engaged in an anti-British campaign in India. The pursuit of world revolution had not been abandoned in Soviet foreign policy, even if it had been downplayed, and the Soviets continued to hope that it would still come about. On this occasion the Soviets were able to avoid the threatened rupture in relations, although they did not take the warning as seriously as they perhaps should have. Curzon clearly wanted to break off relations with the Soviet Union, but the ascension of a Labour government under Ramsay Macdonald forestalled this.

Later in 1923, revolution outside of Russia reared its head for the Soviets again, although in somewhat different context. This time, rather than being accused by another power of revolutionary activity, the Soviets believed that Germany was on the brink of revolution. The Communist Party of Germany (KPD) indicated that a German Revolution was imminent and the Comintern became actively involved in plans to carry it through. Its hopes were to be proved misplaced when the German October of 1923 was aborted and collapsed in failure. With this blow, Soviet hopes for the success of revolution in the wider world were severely diminished. Even so, the Soviet Union did not entirely give up on the line of attempting to spread the tide of revolution beyond Russia; but the Soviet government did take stock of the situation in which it found itself.

The Soviets concluded that the chance of revolution outside of Russia had diminished by 1923. In part, they saw the reason for this in what they termed 'the relative stabilization of capitalism' after the upheaval of the First World War and during the years that immediately followed it. But they also blamed the ineffectiveness of member parties of the Comintern to carry through revolution. The German October, they concluded, had failed at least in part because the KPD was not organized along Bolshevik lines and did not follow rigid revolutionary discipline. Thus it was that the Comintern announced the programme of Bolshevization at its 5th Congress in 1924, which was intended to bring the member parties under greater control, such that they could work in a more effective manner towards the revolution. It also asserted an increased Soviet dominance over the Comintern. While the process of Bolshevization was not designed to be an overnight success, it also served to somewhat diminish the scale and intensity of the Comintern's revolutionary activities, particularly in Europe, as the focus shifted towards party building rather than insurrection.

The drop in revolutionary intensity was of use to the Soviets in their relationship with other powers. In February 1924 Soviet diplomacy made great gains, with *de jure* recognition extended by Great Britain, swiftly followed by France and then by all of the major powers with the exception of the United States. While in part this was connected to the more pro-Soviet Labour government in Britain, and to arguments in French circles that France was missing out on an important trading relationship, recognition in 1924 was nonetheless an important breakthrough for Soviet diplomacy. The extension of recognition was not, however, universally popular.

In October 1924, in the run-up to the British general election, the infamous Zinoviev Letter was published in the British newspaper the *Daily Mail*. The letter claimed to have been sent from Grigorii Zinoviev, the leader of the Comintern, to the Communist Party of Great Britain with instructions to organize propaganda and agitation in Britain and within British colonies. While the letter is now acknowledged to have been a forgery produced by the British security services and Russian émigrés, it displayed the continued suspicion, in some British circles, of the Soviet Union and its intentions with respect to the rest of the world. Despite this, such activity was still the aim of the Comintern, although it had taken something of a back seat in the broader picture of Soviet foreign policy, as indicated by the shift of emphasis that the Soviet government indicated in 1924–25. The Zinoviev Letter, while clearly not instrumental in this shift, nonetheless served to indicate that while the Soviet Union may have achieved diplomatic recognition and a degree of acceptance within the international community, there nonetheless were challenges that needed to be addressed, and other powers remained suspicious of Soviet foreign policy intentions.

It was in this context that a significant change was voiced by the Soviet Government – that of building socialism in one country. In late 1924 Joseph Stalin coined the phrase 'socialism in one country'. The notion was that, while the socialist revolution only having been carried through in one country was insufficient, it was nonetheless the situation in which the Soviet Union found itself. The ideological standpoint, further developed by Nikolai Bukharin in 1925, was that the Soviet Union was the heart of the worldwide socialist revolution and that, as a result, the Soviet Union could not be allowed to collapse, lest that should herald the end of all hopes for the furthering of socialist revolution around the world. While the Left Opposition of Lev Trotsky, Grigorii Zinoviev and Lev Kamenev fiercely criticized the line, it nonetheless became the policy of the Soviet government, although its adoption had arguably taken place some time before its announcement. Revolution was no longer the order of the day, with state building and stability becoming the focus of the Soviet Union. This is not to say that the idea of revolution had vanished, but the line became one of taking opportunities for revolution outside the Soviet Union as and when they arose, rather than playing an active role in creating them.

The statement of 'socialism in one country' is often overplayed. It was significant, and it did mark an ideological shift, but it needs to be viewed as a statement made in reaction to the situation in which the Soviet Union found itself in relation to the world. The conclusion had been reached that revolution outside of Russia was increasingly unlikely, at least in the short term, and that continuing to pursue such a line in foreign policy might well prove to be detrimental to the Soviet Union. Stable relations with foreign powers were vitally necessary for the security, stability and economic development of the Soviet Union, and it was recognized how much these were dependent on states not perceiving that the Soviet Union was working to undermine or overthrow them. Thus, despite the criticism that the Left made of the shift, the logic of why 'socialism in one country' became policy is fairly clear. But it is also important to be clear that the policy was not an out and out abandonment of the revolutionary line: it merely served to put it on ice, and was an admission of the situation in which the Soviets found themselves.

That hopes for revolution outside of Russia had not completely faded was demonstrated by events in China during 1925–27 and in Britain in 1926–27. China had figured in Soviet thinking in the early 1920s, with Comintern assistance in the formation of the Communist Party of China (CPC) and Soviet and Comintern involvement in attempts to fuse it with the Nationalist Kuomintang (KMT) under Sun Yat-Sen after 1922. The united front tactics mirrored the line that the Comintern took elsewhere – that it was easier to work from within a nationalist organization in some contexts rather than attempt to establish a parallel organization. With Sun Yat-Sen's death in 1925, however, the position of the Soviets via the CPC became stronger, and then much weaker. Borodin, the Comintern representative actively discussed strategy with Chiang Kai-Shek, the new leader of the Kuomintang, but friendly relations were soon to come to an end. As Chiang Kai-Shek led the Northern Expedition, following his successful coup in March 1926 in an attempt to unify China, he became suspicious of Soviet intentions with respect to China. He decided to dismiss Soviet advisers from China and to conduct a purge of Communists. By April 1927, China had fallen into civil war between the Nationalists and the Communists, who Chiang Kai-Shek believed were heavily backed by the Soviet Union. By 1928 the Communists had been marginalized and the Kuomintang held sway over China.

The British had noticed the Soviet involvement in China and become concerned about the extent to which this might threaten their interests in the Far East and Central Asia. When Chiang Kai-Shek expelled Soviet advisers, and with the outbreak of the Chinese Civil War, the Chinese communicated intelligence to the British that Soviet intentions were far from benign with respect to the wider world. Some quarters of the British government were becoming increasingly of the same opinion, not least because the Soviets had attempted to become involved in the British General Strike of 1926 and were implicated in Communist-led unrest in India. Events came to a head when the British raided ARCOS (the All-Russian Co-operative Society) in May 1927, and relations between the Soviet Union and the British government were broken off. While this appears dramatic, it is necessary to understand precisely what had happened, and what events had triggered the British decision to seek a rupture in Anglo-Soviet relations.

In May 1926 a General Strike had erupted in Great Britain. It causes lay in the refusal of the coal miners to accept a cut in pay as the protection of their earnings in the wake of the Dawes Plan of 1924. The Soviets played no role in bringing about the strike, but they did attempt to assist the British working class and the British Trade Union movement in what they hoped might have been a resurgence of revolutionary potential. The Soviet government offered a substantial sum of money to the Trades Union Congress (TUC) in order to support the strikers. The TUC refused to accept the money for fear that it would be accused of accepting 'red gold', but the National Miner's Union accepted the payment, and a payment in September of that year. While the General Strike did not turn into revolution, and lasted for only nine days, that the Soviets had been seen to make an attempt to interfere in British domestic affairs caused concern in some British circles, and led to a call for a rupture in Anglo-Soviet relations. The rupture was not forthcoming, but Soviet actions and their interpretation had nonetheless caused some harm to Anglo-Soviet relations. At the same time, the failure of the General Strike to lead to revolution brought about analysis of Soviet foreign policy in Moscow, with Trotsky, Zinoviev and Kamenev crystallizing into the Left Opposition. Their criticisms of the retreat from internationalism in Soviet foreign policy were far reaching, particularly Trotsky's, but clashed with Stalin's views. The Left Opposition were to find themselves ostracized, with Zinoviev being removed as head of the Comintern. The line remained that the world was not ripe for revolution.

The calls for a rupture in relations with the Soviet Union did not, however, go away. In early 1927 there was almost persistent talk of a rupture, but a pretext for it was found to be lacking. A basis for a shift in diplomatic relations was to be found, though, in the events of May 1927. Information provided by the Chinese to the British Security Service (SIS) indicated that the Soviets were using their trade delegation and ARCOS as a basis for illegal revolutionary activity and had in their possession an illegally obtained military training manual and the means to produce copies of illegally obtained documents. On 12 May 1927 British police raided the premises of ARCOS, ostensibly in search of stolen documents. They found little of any great significance, and nothing that the British weren't already aware of, but enough to spin a story to the British public and to Parliament that the Soviets were using ARCOS as a base for the conduct of espionage and revolutionary activity throughout the British Empire. The Soviet Union attempted to make the point that the British had broken the rules of diplomacy, particularly in arresting Lev Khinchuk, head of the Soviet Trade Delegation in London, who was protected by diplomatic immunity. The protests fell on deaf ears and relations between Great Britain and the Soviet Union were broken off in the aftermath of the raid.

While the ARCOS raid may have been little more than the creation of a pretext for a rupture in Anglo-Soviet relations, it was of significance. Firstly, it displayed that the British remained concerned about Soviet activity directed towards them, and had found that they had failed to persuade the Soviets that revolutionary activity needed to be stopped if a diplomatic relationship was to continue. That it coincided with British moves against the Comintern in India is striking. Secondly, and more importantly, it triggered a war scare in the Soviet camp, which was quickly followed by a radical change in policy. The rupture of relations with Great Britain, which would last until 1929, caused a fear of war to rise in the Soviet Union. Reading the rupture as heralding a return to capitalist encirclement, echoing the fears of the Civil War period, the Soviets became convinced that Britain, France and China would engage in military action against the Soviet Union. While the immediate fear of war subsided, the notion that war was on the horizon was cemented in the Soviet mind, particularly in Stalin's, and the Soviet Union made a series of changes in response.

1928: the Left Turn

By 1928, Joseph Stalin had cemented his position as *de facto* dictator of the Soviet Union. Once in firm control, he initiated a dramatic reorientation of Soviet policy in both the domestic and foreign fields. In domestic policy he launched the Great Break, with its attendant collectivization of farms and crash industrialization. Reversing NEP, which was seen to be failing to deliver the rates of economic growth that the Soviet Union needed in a climate of a threat of war from the capitalist powers, Stalin introduced a centralized economic plan for the Soviet state. While this by no means removed the need for foreign trade, there was a shift in emphasis, not least because the Soviets had lost a major trading partner in Great Britain and the capitalist world was perceived to be descending into economic crisis. The Soviet economy was reoriented to provide greater efficiency, with collectivization of farming freeing up agricultural labour for the industrial sector and with the launch of centralized planning under the auspices of the First Five Year Plan of the industrial economy. Through the implementation of these policies, the Soviet Union began the process of gearing its economy towards rearmament and, ultimately, the ability to fight a war.

The changes were not only felt in domestic policy. The fear of war, and the rupture with Great Britain, had pushed the Soviets into a diplomatic semi-isolation. The rupture with Britain was viewed by other powers as an indication that the Soviet Union still clung to a revolutionary foreign policy and needed to be dealt with cautiously.

The Comintern's policy also shifted dramatically in 1928, in response to the events of 1927 and the deepening of a global economic crisis. With the expulsion of Soviet advisers from China and Chiang Kai-Shek's rooting out of Communists, the Comintern concluded that alliances with nationalist and social democratic groups could not continue. The Comintern leadership felt betrayed by the Kuomintang, and believed that it was seeing ineffectual, and possibly harmful, alliances in Europe, and elsewhere in Asia. The instruction was that all such links should be severed and that social-democratic tendencies within Comintern member parties should be eradicated. What emerged was a doctrine of 'social fascism' in which liberal social democratic and nationalist parties were damned as the facilitators of the rise of the radical Right, or as allowing the persistence of compromise with colonial powers. At the same time, Comintern tactics shifted to a doctrine of 'class against class', similarly breaking with former alliances and denouncing non-Communist political parties as bourgeois and reformist rather than revolutionary. Gone was any attempt to accommodate or work with other groups in Comintern thinking.

This ultra-Left shift was packaged within the notion of the Third Period. Announced by Nikolai Bukharin at the 6th Comintern Congress in the summer of 1928, although originating as an idea before that point, the argument was that a new stage in the revolutionary continuum was being entered. The First Period had been that of revolutionary upheaval – the Russian Revolution and its immediate aftermath – which was then followed by a period of capitalist stabilization. By the late 1920s, the argument was, a new stage had been reached in which capitalism was entering into its death throes and the world was ripe for revolution. With a deepening economic crisis occurring around the world at the time, the logic of this thinking was apparent, even if the revolutionary hopes may have been misplaced. Even so, the potential for revolution to come from the political Right, as well as the Left, in times of severe economic downturn was made plain.

The drastic move to the Left put the Comintern in a somewhat paradoxical position. On the one hand, the invective and the argument of a new age of revolutionary cataclysm came across as the adoption of a fiercely revolutionary stance which contrasted strongly with the moderation of the mid 1920s. On the other hand, the Comintern and its member parties moved so far to the left and pushed away other groups, so that it effectively moved to the political margins and was largely ineffective in pushing through further efforts towards revolution. While it remains unclear whether this was deliberate, in the climate of the late 1920s it was certainly advantageous to Soviet diplomatic efforts.

The Left Turn was less keenly felt in Soviet diplomacy. While the fear of war remained palpable, and indeed impacted on Soviet diplomacy, there was no sudden change of line. Normalization and stability remained the focus. Efforts were entered into to restore the relationship with Great Britain and to bring the Soviet Union further into line with the international community. Most important, however, was that, in the wake of 1927, Soviet diplomacy became almost entirely concerned with Soviet security.

So it was that the Soviet Union became a signatory to the Kellogg–Briand Pact, which sought to outlaw war as a means for states to settle their differences. The pact had its origins in April 1927 as an agreement between France and the United States, but the Americans were keen to turn it into a multilateral pact. The initial invitations for signatories to the pact excluded the Soviet Union, not least as a result of the rupture with Great Britain and the fact that the United States had still not granted diplomatic recognition to the Soviets. Some in Moscow read the omission of the Soviet Union as an indication that the Kellogg–Briand Pact included the tacit formation of an anti-Soviet bloc. It was the French, though, who extended the invitation to the Soviets to become signatories. Amid his own calls for universal disarmament, Maxim Litvinov, acting as *de facto* Foreign Commissar, signed the Pact on the Soviet Union's behalf. Not only was this a major diplomatic success for the Soviet Union, it also allowed it to publicly affirm a Soviet desire for peace.

Even so, the Soviet Union remained somewhat isolated diplomatically. The situation worsened in 1929 as the relationship established at Rapallo with Weimar Germany began to falter. The Young Plan of 1929 set the final amount of war reparations to be paid by Germany, and the Weimar government accepted the plan in return for the allies' evacuation of the Rhineland by 1930, rather than by 1935 as the Treaty of Versailles had originally stipulated. This heralded a German move towards the West, the relationship with the Soviet Union now being less important than it had been. The Soviets viewed this as yet another attempt to draw Germany in an anti-Soviet bloc.

The relationship with Britain and France remained troubled, but late in 1929 the Soviets were able to restore diplomatic relations with Great Britain, even while issues surrounding propaganda and debt with both Britain and France remaining unresolved. It should be noted, however, that this had much to do with a British desire to exert some degree of pressure on the Soviets to desist from anti-British propaganda – having discovered after the rupture of relations that they had lost an important means of control – rather than necessarily ushering in a new era of normalization of the Soviet Union's diplomatic relations.

Conclusion

Soviet foreign policy developed considerably during the 1920s. Most notable was the development of the two strands of policy – one aimed at the export of revolution to the world the other at the normalization of relations with other powers. What emerges here is a clash between ideals and the imperatives of state management in the situation in which the Soviets found themselves. Just as they had found immediately following the Russian Revolution, there was a need for the Soviet state to be engaged in diplomacy with other powers and, with the shift to NEP, a very real need for a stable basis for foreign trade. Additionally, what can be seen to have developed was a clear notion that the security of the Soviet Union was paramount. While at the beginning of the 1920s that security was predicated on building a relationship to stop an anti-Soviet bloc emerging, by the end of the decade it was apparent that thinking was starting to move towards the pursuit of multilateral arrangements that were aimed at avoiding the outbreak of a war into which the Soviet Union did not wish to be drawn.

At the same time, the commitment to bringing about world revolution did not entirely go away, but became subordinated to the needs of the Soviet state. The Comintern, despite the upset that its activities caused during the 1920s for Soviet diplomatic efforts, played second fiddle to the Soviet pursuit of normalization. While this did not always sit well with observers or with those within the Soviet government, there was a tacit admission that the prospects for world revolution were fading, particularly after 1923. That renewed prospects for revolution seemed to appear towards the end of the 1920s was picked up by the Comintern, but the revolutionary line in foreign policy remained secondary to the primary concern of the period – the security of the Soviet state. The Comintern by no means faded away, but the Soviet Union had other concerns which it addressed by seeking stable relations with foreign powers that were not upset by the activities of the Comintern and by developing the Soviet economy towards greater efficiency and the development of industry.

As the Soviet Union entered the 1930s, new challenges were on the horizon, to which it would need to respond. While some aspects would be new, there was also a great deal of continuity, with security remaining the paramount concern in Soviet foreign policy thinking.

Further reading

Carr, E. H., *The Russian Revolution from Lenin to Stalin, 1917–1929* (London: Macmillan, 1979).

Carr, E. H., *Socialism in One Country* (3 vols, London: Macmillan, 1958–64).

Fischer, L., *The Soviets in World Affairs: A History of the Relations between the Soviet Union and the Rest of the World, 1917–1929* (2nd edn, Princeton: Princeton University Press, 1971).

Gorodetsky, Gabriel (ed.), *Soviet Foreign Policy, 1917–1991: A Retrospective* (London: Cass, 1994).

Gorodetsky, G., *The Precarious Truce: Anglo-Soviet Relations 1924–27* (Cambridge: Cambridge University Press, 1976).

Jacobson, J., *When the Soviet Union Entered World Politics* (Berkley, CA: University of California Press, 1994).

Kennan, G., *Russia and the West under Lenin and Stalin* (London: Hutchinson, 1961).

Kocho-Williams, A., *Russian and Soviet Diplomacy, 1900–1939* (Basingstoke: Palgrave, 2012).

McDermott, Kevin, and Jeremy Agnew, *The Comintern: A History of International Communism from Lenin to Stalin* (Basingstoke: Macmillan, 1996).

Melgrani, P., *Lenin and the Myth of World Revolution* (Atlantic Highlands, NJ: Humanities Press International, 1989).

O'Connor, T., *Diplomacy and Revolution: G. V. Chicherin and Soviet Foreign Affairs, 1918–1930* (Ames: Iowa State University Press, 1988).

Rees, T., and Thorpe, A., *International Communism and the Communist International 1919–1943* (Manchester: Manchester University Press, 1998).

Ulam, A., *Expansion and Coexistence: Soviet Foreign Policy, 1917–1973* (New York: Holt, Rinehart and Winston, 1974).

Uldricks, T., *Diplomacy and Ideology* (London: Sage, 1979).

Volkogonov, D., *The Rise and Fall of the Soviet Empire* (London: HarperCollins, 1998).

Wesson, R. G., *Soviet Foreign Policy in Perspective* (Homewood, IL: Dorsey Press, 1969).

White, S., *Origins of Détente* (Cambridge: Cambridge University Press, 1985).

4 Soviet foreign policy under Stalin in the 1930s

During the 1930s the Soviet Union continued to place security at the centre of its foreign policy. The sense of an impending war continued to pervade Soviet thinking, with the economy becoming increasingly geared towards rearmament, and persistent attempts to avoid the Soviet Union's being drawn into a war. The Soviet Union faced challenges from both East and West during the 1930s, but it was after the rise of Nazi Germany in 1933 that the Soviets showed their full commitment to staying out of a war in Europe for as long as they possibly could. They would ultimately achieve the security they desired through the conclusion of a non-aggression pact with Nazi Germany in August 1939.

Despite the fact that it was Soviet security that was the main priority, there remains controversy as to how the Soviets hoped to achieve it. Much has been written in the discussion as to what were the true aims of foreign policy during the 1930s. The debate not only takes into account the seeming contradictions of Stalinist foreign policy but also raises questions as to who was in control of foreign policy at the time. It breaks down into several major camps, largely split between those who argue that the Soviet Union was committed to collective security as a means to avoid war, those who are of the opinion that the Soviets desired rapprochement with Germany, and those who see Soviet policy in the 1930s not so much as an adherence to a grand design but as the product of in-fighting and opportunism.

Even so, much of this controversy remains focused on Soviet policy towards European powers, looks backwards from the Nazi–Soviet Pact of 1939, and does not always take into account the Soviet Union as a global power. In order to understand Soviet foreign policy during the 1930s it is necessary to look at the multiple aspects of the Soviet position in world affairs and make an assessment of how policy developed and what the challenges were that the Soviet Union faced during the decade.

There was a change in personnel in Soviet diplomacy, and a marked shift in policy, during the 1930s. In July 1930 Maxim Litvinov was appointed Foreign Commissar. Although he had effectively held the post since 1928, while his predecessor, Georgii Chicherin, was ill, his appointment was significant for the direction of foreign policy. Litvinov was a known anglophile and had a British wife, and had been Deputy Commissar for the West during the 1920s. This led him to a stance from which he viewed Soviet foreign policy concerns as being chiefly orientated towards relations with European powers. He was also to become the formulator, and champion, of the Soviet Union's drive for collective security after 1933.

Collective security was a policy that had at its heart the aim of preventing a war breaking out in Europe, into which the Soviet Union would inevitably be drawn. The mechanism was to be a series of bilateral and multilateral treaties which would prevent war from breaking out. The state that this system was intended to constrain was Nazi Germany, Litvinov and other Soviet officials being well aware of Hitler's expansionist intentions to seek *Lebensraum* (living space) within the Soviet Union, and alarmed by Hugenberg's proposals for German expansion, made at the World Economic Conference in London in June 1933. Collective security became the official Soviet foreign policy line after 1933 and held until August 1939, even though it was to prove ultimately unsuccessful. The reasons for its adoption and for its failure need to be unpicked in the light of the 1930s and the challenges that the Soviet Union faced in maintaining security. What should be considered is where the threats to the Soviet Union lay and how Soviet policy evolved in their light.

The German threat

In 1933 the Soviet Union watched with trepidation as Hitler took power in Germany. Stalin and other members of the Soviet government were under no illusions as to the enmity that Hitler expressed towards the Soviet Union and were well aware of the territorial designs that had been outlined in *Mein Kampf*. Nazi Germany was a serious threat to the Soviet Union, but also to peace in Europe.

One of the first causes of concern for the Soviets was the statement made at the World Economic Conference in London by Alfred Hugenberg, the Economics Minister of the Third Reich. In his statement he made clear the notion that Nazi Germany would seek expansion towards the east in pursuit of *Lebensraum*, and had its sights set on Soviet territory. This greatly concerned the Soviets, but they were further worried by the fact that the other powers did not indicate that they necessarily saw this as problematic. While the Soviets may well have attached more significance to the statement than did other powers, and indeed more than they should have done, the fear of potential German expansion eastwards was nonetheless palpable for the Soviets. However, the Soviets feared not only a loss of territory; they were also concerned that German actions would lead to a war in Europe which the Soviets could not avoid being drawn into. At a time when the Soviet economy and society needed peace in order to develop, war was not something that the Soviets wished to countenance, even if they had accepted that it was on the horizon.

To counter German expansion and the threat of war in Europe, the Soviet Union pursued a policy of collective security. Espoused by Foreign Commissar Maxim Litvinov, though by no means an original idea, the policy rested on the notion that the creation of a system of bilateral and multilateral treaties would make Germany unable to take action in Europe that would lead to war. Hence the Soviet Union's security would be guaranteed. So it was that, after the rise of Hitler, the Soviets embarked upon a diplomatic campaign to bring them into closer alignment with other powers.

One of the first marked steps of collective security was Soviet membership of the League of Nations. Joining in September 1934 (notably after both Japan and Germany had left), the Soviets engaged in the League as a part of the campaign towards collective security, even to the extent that Litvinov was criticized for spending too much time in Geneva. The problem with Soviet membership of the League of Nations, however, was that the League proved to be quite ineffective in dealing with the crises of the 1930s – notably following the Japanese invasion of Manchuria in 1931 (discussed below) and the Italian invasion of Abyssinia in 1935. The League was toothless; its membership did not include the United States, and with the departure of both Japan and Germany it was in a weak position. Even so, the Soviets saw the League as important in relation to the push for collective security, not least because the spirit of the League matched Litvinov's vision of a means to constrain Nazi Germany, even if he retained a degree of scepticism as to whether it would be effective.

Soviet entry into the League of Nations allowed the Soviets a platform from which they could proclaim their commitment to peace and attempt to develop a system of collective security. The problem that the Soviets encountered, though, lay not only in the weakness of the League but also in finding partners willing to enter into agreements with them. Despite the Soviet emergence from isolation, other powers remained suspicious of Soviet intentions and capabilities, or were unwilling to commit to an agreement that could draw them into a war. The two most significant powers in Soviet efforts were Great Britain and France, with whom the Soviets sought to conclude a triangular security relationship against Germany, but both of whom were wary of the Soviets and seemed content to appease Hitler during the middle and late 1930s.

This is not to say that Soviet efforts towards collective security came to nought. In 1934 and 1935, France and the Soviet Union grew closer to one another as a result of a shared fear of Nazi Germany. After the death of the French Foreign Minister Barthou almost saw Pierre Laval conclude a Franco-German rapprochement, Litvinov was able to persuade Laval into concluding a mutual assistance treaty with the Soviets in April 1935. The treaty declared that assistance would be provided in the event of an unprovoked attack by a European state, but was to prove much less effective than the 1893 Franco-Russian alliance, which had contained specific details about military assistance. The treaty was problematic in other respects, the French insisting that their duty to assist the Soviet Union would be conditional on any assault being recognized as an act of aggression by the League of Nations; contained no promise of support to the Soviet Union in the event of an attack from Japan; and took the divided French government over a year to ratify. There was also an unresolved issue that stemmed from the fact that Germany and the Soviet Union did not have a common border, so that any Soviet assistance to France would be contingent on Poland or Romania allowing Soviet troops to cross their territory. At most, the treaty represented a basis for a future alliance between the Soviet Union and France.

Shortly after concluding the Franco-Soviet treaty, the Soviets concluded a similar agreement with Czechoslovakia. On 16 May 1935 a mutual assistance treaty was drawn up which promised Soviet support to the Czechs in the event of an attack from another power. However, the devil lay in the detail that the Soviets were obliged to support Czechoslovakia only if the French honoured their obligations under their own pact with the Czechs, and again there was the issue of the lack of a common border between the Soviet Union and Czechoslovakia. While neither pact would prove effective in preventing German expansion, they nonetheless served to affirm the Soviets' drive towards collective security and their position as its champions.

With the turn towards a policy of collective security, the Comintern line was also changed. What emerged was an aspect of, or partner policy to, collective security in the form of the United Front. In light of the Soviet fear of war and the decision to seek security in the 1930s through diplomacy, the Comintern could not be allowed to upset Soviet efforts to maintain peace. Not only did the ultra-left policies of the Third Period need to be jettisoned, but a new, conciliatory policy line was to be adopted. Accordingly, the United Front was announced by Georgi Dmitrov, leader of the Comintern, at the 7th Comintern Congress in July 1935. The line was the opposition of Fascism through the adoption of Popular Fronts which drew together all anti-Fascist elements. Gone was the rhetoric of social Fascism and class against class, to be replaced by a call for unity in the face of a common enemy. In part this was conceived as an attempt to prevent other powers from supporting the Fascist powers – Germany, Italy and, as far as the Soviets were concerned, Japan – against the Soviet Union, and stemmed from the *de facto* situation that had emerged in France during 1934, when French Socialists and Communists had agreed to cooperate in opposing Fascism. The Comintern's new line did serve to quell national struggles to some extent and to appease other powers as the intensity of its revolutionary line eased, but there were problems in overcoming the wounds that had been caused by the prior damning as social fascists of those with whom the Communists now sought to ally. Even so, the policy can be seen as an aspect of collective security that sought to limit the danger of war in Europe and the spread of Nazi Germany.

With the shifts in Soviet policy clearly articulated, and with some ground gained in its pursuit, the Soviets were forced to deal with challenges to their alliances and to entertain alternatives to the seeking of an alliance against Hitler. The first major issue that the Soviets had to contend with was the German militarization of the Rhineland in March 1936. The Locarno Treaty of 1925 had secured the territory as a demilitarized buffer between France and Germany, and allied forces had departed in 1930, after agreement with the Weimar government. When Hitler sent troops into the Rhineland, the reaction of some in the French government was to call for a military response to force the Germans to withdraw. Britain, however, persuaded France that such a course of action was not in its best interests, as the Rhineland was German territory and, as such, military action would be construed as an act of war and would violate the principles of self-determination enshrined in the Versailles Treaty. Accordingly, no action was taken against Nazi Germany's move, and France and Britain began the process of appeasing Hitler.

From the Soviet point of view, Nazi Germany's move into the Rhineland, and British and French inaction in relation to it, was problematic for collective security. Not only did it highlight that international treaties and pacts could not necessarily be depended on as a means to preserve peace and contain German expansion, it also served to demonstrate Hitler's disregard for the Franco-Soviet treaty of 1935. Further, when Germany followed militarization with the construction of fortifications along the Siegfried Line, a German defensive line of tank traps and bunkers running between the Netherlands and Switzerland. France was left in a similar position to the Soviet Union, should assistance need to be rendered to Czechoslovakia or to the Soviet Union, because it would encounter great difficulty in advancing into German territory. Thus, in militarizing the Rhineland in early 1936 Nazi Germany greatly shook Soviet confidence in collective security, causing the Soviets to become alarmed by the Franco-British appeasement of Hitler and to conclude that, as Hitler had achieved his stated aims in the West, he would now move eastwards.

The Soviet Union and the Spanish Civil War, 1936–38

A further challenge arose for the Soviets in July 1936, with the outbreak of the Spanish Civil War. Following several weeks of sporadic troubles, the Fascist General Francisco Franco launched a military coup against the Spanish Republic. Spain collapsed into civil war as the Republic, itself a popular front dominated by socialists, resisted the nationalist rebellion of Fascists and conservatives. Britain and France immediately called for a policy of non-intervention from outside powers, and a Non-Intervention Committee (NIC) was established in London. Nazi Germany, Fascist Italy and the Soviet Union all agreed to abide by the agreement not to intervene in the conflict, but they promptly went back on their word. Mussolini extended major military aid to Franco, while Hitler provided a lesser level of support. Stalin's move to support the Spanish Republic was somewhat more cautious, more secretive and had a slightly sinister edge to it.

In making their decision to intervene the Soviets found themselves on the horns of a dilemma. On the one hand, the Spanish Civil War was a conflict against Fascism that the Soviets had sworn to uphold, and if Fascism prevailed in a swift victory in Spain, then it might spread to the rest of Europe and Hitler might well turn eastwards towards the Soviet Union sooner, rather than later. On the other hand, the Soviets had agreed with the NIC not to intervene in the conflict, and any betrayal of that trust would cause harm to the Soviet drive for collective security and any potential alliance with Britain and France. Additionally, the Soviets feared that a decisive victory for communism in Spain would push Britain and France into an anti-Soviet alliance with Germany.

In September 1936 the Soviets decided on a limited and secret intervention in Spain. This allowed them to fight Fascism and keep Germany busy in Spain, while at the same time being relatively invisible to Britain and France and not agitating for a communist revolution. The limited secret intervention, known as Operation X, was coupled to the opening of a Soviet Embassy in Madrid. The intervention was directed by the NKVD (People's Commissariat of Internal Affairs), but channelled through the Comintern. The first step was assistance to the Spanish Republic in defending Madrid. Soviet military advisers were sent, but no actual Soviet troops, although arms were supplied. Instead, the Comintern directed large numbers of foreign volunteer combatants in the form of the International Brigades between 1936 and 1938. In doing so, the Soviet Union avoided direct confrontation with another power and to some extent was able to publicly preserve the notion that it had not intervened in the conflict and gone against the agreement with the NIC.

The Soviet involvement in Spain shifted, however, in 1937. Soviet military support to Spain largely ceased, even if some degree of economic aid continued and the International Brigades continued to fight on the side of the Republic. The two sides in the Civil War had become somewhat deadlocked in their conflict; the chance of a Republican victory still remained in 1937, but it had become clear that this could only be achieved if the Soviets made a decisive move to render sufficient military assistance to the Republican effort. The Soviets were unwilling, and unable, to make such a move in 1937. There was a fear of sparking war with the Fascist powers of Europe, challenges in moving troops and armaments into Spain, and introversion caused by the purges within the Soviet Union. Further, the Soviets damaged the Republic's efforts during the summer of 1937, when Stalin ordered that the Communists should turn on Trotskyite and Anarchist elements, thus almost causing a civil war within a civil war.

By 1938, the Soviets had all but abandoned the Spanish Republic. The Spanish gold reserves, deposited in Moscow during 1937, were depleted and the flow of arms dried up. Solidarity, demonstrated earlier in the conflict in public parades and newspaper articles, ceased during 1938. By the end of the year, the International Brigades were ordered to leave Spain and were disbanded. The Soviets, it seemed, had given up on Spain and abandoned the Republic to Franco's eventual victory in 1939. It is apparent that the Soviets disengaged from the Spanish Civil War because they were unprepared to commit the necessary military force to assist the Republic in its fight against Fascism. The reasons lay partly in the Soviet drive for collective security and its failure to have achieved much in terms of viable commitments from other powers. The Soviets did not intend to invite war upon themselves via support for Spain. At the same time, the Soviets became focused on the rooting out of internal enemies as Stalin's purges unfolded. Further, as the Spanish Civil War unfolded, the Soviets also became involved in supporting China against Japan and fighting a war on their own borders in the Far East. They were also becoming increasingly worried about the prospects for Soviet security, and what appeared to be the ever-increasing proximity of war.

The Kandelaki Affair

With the Soviets' realization that there was little enthusiasm for collective security from other powers, they began to examine their options for conserving their own security. While the Soviets had pursued collective security, they had also been aware of other avenues that might be followed, particularly in terms of finding a means of achieving Soviet security through rapprochement with Nazi Germany. Within the Soviet government, Vyacheslav Molotov was the chief proponent of accommodation with Germany, arguing that the Soviet Union should not be constrained in its foreign policy action by agreements with other powers. Rapprochement with Germany, however, did not gain traction until the conclusion of the Nazi–Soviet Pact in August 1939, but the period between 1935 and 1937 displayed a Soviet attempt to move towards a closer relationship with Germany.

The manifestation of this surrounds German–Soviet trade discussions and whether there was any hope in the Soviet camp that they could be turned into a political arrangement. The key figure here was David Kandelaki, the head of the Soviet Trade Delegation in Germany, and much of the discussion turns around several meetings that he had with Max Schact, the German Economics Minister. Kandelaki and Schacht met in late 1935 and on at least two occasions in 1936 and 1937. The first meeting took place in December 1935, and took the form of a trade negotiation which signalled to the Soviets that some form of accommodation with Germany might yet be possible. A more significant meeting took place on 24 December 1936, and although Schacht's report attested that he had made it plain that further trade could only be conditional on Soviet guarantees concerning agitation outside of the Soviet Union, the report from the Soviet Ambassador, Iakov Surits, to Moscow indicated that Schacht was attempting to ascertain whether Moscow was open to a potential political discussion. Chief among German concerns, it seemed, was Soviet withdrawal from Spain, abandoning support for the French Popular Front government and an end to a policy that aimed to encircle Germany.

The Soviets gave a clear indication that they were happy for talks between Kandelaki and Schacht to continue, with Litvinov even giving instructions as to how Kandelaki was to proceed. It is apparent that Moscow saw an opportunity to change the relationship with Germany, even if Litvinov remained unhappy about the abandonment of collective security that this might entail. Kandelaki accordingly met with Schacht once more, at the end of January 1937. Schacht indicated that there could be further discussions, but that these could only be conducted via a meeting between the German Foreign Minister, Konstantin von Neurath and the Soviet Ambassador to Germany, Iakov Surits. Further talks did not take place, Hitler refusing to countenance the idea of political arrangement with the Soviet Union. The opportunity for normalization of relations between the Soviet Union and Germany had passed, but it is significant that the Soviets had made an effort to achieve it. The upshot was that Soviet–German relations entered a period of hiatus, and the individuals involved in attempting to improve them largely disappeared from the political scene.

Stalin's purges and foreign policy

With tension in Europe, Soviet involvement in Spain, and both collective security and rapprochement with Germany faltering, the internal politics of the Soviet Union dealt a harsh blow to the realization of foreign policy objectives. The issue here was Stalin's purges and their impact on Soviet foreign policy.

Following the assassination of Sergei Kirov in 1934, the Soviet Union entered an era of state-driven terror. Traitors, spies and counter-revolutionaries were rigorously sought out, arrested and sentenced for their crimes, real and imaginary. In 1936 the scale of the repression increased, with foreign-linked conspiracies becoming a prominent theme in accusations levelled against individuals. Huge numbers became victims of the purges that raged between 1936 and 1938, while a series of show trials of prominent individuals were acted out. The world viewed the purges with some distaste, but they also created a significant handicap in the conduct of Soviet foreign policy. While this may have been symptomatic of the purges rather than the design, it nonetheless bears consideration.

The main area in which this was the case was the purge of the Soviet Diplomatic Corps and of the Red Army. Soviet diplomats were recalled, some of them being arrested and shot following accusations of espionage and working with Fascist elements against the Soviet Union. During the course of the purges approximately half of the senior-level officials and ambassadors were removed from their positions. The purge of the Diplomatic Corps left situations vacant in a number of capital cities, exposing not only the extent of the purges within this group, but also making inter-state negotiations problematic. Furthering this problem, a new wave of officials entered the Narkomindel who lacked experience and were unable to function independently. Foreign diplomats and politicians remarked that the Soviet Diplomatic Corps had been seriously damaged, to the extent that it was almost impossible to conduct normal relations with the Soviet Union without engaging with high-level officials in Moscow. Clearly, at a time of global tension, and when Soviet diplomatic efforts were foundering, this was counter-productive.

Perhaps more problematic for the Soviets, though, was the purge conducted in the Red Army during 1937. Amid accusations of having rendered assistance to Germany, 70 per cent of the Officer Corps were executed, including senior officers, amongst them the central figure of Marshal Tukhashevky. The purge of the Red Army's officers was clearly deleterious to the efficacy of the Soviet armed forces, not least because it removed experienced commanders and damaged morale and discipline. That this was the case was not lost on other powers, notably Great Britain, who questioned Soviet military capabilities when considering whether to enter into an alliance with the Soviets against Germany. The British concluded that the Soviets had put themselves into a position where they were ill prepared for war. This became a particular issue when Germany started to make expansionist moves in 1938.

Germany moves East: Austria, Czechoslovakia, the Munich Agreement and the genesis of the Nazi–Soviet Pact

In March 1938 Germany annexed Austria. Britain and France, despite Austrian appeals for help, stood by and allowed the *Anschluss* to take place, concluding that only the use of force could have dissuaded Hitler. From the Soviet point of view, the *Anschluss* demonstrated German expansionist aims and pushed Germany further towards Eastern Europe and the Soviet Union. While this was concerning for Moscow, not least because it extended German influence, a greater challenger reared its head in September 1938 when Germany made a move into Czechoslovakia, with the intention of annexing the Sudetenland.

The upshot of the move was the Munich Conference, which involved Britain, France and Germany, with the Italians acting as intermediary. The Soviets were not invited to Munich, despite their treaty with the Czechs, and they took this as a snub. The outcome of the Conference was that Britain and France pressured Czechoslovakia into ceding the territory to Germany, while Germany made assurances not to expand further. Neville Chamberlain, the British Prime Minister, believed that he had secured a promise from Hitler that would guarantee peace in Europe, but the view from Moscow was somewhat different.

The Soviets emerged from the aftermath of Munich as the only power that had not been held to an agreement with respect to Czechoslovakia. As France had failed to support the Czechs, the Soviets had been under no obligation to do so. Even so, it is apparent that the Soviet Union would have struggled to come to Czechoslovakia's aid, not least because of questionable Soviet military preparedness, but more importantly because such assistance would have required Soviet forces to cross Poland or Romania, and neither power seemed likely to allow that to happen. The Soviets, however, were keen to point out that they had not violated any agreement, even if it was becoming increasingly apparent that Soviet desires to achieve a system of collective security were unlikely to be unrealized.

The Soviet Union, after the Munich Conference, became concerned that the strategy adopted by Britain and France indicated their intention to appease Hitler to the extent that he would move eastwards, towards Soviet territory. It also indicated to them that Britain and France were not committed to the construction of a tripartite alliance against Germany that included the Soviet Union as a partner. Even so, September 1938 did not mark the end of Soviet efforts to convince the British and French to enter into such an alliance. While Munich dealt a severe blow to Soviet foreign policy, it most certainly did not mark an end to collective security as an aim, even if hopes of achieving it were now dim.

Soviet diplomacy immediately after Munich remained focused on the pursuit of a tripartite alliance with Britain and France. One reason for this was that a rapprochement with Germany seemed extremely unlikely in the autumn of 1938, and so an alliance against Nazi Germany presented itself as the only way that the Soviets might guarantee their security. Negotiations between the Soviets and the Anglo-French camp continued, but to little avail.

The situation for the Soviets became worse when Hitler broke the agreement made at Munich and moved to annexe the remainder of Czechoslovakia in March 1939. Once again, Britain and France failed to act, preferring to appease Hitler. Stalin made a speech on 10 March in which he highlighted the notion that an imperialist war in Europe had already begun, but Britain and France refused to hold to their agreements, or to be much interested in the prevention of war. To some extent, Stalin was making the final plea to the British and French to enter into an alliance with the Soviets, with the tacit threat that if they did not, then the Soviet Union might turn towards agreement with Germany.

The problem for Stalin was that in March 1939 there was no apparent potential for a German–Soviet agreement, and so his threat was somewhat empty. Even so, the British and French did re-examine their assessment of the suitability of the Soviet Union as an ally. Negotiations between Maxim Litvinov and the British Ambassador to Moscow opened in mid-April 1939 and a Soviet offer for a formal Soviet–British–French pact was made on 16 April. However, the lack of Soviet preparedness for war continued to present a stumbling block, as did Soviet calls for reciprocity in any agreement with respect to military aid and Soviet desires for some adjustment of territorial guarantees that the British and French had made with other powers. There was also some fear that the Soviets would seize territory in Eastern Europe. Britain and France concluded that they were not keen to enter into a tripartite alliance with the Soviets, not least because any such agreement in the spring of 1939 might have precipitated war with Germany. The Soviet drive for collective security appeared to have failed.

The policy he had espoused having proved to be unworkable, Foreign Commissar Maxim Litvinov was dismissed, being replaced by Vyacheslav Molotov on 3 May 1939. While there was a clear difference between the two men in terms of their foreign policy outlook, the change did not herald an immediate change in Soviet foreign policy. Rather, it signalled that the Soviets were open to offers, whether they came from Nazi Germany of from the Anglo-French bloc. The rather stark signal prompted some movement from the British, who responded on 8 May to the Soviet proposal of 16 April. While this did not lead to agreement, it kept the door open for further negotiations. Even so, it was too little too late.

However, the British and French moved slowly towards constructing such an alliance, while again signalling to the Soviets that they were not particularly committed to achieving it. In June, France and Britain made their final move and agreed to send a delegation to Moscow for talks. While Anthony Eden, an experienced diplomat, offered to lead the delegation, Chamberlain instead sent a more junior Foreign Office official, William Strang. The Soviets interpreted this as a further indication of the British lack of enthusiasm for an alliance, and the discussions continued through July without achieving anything concrete. When the Soviets made the proposal that military talks should be opened, the British and French sent a further delegation, but it did not arrive until 10 August, after delays and a sea journey, and was headed by officials who were not empowered to conclude an agreement with the Soviets. While the Anglo-French delegation negotiated over the finer points of a potential alliance and the talks stalled, the Soviets were receiving signals from Germany that an agreement might be entered into.

The Germans made their move towards the Soviets on 11 August, the day after the Anglo-French delegation began talks about a military alliance. Joachim von Ribbentrop, the German Foreign Minister, informed Georgii Astakhov, the Soviet Deputy Ambassador in Berlin, that there was no reason why Germany and the Soviet Union could not come to an agreement to respect each other's interests. The Soviets signalled that they were open to discussing formalizing such an arrangement, and on 15 August Ribbentrop made plain his desire to visit Moscow with a view to concluding an agreement. The Soviets at this point asked if the Germans were open to a non-aggression pact and a confirmation that the Baltic States lay in the Soviet sphere of interest. The Germans answered that they were prepared to make such an offer, and Ribbentrop went to Moscow to conclude a pact between the two powers. He was in Moscow for twenty-four hours, during which time the Nazi–Soviet Pact was concluded, signed by Molotov and Ribbentrop, and a secret protocol detailing territorial rearrangement agreed. This final move was to take place on 23 August 1939, just a week before Hitler planned to make a move on Poland.

The Nazi–Soviet Pact and its implications

On 23 August 1939 the Soviet Foreign Commissar, Vyacheslav Molotov, and German Foreign Minister, Joachim von Ribbentrop, signed a pact of non-aggression. The agreement was to last for ten years, but neither side realistically believed that it would run its full course. It was a fairly brief document and neither side pledged military cooperation, although a basis for mutual economic arrangements was indicated in it. Importantly for the Soviet Union, the Pact guaranteed security against being drawn into a war that was now about to erupt. It also contained a Secret Additional Protocol which detailed the territorial rearrangement based around German and Soviet spheres of interest in Eastern Europe and the Baltic that would come into effect in the event of the outbreak of war. This gave the Soviets an extension of their borders to the west, providing a buffer against Germany and thus granting them further security, but it was not without its problems.

Much has been made of the Nazi–Soviet Pact and the fact that two powers that were vehemently ideologically opposed to one another entered into an agreement on the eve of the Second World War. What is important to understand is that, with the failure to reach agreement on an alliance with Britain and France, the Soviets had no real alternative to such an agreement, other than to stand alone against the threat of German military advances to the east. In a speech to the Supreme Soviet on 31 August 1939 Molotov explained the Pact as fitting with the Soviet Union's security policy, and indeed pointed out that it was not necessarily an arrangement that ran counter to the Soviet pursuit of collective security. While the point rang true that guaranteeing security was congruent with the broader scheme of Soviet policy, some were less than convinced that a Soviet agreement with Nazi Germany was not, in fact, a radical *volte face*.

Other powers reacted with horror to the Nazi–Soviet Pact, the British in particular demonstrating that they were concerned about what it meant. The Pact meant that Hitler would not be drawn into a two-front war, should he make further advances in Europe, and the Soviet Union would sit on the side lines. More problematic was the Secret Protocol, of which the British, surprisingly, were aware, and the threat that it posed to Eastern European states to which Britain had made guarantees, notably Poland.

Soviet actions reinforced the notion in some quarters that the Soviet Union could not be trusted, was inherently expansionist in intent and without scruples as to the powers it was prepared to deal with. The price, it would seem, for achieving security on the eve of war was that the Soviet Union was returned to the status of a pariah.

Japan, China and the Far East

While the Soviets faced a serious challenge to their security in Europe, they also had to contend with the threat posed by an expansionist Japan. After Chiang Kai-Shek had expelled Soviet advisers from China in 1927, the Soviets had severed relations with the Kuomintang government. The relationship had worsened after the Kuomintang authorities in Manchuria launched raids on Soviet consulates along the Chinese Eastern Railway in May 1929, and then seized the railway in July. The Soviet reaction was to dispatch the Red Army to deal with the problem, and in November 1929 Manchurian forces were defeated and forced to withdraw. Manchuria was then placed under joint Soviet and Chinese administration in December 1929, heralding an improved relationship between the Soviets and the Kuomintang, although the Soviets were not able to turn this into a full restoration of the diplomatic relationship with China. Even so, the Soviets were content that the Kuomintang regime was a sufficient block to Japanese expansion, and did not attempt to push further into Manchuria.

When Japan invaded Manchuria in 1931 and established the state of Manchukuo, the Soviets were rightly concerned about security and Japanese intentions. The Manchurian Crisis was handled ineffectively by the League of Nations, Japan refusing to respond to calls to leave Manchuria and ultimately leaving the League. Conceding that they had lost any control they had held in Manchuria, the Soviets' response was to answer firmly, but not aggressively, to the Japanese threat to its far eastern territory and to its interests in Outer Mongolia. The Soviet Far Eastern Army was reinforced, and a declaration published in *Izvestiya* on 4 March 1932 stated that the Soviets had done all in their power to sustain relations with Japan, despite the violation of Soviet interests in Manchuria, and warned that anti-Soviet statements would not tolerated. It also indicated to the Japanese that the Soviets were aware of Japanese plans to launch an assault on the Soviet Union.

While this left the Soviets without the restoration of their interests in Manchuria, it also highlighted that they were keen to avoid conflict with Japan. Subsequent events displayed that the Soviets were even prepared to go so far as appeasing Japan. When the Japanese violated Soviet rights on the Chinese Eastern Railway, the Soviets chose not to react, as they realized that they were powerless to achieve anything in Manchuria. Instead, some time after, they offered a non-aggression pact to Japan in order to attempt to defuse the potential for a Japanese encroachment on Soviet interests in Outer Mongolia or into the Soviet Union in the east. The Japanese refused this offer in December 1932, on the grounds that they and the Soviet Union still had unresolved disputes. Even so, the Soviets had indicated that Japan could go no further without becoming embroiled in military conflict with the Soviets.

The Soviets were not convinced that they had decisively stopped Japanese expansion towards their territory, and a renewed overture to China was made in late 1932 in order to ensure that China and Japan would not become allies. Relations between the Kuomintang government and the Soviet Union were restored, despite the fact that the Soviets were actively assisting the rebel Communist Chinese government under Mao Zedong, which had been established in Kiangsi province in southern China and which the Kuomintang was seeking to depose. The Chinese, however, had been further convinced of Japanese expansionist desires with the attack on Shanghai in 1932, and were prepared to establish a link with the Soviets on the basis of common enmity towards Japan.

China was not the only power that forged a diplomatic relationship with the Soviet Union on the basis of having a common enemy in Japan. The United States, which was enjoying increased trade with the Soviet Union, even though it had failed to extend recognition to the Soviets since the Russian Revolution, decided to recognize the Soviet Union in late 1933. Noting American opposition to Japan, and Secretary of State John Stimson's declaration that the Japanese invasion of Manchuria violated the Nine Power Agreement, both Litvinov and the Soviet press indicated that a relationship between the United States and the Soviet Union would make efforts to preserve peace in the Far East more manageable. While not entirely envisaging it as part of the plan of collective security, Litvinov was clearly thinking along these sorts of lines as a means to block the Japanese threat. So it was that in November 1933 Soviet–American relations had their beginning, ending a state of non-recognition that had persisted since the Russian Revolution. By the end of 1933 the Soviets had effectively emerged from diplomatic isolation.

Even so, the Japanese challenge to the Soviets did not go away, even if Great Britain had concluded that the Soviet Union was perfectly able to contain Japanese expansionism. In 1935 the Soviet leadership showed that they were disquieted by the situation in the Far East. Despite the accommodation with the United States, the relationship had failed to bring about a means to prevent Japanese encroachment into northern China. Worse still, from the Soviet point of view, was that the Kuomintang government had reached an agreement with the Japanese after the events of 1931–32 and moved to focus militarily against Mao Zedong's Communist government in southern China. In 1934 the Communists were forced out, and embarked on the infamous 'Long March' north which ended with the formation of a Communist state in north-western China. Clearly, the Soviets were troubled by Kuomintang action against the Chinese Communists, but so too were they concerned that Japanese militarism, if left unchecked, might turn to focus on the Soviet Union and its interests.

The Soviet reaction was to try to appease Japan, while at the same time precipitating war between Japan and China. In 1935 the Soviet Union sold the Chinese Eastern Railway to Japan, while at the same time encouraging the formation of a united front between Chinese Communists and the Kuomintang to make a joint stand against Japan. While the relationship was not entirely stable, Chiang Kai-Shek striving to unify China through 1936 and block the Communists, the alliance was in keeping with the Comintern's adoption of the United Front at the 7th Comintern Congress in 1935.

The timing of the creation of a Chinese United Front against Japan coincided with Japanese moves into Inner Mongolia, which led to small-scale skirmishes with Soviet troops on the border with Outer Mongolia later in the year. Pledging Soviet assistance to Outer Mongolia in the event of a Japanese attack, the Soviets concluded a mutual assistance treaty with Outer Mongolia in March 1936. The treaty reaffirmed Chinese control over the territory, and served as a display of Soviet confidence in their ability to deal with Japan that impressed Western powers. In November 1936 Japan and Nazi Germany concluded the Anti-Comintern Pact, which gave rise to further Soviet fears about security in the Far East. The prospect of war in the Far East was clear to the Soviets, but they were hopeful that it would be a war on Chinese territory rather than on their own. The Soviets would see their hopes become reality in the following year.

By 1937 Sino-Japanese relations had deteriorated severely, and on 7 July 1937 Japan launched an assault on China. The Japanese struck quickly and decisively, but then became embroiled in a protracted conflict with China. The Soviets were pleased that this was the case, as Japanese military involvement in China meant that the threat to the Soviet Union's own territory was greatly reduce. Accordingly, the Soviets took steps to ensure that China could continue to fight Japan. The Chinese Communists were instructed to strengthen their relationship with the Kuomintang, even allowing themselves to be subordinated to Chiang Kai-Shek's regime. More significantly, in August 1937 the Soviets concluded a treaty of friendship with the Kuomintang government and started to send arms and military advisers and to extend credit to China, all of which ensured that the conflict would continue.

Although the Soviets had succeeded in pitching Japan against China and in prolonging the conflict, there were still Soviet clashes with Japanese forces. In June 1937 Soviet troops had occupied Kanchazu Island in the Amur River, encroaching on Japanese territory. The Soviets were shelled by artillery and forced to withdraw. There were further clashes on the Japanese–Soviet border in the summers of 1938 and 1939. In July 1938 Manchurian forces attempted an invasion of the Soviet Union, only to be defeated at the Battle of Lake Khasan. Despite the defeat, the Japanese made a further attempt in May of the following year, and were defeated decisively by Soviet and Mongolian forces at Khalkin Gol in August. The defeat of the Japanese in this undeclared border war kept Japan and the Soviet Union from further conflict, and led to the conclusion of the Japanese–Soviet Nonaggression Pact in April 1941 which assured that further Japanese aggression would be directed southwards rather than towards the Soviet Union.

Conclusion

The Soviet Union faced challenges to its security from both Europe and Japan, and pursued much the same line in both instances – it sought security. How that security was achieved differed in each case, not least because the external factors were not the same. What is clear, though, is that in its pursuit of security there were constants on Soviet foreign policy thinking.

While much can be made about what the true intent of Soviet foreign policy was in the 1930s, it is clear that the Soviets tried to achieve security through mutually beneficial alliances, with the intention of containing aggressor states. When this did not work, they pursued other options – pushing Japan into a war with China, and in Europe finding accommodation with the aggressor. While not without their problems, both strategies led to the same conclusion – when war broke out in September 1939, the Soviet Union was not dragged into the fray. If one takes the view that avoiding war was the aim of Soviet foreign policy, then, on balance, that policy would seem to have been successful.

When one drills down, however, one sees that while there was a constant aspect to Soviet foreign policy over the decade, it was in fact a policy that seemed to conform to little in the way of a grand plan. Part of this had to do with the unwillingness of other powers to subscribe to Litvinov's collective security policy, some of it was the product of different interests within the Soviet hierarchy, while still other reasons can be found in the fact that Soviet foreign policy became reactive to a series of events on the international stage. It is therefore difficult to account for Soviet foreign policy in particularly simple terms, as it lacked consistency of approach, even if there was a single goal – the security of the Soviet Union in the coming war.

Further reading

Carr, E. H., *The Comintern and the Spanish Civil War* (London: Macmillan, 1984).

Cattell, D., *Soviet Diplomacy and the Spanish Civil War* (Berkley: University of California Press, 1957).

Gorodetsky, G., *Grand Delusion: Stalin and the German Invasion of Russia* (New Haven: Yale University Press, 1999).

Haslam, J., *The Soviet Union and the Struggle for Collective Security in Europe, 1933–39* (London: Macmillan, 1984).

Haslam, J., *The Soviet Union and the Threat from the East, 1933–41: Moscow, Tokyo and the Prelude to the Pacific War* (London: Macmillan, 1992).

Hilger, G., and Meyer, A., *The Incompatible Allies: A Memoir–History of German–Soviet Relations* (New York: Macmillan, 1953).

Hochman, J., *The Soviet Union and the Failure of Collective Security, 1934–1938* (Ithaca, NY: Cornell University Press, 1984).

Iriye, A., *The Origins of the Second World War in Asia and the Pacific* (London: Longman, 1987).

Kocho-Williams, A., 'The Soviet Diplomatic Corps and Stalin's Purges', *Slavonic and East European Review* vol. 86 no. 1 (2008).

Kowalsky, D., *Stalin and the Spanish Civil War* (New York: Columbia University Press, 2004).

Lensen, G. A., *The Damned Inheritance: The Soviet Union and the Manchurian Crises, 1924–1935* (Tallahassee: Diplomatic Press, 1974).

McDermott, K., and Agnew, J., *The Comintern: A History of International Communism from Lenin to Stalin* (Basingstoke: Macmillan, 1996).

Moore, H., *Soviet Far Eastern Policy, 1931–1945* (Princeton, NJ: Princeton University Press, 1945).

Morley, J., *Deterrent Diplomacy: Japan, Germany and the USSR, 1935–1940* (New York, Columbia University Press, 1976).

Nekrich, A. M., *Pariahs, Partners, Predators: German Soviet Relations, 1922–1941* (New York: Columbia University Press, 1997).

Payne, S., *The Spanish Civil War, the Soviet Union, and Communism* (New Haven, CT: Yale University Press, 2004).

Pons, S., *Stalin and the Inevitable War: 1936–1941* (London: Frank Cass, 2002).

Raack, R., *Stalin's Drive to the West, 1938–1941: The Origins of the Cold War* (Stanford, CA: Stanford University Press, 1995).

Radosh, R. (ed.) *Spain Betrayed: The Soviet Union in the Spanish Civil War* (New Haven, CT: Yale University Press, 2001).

Ragsdale, H., *The Soviets, the Munich Crisis and the Coming of World War II* (Cambridge: Cambridge University Press, 2004).

Roberts, G., *The Soviet Union and the Origins of the Second World War: Russo-German Relations and the Road to War, 1933–1941* (Basingstoke: Macmillan, 1995).

Steiner, Z., 'The Soviet Commissariat of Foreign Affairs and the Czechoslovakian Crisis in 1938: New Material from the Soviet Archives', *Historical Journal* vol. 42 no. 3 (1999).

Stone, G., *Spain, Portugal and the Great Powers, 1931–1941* (Basingstoke: Palgrave, 2005).

5   The Soviet Union and the Second World War

On 1 September 1939 Hitler ordered the invasion of Poland. An ultimatum was issued by Britain that German troops should retreat, but when it went unanswered the Second World War erupted on 3 September. From the perspective of the Soviet Union, the Second World War breaks down into two distinct phases: the period between the conclusion of the Nazi–Soviet Pact and the German invasion of the Soviet Union in the summer of 1941; and the Great Patriotic War fought against Germany from June 1941 to May 1945. During the first phase, the Soviets annexed territory under the conditions of the Secret Protocol to the Nazi–Soviet Pact, which included waging war against Finland, and engaged in trade and further negotiations with Nazi Germany. After June 1941 they were locked in a fierce conflict on the Eastern Front as well as being members of the Grand Alliance with Britain, France and the United States.

After the Pact: the Soviet annexation of territory and the Winter War with Finland, 1939–40

While foreign powers saw the Nazi–Soviet Pact as problematic, there were distinct challenges for the Comintern. In one move, the Soviets brought an end to the Comintern line of anti-Fascism that had been pursued since the 7th Comintern Congress in 1935. In the eyes of some within the Comintern, Stalin had made a deal with the devil, and this was unforgivable. Some left the Comintern, but many remained. Those who stayed found that instructions about the modification of the Comintern line were forthcoming, particularly when the Second World War broke out on 3 September 1939. Anti-Fascism was to be dropped, with references to it removed from Comintern literature, and the Second World War was to be opposed as an imperialist war. The Comintern was ordered to take a stance of sedition, and in some instances to engage in sabotage against the war effort. Other powers, particularly Britain, were concerned at such instructions, although they seem to have had little real impact. The same was not the case for other changes that followed the Nazi–Soviet Pact.

Almost as soon as the ink was dry on the Pact, the Soviets began taking steps to exploit the gains that it offered them. On 24 September 1939 the Estonian Foreign Minister was forced to sign a mutual assistance pact with the Soviets which included Soviet rights to establish military bases in Estonian territory. Immediately after this, the same agreements were forced on Latvia and Lithuania. With German agreement that the Baltic States were within the Soviet sphere, there was no way that the Soviets could be resisted. Following this, the Soviets orchestrated the deportation of large numbers of Estonian, Latvian and Lithuanian citizens to Siberia and Central Asia, removing elements that they saw as anti-Soviet. When rigged elections were staged, the Baltic States unanimously elected to become a part of the Soviet Union, and in June 1940 the Soviet Union annexed the States and made them republics of the Soviet Union. While this state of affairs was never recognized by the United States or other Western powers, the Soviets cemented their rule over the Baltic States until the latter years of the Soviet Union.

It was not only the Baltic States that the Soviets moved into. Following the German domination of Western Poland, the Soviets occupied the Eastern portion that had been promised them under the Secret Protocol. They moved further to secure the territory that had been placed in their sphere of interest, largely without having to resort to armed conflict. There was one area, though, where the story was different. Finland, which had been a part of the Russian Empire before the Revolution and also has a Baltic coastline, had been agreed under the Secret Protocol to be within the Soviet sphere of interest. The Finns, however, provided much more resistance to the Soviet attempt to turn the agreement with Germany into a reality. In October 1939 the Soviets demanded that the Finnish–Soviet border in the Karelian Isthmus be moved a significant distance to the north. The logic for this was clear from the Soviet point of view, as the border up to that point lay approximately 20 miles from Leningrad and thus there was little buffer in proximity to the Soviet Union's second city. The Soviets also demanded to be granted leases of the ports of Pestamo and Hango, with the intention of using them as military bases. The Soviets did not initially attempt to do this either by force or through the methods employed in the Baltic States, but instead made an offer of part of Soviet Karelia. The Finnish government rejected the proposal on the basis that it was deleterious to Finnish security. Negotiations between the Soviets and the Finns broke down, and Molotov announced the end of the Soviet–Finnish Non-Aggression Treaty on 28 November. On 30 November the Soviets launched an attack along the length of the Soviet–Finnish border and bombed Helsinki, beginning the Winter War.

The Soviets did not anticipate that the Finns would provide much in the way of resistance, and expected that the conflict would be resolved quickly. They were to find, however, that they had misjudged the situation, as the Finnish army outfought Soviet troops, who were ill prepared to fight in the conditions of an Arctic winter. In order to mitigate initial failures, the Soviets created a puppet government under Otto Kuusinen, a senior Finnish official in the Comintern, with whom they concluded a treaty. The eruption of war, and the subsequent attempt to annexe territory under the auspices of a puppet government, was viewed with consternation by foreign powers – the Soviet Union was expelled from the League of Nations on 14 December 1940, and Great Britain considered military intervention.

Despite the resistance and the international outcry, the Soviets continued to try to push further into Finland. While the Finns had held the Soviets fast up to and during January 1940, in February the Soviet launched a sizeable offensive across the Finnish defence of the Karelian Isthmus, the Mannerheim Line. Even so, the Soviets were not able to secure victory, and with the threat of war with Britain mounting, Stalin decided to back down. The Soviets concluded a treaty with Finland which largely followed the position that had been outlined in the Soviet demands during October 1939, and most of Karelia and most ports and military bases in Finland passed to the Soviet Union.

The Soviets did not secure the victory that they had hoped for over Finland, although they did manage to push the border further away from Leningrad. But it had come at some considerable cost. The Red Army sustained over 200,000 casualties, including approximately 50,000 dead. Soviet ineffectiveness against the Finns also served to highlight to other powers that the Soviets did not possess an effective army, which confirmed the scepticism of the late 1930s and made the Germans confident about their chances, should they attack the Soviet Union.

German–Soviet relations 1939–41: the road to war

Initially, after the conclusion of the Nazi–Soviet Pact relations between Germany and the Soviet Union were cordial, with significant efforts made on both sides to develop trade between each other. This situation did not last for long, however, with Hitler making plain in November 1939 that Soviet expansion into the Baltic States, despite the fact that it had been agreed under the Secret Protocol, might prove problematic for Germany and that the Nazi–Soviet Pact was worth holding to only so long as it was expedient for Germany to do so. While relations continued to be relatively friendly throughout 1940, Hitler seems to have decided in July 1940 to attack the Soviet Union the following year, following the swiftness of the German domination of France. By the end of August 1940 a plan of attack had been drawn up, and on 18 December 1940 Hitler signed what was to become Operation Barbarossa – a plan for the invasion of the Soviet Union in May 1941 with the intention of its destruction inside five months.

The Soviets were not aware of Hitler's decision to invade the Soviet Union. The relationship between the two powers continued to appear relatively friendly, although it was not without its strains. The Three Power

Pact, which cemented the Axis between Germany, Italy and Japan, was concluded in September 1940. The Soviets were concerned about what they viewed as a possible move to encircle the Soviet Union. Ribbentrop assured Molotov that the Pact was aimed solely at the United States, not the Soviet Union, and Ribbentrop even briefly considered adding the Soviet Union to what would have become a Four Power Pact. He communicated the possibility of such a move in a letter to Stalin on 13 October 1940 in which he detailed German policy with respect to all matters that concerned the Soviet Union, and made allusion to a potential Four Power Pact. Molotov was dispatched to Berlin for discussions with the Germans.

Molotov spent two days in Berlin in November 1940, during which time he met with a number of senior German officials, among them Goering, Ribbentrop and Hitler. While Hitler waxed lyrical about the Four Powers dividing the world, the most significant meeting was with Ribbentrop on 13 November, held in an underground shelter during a British air raid. Molotov indicated that the Soviets were interested in becoming part of a Four Power Pact, provided that Soviet interests were included in the agreement. In outlining Soviet desires, Molotov attempted to press for further concessions in the Balkans, which the Germans had expressed disinterest in during 1939, but now seemed unwilling to allow to fall into the Soviet sphere of interest. Ribbentrop suggested to Molotov that the Soviets might pursue interests elsewhere, particularly if they were to move towards Persia, Afghanistan and India. In short, Ribbentrop was attempting to persuade Molotov to ignite a conflict with Britain in Central Asia.

Molotov and Ribbentrop agreed nothing concrete during the meeting, but two weeks later the Soviets made a response to the offer of the Four Power Pact that had been outlined during the November meeting. The Soviets never received a reply, but this did not signal an end to the relationship, even if Hitler was on the verge of signing the order for the invasion of the Soviet Union in 1941. The treaty of January 1941 secured German–Soviet trade, with the Soviets contracting to supply large quantities of raw materials to Germany. The relationship began to run onto rocky ground, however, when Germany advanced into Romania in March 1941, ostensibly in response to British operations planned in Greece. This move threatened the Soviet desire to maintain the security of Bulgaria and the Turkish Straits, and when Bulgaria was added to the Three Power Pact and occupied by Germany in March 1941 the Soviets raised a huge cry.

The situation worsened with the German domination of Yugoslavia. On 25 March 1941 Yugoslavia joined the Three Power Pact. This prompted fierce protests in Yugoslavia and resulted in a military coup and rejection of the Pact on 27 March. The Soviets concluded a friendship and non-aggression treaty with the Yugoslav regime on 5 April, one day before Hitler invaded and crushed the regime. While Stalin had hoped to deflect German aggression away from the Soviet Union by bolstering Yugoslav resistance, he had misjudged German military strength, while at the same time enraging Hitler. Stalin realized this latter fact, and took steps to address the situation. Accordingly, the Soviets appeased Hitler by delivering on their trade obligations and breaking off their relations with Yugoslavia, Greece, Norway and Belgium. While the Soviets made the argument that these states had lost sovereignty as a result of German occupation, Hitler concluded that the time was ripe to launch his attack on the Soviet Union.

June 1941: the Nazi invasion of the Soviet Union

At 3 o'clock on the morning of 22 June 1941, Nazi Germany launched the invasion of the Soviet Union. Operation Barbarossa had begun a month later than initially planned, largely because German tank units had been engaged elsewhere, but Hitler remained confident that he could destroy the Soviet Union by the end of the year. While he was to be proved wrong, the Soviets were taken seemingly unawares by the attack, and Stalin withdrew until 3 July 1941 before calling for a Soviet counter-attack.

The German invasion of the Soviet Union had been planned for some time, although the Soviets remained unaware of the fact because German–Soviet relations continued to function. As the relationship deteriorated in the spring of 1941, so reports of German troop movements towards the Soviet border increased, but still the Soviets took little action to reinforce their forward positions. Even intelligence passed from Britain in the weeks and days before the invasion, coupled to Soviet intelligence reports, failed to put the Soviets into a position of alert. Stalin, it seemed, was in denial as to the reality of the situation he faced.

Even so, the reality might, it seems have been different. Molotov argued that the Soviets were aware, but were fearful that fortifying their forward positions would lead to an earlier German attack. Others have pointed to the fact that Germany would first swamp the buffer zone created by the territorial gains under the Secret Protocol to the Nazi–Soviet Pact, and that it was the Soviet intention for these areas to bear the initial brunt of the assault. Some have suggested that allowing invasion, with the intention of retreating and regrouping was a deliberate strategy on the part of the Soviets, and it has been argued that the Soviets had already drawn up a plan to attack Germany when the invasion happened.

The Soviets' apparent lack of preparation was seen not just in the delayed response from Stalin, but also in the speed with which German troops swarmed into and occupied Soviet territory. In the first six weeks of the conflict, the Soviet Union lost all of the territory gained under the Secret Protocol to the Nazi–Soviet Pact, and sustained heavy casualties and loss of equipment. Despite this, by the end of 1941 the Soviets had stemmed the tide of the German invasion and would begin to first hold, and then push the Germans back during the course of 1942 and 1943. Key to this was not only the resilience of the Soviet economy and the determinedness of the population to defeat Nazi Germany, but also in the Grand Alliance forged between the Soviet Union, Great Britain and the United States of America.

The course of the war

As German troops flooded into Soviet territory in the summer of 1941, the Soviets seemed to be in disarray. Most of the Soviet air force was lost on the ground in the first few days of fighting, and confusion hampered the organization of resistance. On 3 July, emerging from his seclusion, Stalin called for a Soviet counter-offensive, instructing his commanders to push forward into enemy territory. While these moves yielded little in terms of pushing back the front, successive breakouts from encirclement and a steady retreat held the German advance at a pace that was somewhat less than Hitler had intended.

Operation Barbarossa, Hitler's plan for the invasion of the Soviet Union with the intention of forcing its collapse by the end of 1941, initially appeared to be working. It began to falter in October 1941, however, when Soviet troops provided fierce resistance to the German push towards Moscow at Smolensk. Although Smolensk did fall to the Germans, the Soviets held up the invaders' advance. Following Smolensk, German tanks struggled to move in the muddy conditions they encountered, although when the ground froze in November 1941 the German pace picked up. By the end of November, the Germans had reached both Moscow and Leningrad, although they had arrived too late to fulfil the plans laid out in Operation Barbarossa.

Germany laid siege to Leningrad, but failed to take it, despite bombardment and severe food shortages during the 900-day long siege. Similarly, Moscow was successfully defended through the winter of 1941–42, with Soviet forces pushing back a German army that was ill prepared for the harsh conditions of winter. While this marked a Soviet success, and signalled a counter-offensive strategy that seemed to yield some results, Germany was not in retreat. In the spring of 1942, Hitler focused on attempting to hamper the Soviet war effort by preventing the Soviets from accessing grain from Ukraine and oil from the Caucasus. Soviet resistance was fierce, and the rugged terrain of the Caucasus proved difficult for the Germans to fight in, but still they pressed on. Then, in the summer of 1942, Hitler made a push towards Stalingrad, with the specific aim of capturing the Soviet oil fields that lay to the east of the Volga. The offensive began on 28 June 1942 and the fighting quickly moved towards Stalingrad. Stalin's orders of 28 July were plain – not a single step backwards could be taken. On 5 August Stavropol fell to the Germans, and on 9 August Krasnodar suffered the same fate. During the same time, German troops reached Stalingrad and commenced a slow advance that would continue through August and September as they fought their way through the streets of the city. The Soviets, however, provided fierce resistance, and turned the tide in the middle of October, before launching a counter-offensive on

19 November. This led to the encirclement of the entire German Sixth Army under Friedrich von Paulus. Ordered to wait for reinforcements, which were unable to break through, von Paulus eventually surrendered on 2 February 1943. In the wake of their victory, the Soviets pushed forward along the length of the Eastern Front.

After Stalingrad, which can be seen as a turning-point in the Great Patriotic War, the Soviets pushed westwards. They clashed fiercely with the Germans at Kursk in July 1943, the largest tank battle in history, and emerged with a decisive victory. After Kursk, the Soviets pushed inexorably westwards, with the pace increasing through 1944 and into 1945. By April 1945 the Red Army had liberated the entirety of Eastern Europe from German occupation and had reached Berlin. On 22 April, Hitler's birthday, the Soviet bombardment of Berlin began. By 8 May 1945 (9 May Moscow time), Berlin had fallen to the Red Army and Nazi Germany had been defeated. The Great Patriotic War had seen the Soviet Union victorious.

Even so, the war was not entirely over for the Soviet Union. Stalin had pledged to the United States that, following the defeat of Germany, the Soviet Union would enter the war against Japan within ninety days. The Soviets held to their bargain, advancing into Japanese territory in early August 1945, just as the United States' bombing of Hiroshima and Nagasaki dealt the blows that would ensure Japanese surrender. Soviet military action was brief, with the Soviets playing little role in the defeat of Japan. Despite this, when Japan surrendered and the Second World War ended, Soviet forces occupied Japanese territory, notably North Korea and Sakhalin Island.

The Soviet Union emerged victorious from the Second World War, but it was not without cost. A bitter fight for survival had resulted in the deaths of 27.5 million Soviet citizens, approximately half of whom were civilians. Soviet resilience in the face of invasion, partisan warfare, the strength of the Soviet economy and foreign assistance had brought a victory over Germany that buoyed the dealings of the Soviet Union with foreign powers and saw the Soviet Union emerge as a significant power in the post-war world.

The Grand Alliance

While the Soviets were to emerge as victors, not least as a result of the resilience of the Soviet economy and population, the alliance forged with Britain and the United States was of great importance. This alliance was not born out of any friendship, but of necessity, and would not form a basis for cooperation after the defeat of Germany. Nonetheless, in the face of a common enemy the three powers were able to find a way to pursue common objectives, even if their desires for the post-war world differed.

The first indication that such an alliance might be created was contained in Winston Churchill's speech on the evening of 22 June 1941 in which he indicated that Britain would extend its support to the Soviet Union in the fight against Germany. Even so, and despite parts of the speech appearing in the Soviet press, the Soviet government made no formal response. On 7 July 1941 Churchill wrote to Stalin offering support and praising the Soviet resistance to the German invasion. On 13 July, on the basis of Churchill's offer, the British Ambassador to Moscow, Sir Stafford Cripps, and Molotov signed a formal alliance.

Almost immediately, on 18 July, Stalin wrote to Churchill asking for Great Britain to open a second front against Germany, in either northern France or the Arctic. He argued that both the British and Soviet war efforts would benefit from such a move, although Churchill was less enthusiastic. Even so, the second front became a persistent aspect of Stalin's demands to the British and would colour the relationship almost from the outset.

The United States, even though it was not at this stage a belligerent power in the Second World War, came into the alliance shortly after Britain and the Soviet Union had agreed to cooperate against Germany. Harry Hopkins – United States Secretary of Commerce from 1938 to 1940 and a close adviser to the United States President, Franklin Roosevelt, and attendee at the wartime conferences – persuaded Roosevelt to allow him to go to Moscow in order to discuss rendering support to the Soviet Union. On 29 July Hopkins offered Stalin immediate and long-term assistance in the fight against Germany. Stalin asked for war materials such that the Soviets could stand against Germany, and gave more detailed information about Soviet military capabilities than had ever been given to any outsider. On returning to the United States, Hopkins briefed Roosevelt, who extended Lend-Lease aid to the Soviet Union, which would prove to significantly strengthen the Soviet war effort. The Soviet Union, a little over a month after being invaded by Germany, had become a part of a tripartite alliance against Hitler that would be victorious in war. Contrary to Soviet efforts before the outbreak of hostilities, however, this was an alliance to fight a war, not to prevent one.

With the framework of the Grand Alliance in place, the Soviets attempted to use it to their advantage, only to find that it did not offer everything that they had hoped it might. When, following Soviet defeats during the summer of 1941, Stalin again asked Churchill, on 4 September 1941, to open a second front in Northern or South-Eastern Europe, he was to find that help was not forthcoming. When Stalin asked again on 15 September, Churchill once more refused, on the basis that the Soviets were asking for more than the allies could give. Stalin was clearly seeking support, however, and while a second front was not opened as he requested, Britain and the United States concluded an agreement to give large quantities of supplies to the Soviet Union from October 1941. While significant aid did not reach the Soviet Union until early 1942, the agreement did much to assuage Soviet fears and to raise morale.

Having received guarantees of support, the Soviets began the process of bargaining with the British and Americans over the shape of the alliance, and also the shape of the post-war world. On 16 December, in a meeting between Anthony Eden, the British Foreign Secretary, and Stalin, a Soviet draft treaty for an alliance against Nazi Germany was discussed. The main thrust of the agreement was that neither party would conclude a separate peace with Germany, but there was an additional secret protocol. The Soviets, it seemed, had been buoyed up by the Secret Protocol to the Nazi–Soviet Pact, and remained unconcerned that Britain had been enraged at Soviet territorial gains under its auspices. The secret protocol that Stalin offered to the British was linked to the earlier agreement with Germany, as it sought to have the British recognize the Soviet territorial gains of 1939. The draft treaty also proposed the partitioning of Germany, with the Rhineland and Bavaria possibly becoming separate states, the restoration of Austrian independence and the drawing of Poland's western border along the line of the Oder River. While Eden refused to agree to Stalin's requests, on the basis that Roosevelt would not allow such territorial decisions and that Churchill would need to be consulted, Stalin had revealed some of his key aims in the war, and he would doggedly pursue them throughout the remainder of the allied relationship. What Stalin wanted was clear – the Soviet buffer zone established in Eastern Europe in 1939, the concessions that had been asked of Ribbentrop by Molotov in 1940 and the complete destruction of Germany as a significant threat in Europe.

Despite the British refusal to agree to his terms, Stalin did not turn his back on the alliance, nor did his partners, even if the alliance was on a less than entirely firm footing. After the United States entered the Second World War following the Japanese attack on Pearl Harbor in December 1941, Roosevelt went to great lengths to build a personal relationship with Stalin. Part of Roosevelt's approach was to try to convince Stalin to trust the Western powers, and he sought to do this by banking on the fact that Stalin would return him the same courtesy of trust and would not seek to annexe territory in Eastern Europe. While he showed a degree of naivety here, it was clear that he believed that the relationship between the Soviet Union and the United States could become cordial.

The relationship with Britain continued, however, to be fraught. In the spring of 1942 sizeable supplies began arriving from Britain and the United States. The major route for these was to the north of Norway, and became problematic in March 1942 when German naval vessels and aircraft began to attack allied convoys. When, in July 1942, a convoy that had been dispatched from Iceland delivered only approximately one-third of its cargo, having lost all but one of the ships en route, and Britain decided to cancel the next shipment, Stalin concluded that the British desire to support the Soviets was waning in the face of German aggression, and that the British remained somewhat anti-Soviet.

That there were difficulties in the Anglo-Soviet relationship was made apparent on Molotov's visit to London in May 1942. To some extent, the visit picked up from the meetings during Eden's visit to Moscow during December 1941. Again, the Soviets attempted to push the British to recognize Soviet territorial gains under the Nazi–Soviet Pact, and were once more refused. Abandoning the pursuit of this line, on 26 May 1942 Molotov instead concluded an alliance with Britain that gave no territorial concessions and had a duration of twenty years. While this appeared to settle matters, Molotov then immediately pressed the British, yet again, to open a second front. Churchill made the point that Britain was not in a position to make such a move, and doubted that it would have a real impact on the removal of German forces from the Eastern Front. Denied yet again on the second front, Molotov turned to Roosevelt in the hope that the United States could put pressure on the British. Roosevelt not only allowed Molotov to inform Stalin that a second front could be expected during 1942, he also pledged 120,000 men to its achievement. Much of the manpower was to be British, and Churchill rejected the proposals. Still, despite being dogged by repeated Soviet requests for a second front, which were met with refusal, the Grand Alliance endured.

As it turned out, the British and Americans had planned to open another front against Germany, but not in the regions that Stalin hoped for. During meetings held in Moscow in August 1942 between the Soviets, Churchill and the United States Ambassador, Averill Harriman, Stalin was informed of the planned allied campaign in North Africa. Stalin was interested, although still it did not entirely satisfy him. It appears that Stalin was most keenly interested in the opening of a second front in Europe, and the allied failure to give him what he wanted led him to distrust his allies.

In 1943, after Soviet successes against Germany, and as the war turned after the Soviet victory at Stalingrad, Churchill and Roosevelt met at the Casablanca Conference in January. As Stalin was not present, the discussion focused on allied activity in the Mediterranean – accordingly it was this area that was the main thrust of allied activity during 1943 – and delaying the opening a front in Northern France. Stalin was informed of their decisions on 26 January. Already less than certain of his allies, Stalin was becoming ever more suspicious of their commitment to the Soviet Union.

During the spring of 1943 Stalin's distrust of the West became increasingly noticeable. Both Ivan Maisky, Soviet Ambassador to London, and Maxim Litvinov, former Foreign Commissar and Ambassador to Washington, were recalled to Moscow. Veteran diplomats were no longer the men that Stalin wanted to represent him in the West. Instead, he made clear his intention to deal with Churchill and Roosevelt himself, and summitry became the means by which Soviet diplomacy was conducted. The triggers for this move appear to have been not just the Casablanca Conference, but also the suspension of convoys to the Soviet Union by the Allies in April 1943 and the breaking of relations with the Polish government in exile, led by Sikorski in London, in the wake of the revelations of a massacre of 15,000 Polish officers and soldiers at Katyn in 1940.

It was only later in 1943 that a meeting of the three allied leaders was agreed upon. The meeting was to be held at Tehran in November 1943, but was presaged by a meeting of foreign ministers in Moscow in October. At this meeting the Soviets again pressed for a second front to be opened by the spring of 1944. Plans were afoot for Operation Overlord, a cross-channel invasion by Allied forces, but Churchill remained unwilling to commit to it as early as the spring of 1944. When the 'Big Three' met together for the first time, at Tehran in late November 1943, Stalin showed that he distrusted Churchill more than Roosevelt and with whom he met privately before the Conference began. In their meetings Stalin made it plain that he would demand all territory that the Soviet Union had gained under the Nazi–Soviet Pact in 1939, outlined his desire that the Polish borders be moved westwards in the east and set at the Oder River in the west, and set out a plan for the partition of Germany. Somewhat naively, Roosevelt agreed with Stalin's position on Poland and Germany and agreed the territorial concessions, not least because he believed that the Baltic States would voluntarily express a desire to remain part of the Soviet Union. Stalin was even able to persuade Roosevelt into supporting the argument for Operation Overlord to be launched in the spring of 1944.

Dealing with almost all of the points that seem to have mattered to him in the course of the Grand Alliance, Stalin believed he had reached agreement on them with Roosevelt. This further cemented his impression that Churchill was set against him and was unwilling to give the Soviet Union what he demanded, and led to the Tehran Conference becoming a battleground between Churchill and Stalin. Stalin had manoeuvred Roosevelt into a position in which he believed that the Soviet Union had been granted its wishes and that he was being given a free hand. Only Churchill seemed to stand in the way.

Even so, Churchill did agree with the proposed Polish borders, and at Tehran the post-war borders of Poland at the Oder River in the west and the Curzon Line in the east were effectively set. Churchill used his agreement on this point to attempt to deal with Stalin, who he believed had misconstrued British policy and attempted to outmanoeuvre him with Roosevelt. In meetings between Stalin and Churchill, the Soviet impression of Britain improved somewhat, not least because Churchill informed Stalin that the invasion of France would take place in May 1944. Accordingly, the Tehran Conference laid out the basic plan that the Allies would pursue for the remainder of the war and made clear that there was agreement between them on some, if not all, points.

Following their success in France after the launching of Operation Overlord in June 1944 and the Soviet victory over Poland in July, the Allies were able to reach further agreement in October 1944. Churchill met with Stalin in Moscow, although Roosevelt had Averill Harriman stand in as an observer rather than attend in person. During the meeting, Churchill made plain his desire to settle Balkan affairs with the Soviets. He made a statement to this effect, and then wrote on a piece of paper the percentages of influence that he sought to agree with the Soviets. Stalin returned the paper with his agreement, and thus was concluded the infamous 'Percentages Agreement', which gave the Soviets 90 per cent influence in Romania in return for 90 per cent British influence in Greece and shared influence in Yugoslavia.

The Grand Alliance was at its high point between this meeting and the Yalta Conference in the Crimea in February 1945. Stalin had found that he could deal with Churchill, believed that Roosevelt had conceded to him what he wanted and was appreciative that the European second front he had wanted had now been opened. By the time the leaders met in February 1945, the defeat of Nazi Germany at the hands of the Allies seemed assured, and Soviet victories had placed most of Eastern Europe under Soviet control.

In the course of discussions at Yalta the first topic was Germany. While there was general agreement that the aim remained the complete defeat of Germany, and that it should be demilitarized and partitioned, a final decision on how to achieve this was deferred to a meeting of foreign ministers, on the basis that the matter was too sizeable to be agreed upon in the context of a brief conference. This was followed by Roosevelt's proposal for the United Nations, an international organization that would act as the arbiter of international politics. The Soviets were prepared to agree to such an organization, although they attempted to gain many more seats in the General Assembly than the United States and Britain were prepared to offer them – the Soviets wanted one seat per Soviet republic, totalling sixteen, but compromised on three. Both the Soviet Union and the United States insisted upon the power of veto over decisions reached by the United Nations. Discussion also turned to the Polish question, and while the earlier agreed borders were affirmed, Britain and the United States showed their concerns about Soviet intentions towards Poland, not least because the Soviets seemed to be backing a pro-Soviet puppet government. Deadlock was almost reached, but was defused by Molotov's proposal that the Lublin government of Poland could be reorganized and free elections could be held. This meant that the Big Three could find agreement, even if it soon became apparent that the Soviets had no intention to holding to their agreement on Poland.

The relationship between the Soviet Union and its allies went downhill fairly quickly after Yalta. Roosevelt died suddenly, in mid-April 1945, and was replaced by the more anti-Soviet Harry Truman. Truman's early attempts to deal with the Soviets largely revolved around appeasing Stalin, which only served to further the extension of Soviet influence in Eastern Europe, which, on 8 May 1945 when Germany was defeated, the Soviet Union effectively dominated. Stalin believed that Roosevelt had been in agreement that this should be the case, and did not foresee that Truman would disagree. Even so, the Soviets were in violation of their agreements at Yalta and the Allies were unhappy with the situation, even if they were powerless to deal with it. Despite the wartime alliance, the Soviets appeared not to have changed, and their actions confirmed in the minds of many that they were not to be trusted. Churchill voiced his concerns, arguing that the Soviet Union had not only constructed puppet governments in Eastern Europe, but had created a situation in which it was completely unclear to the Allies what precisely the Soviets were up to.

The Allies met again at the Potsdam Conference in July 1945, amid the issue of Soviet violations of agreements made at Yalta. Here, the rift between the Soviet Union and the West widened, not least because the issues over Soviet actions in Eastern Europe remained unsolved and because of the revelation by Truman that the United States possessed the atomic bomb. Despite the tensions, Stalin was able to placate Truman by agreeing to join the war against Japan and to the establishment of Council of Foreign Ministers to facilitate further discussions about the post-war world. Agreements were reached at Potsdam between Stalin, Truman and Clement Attlee, the new British Prime Minister, who replaced Churchill during the conference. Zones of occupation were agreed in Germany and Poland, and Stalin was persuaded to relinquish his demand for reparations to be paid to the Soviet Union by Germany. Instead, the occupation zones were to be the sources of reparations. With these agreements in hand, and a deteriorating relationship, the 'Big Three' concluded their final wartime conference.

Conclusion

The Soviet Union did not join the Second World War at its outbreak in September 1939, although it did become embroiled in conflict in pursuit of the territory it had gained under the Nazi–Soviet Pact and its attendant Secret Protocol. Soviet actions in the early days of the war confirmed the suspicions of some that the Soviets were opportunist and interested only in furthering their own power. While to some extent this was a justified view, it ignored the important aspect of the Soviet desire to maintain security above all else, and the push to ensure that the Soviet Union was in a position to deal with a German invasion when it came.

The German–Soviet relationship developed beyond August 1939, largely through trade, although it stopped short of becoming fully cordial. Even so, the Soviets appear to have trusted that if they held to their side of the bargain and fulfilled their trade obligations they would be able to maintain security against war. This was not, in fact the case, and even as the Soviets believed their relationship with the Germans was stable, Hitler drew up his plan for the invasion of the Soviet Union.

The German invasion of the Soviet Union came in the summer of 1941, catching the Soviets seemingly unawares and bringing them into the Great

Patriotic War. In the first six weeks after the invasion, the Soviets moved backwards, losing swathes of territory, before being able to slow the German advance. By the end of 1941, the Soviets had thwarted Hitler's aim to destroy the Soviet Union in a single blow, and had repulsed German forces from Moscow and were holding Leningrad.

The Soviets also had, as an outcome of the invasion, forged an alliance with Great Britain and the United States of America. While that alliance would never be entirely cordial, nor based on mutual trust, the materiel sent by the allies to the Soviet Union was of great significance in aiding the Soviet War effort. As Allied materiel reached the Soviet Union in early 1942, the Soviets were beginning to turn the tide of the war on the Eastern Front. The turning-point came that year with Soviet victory over the Germans at Stalingrad, and the Red Army moved to push the front westwards, ultimately securing victory over Germany in Berlin in May 1945.

The Grand Alliance of the Soviet Union, Britain and the United States was significant in winning the Second World War, and in the discussions on the shape of the post-war world. What is clear is that Stalin had several clear objectives, from which he barely swayed during the course of negotiations. He was adamant that a second front be opened in Europe, that Soviet territorial gains under the Nazi–Soviet Pact be recognized and that Germany be dismembered. He was unable to realize some of these aims at the times that he wanted, but ultimately his aims were met to a great extent, or he at least believed that they had been agreed upon. The Grand Alliance, though, proved to be little more than an alliance in the face of a common enemy, and was not sustainable beyond the war, not least because it was apparent that there was a great deal of mistrust amongst the parties. The mistrust, and the fraught situation at the Potsdam Conference in 1945, seems to have heralded the move towards the global division that became the Cold War shortly after Allied victory in the Second World War.

Further reading

Barros, J., *Double Deception: Stalin Hitler and the Invasion of Russia* (DeKalb, IL: Northern Illinois University Press, 1995).

Bellamy, C., *Absolute War: Soviet Russia in the Second World War* (London: Macmillan, 2005).

Chuev, F., *Molotov Remembers* (Chicago, IL: Ivan R. Dee, 1993).

Feis, H., *Between War and Peace: The Potsdam Conference* (Princeton, NJ: Princeton University Press, 1960).

Gorodetsky, G., *Grand Delusion* (New Haven: Yale University Press, 1999).

Kennedy-Pipe, C., *Stalin's Cold War: Soviet Strategies in Europe, 1943 to 1956* (Manchester: Manchester University Press, 1995).

Kitchen, M., *British Policy Toward the Soviet Union during the Second World War* (Basingstoke: Macmillan, 1986).

Mastny, V., 'Soviet War Aims at the Moscow and Teheran Conferences of 1943', *Journal of Modern History* vol. 47 no. 3 (1975).

Mawdsley, E., *Thunder in the East: The Nazi–Soviet War, 1941–1945* (London: Hodder Arnold, 2007).

Mayers, D., 'Soviet War Aims and the Grand Alliance: George Kennan's Views, 1944–46', *Journal of Contemporary History* vol. 21 no. 1 (1986).

Munting, R., 'Lend-lease and the Soviet War Effort', *Journal of Contemporary History* vol. 19 (1984).

Raack, R. C., 'Stalin Plans His Post-War Germany', *Journal of Contemporary History* vol. 28 no. 1 (1993).

Raack, R. C., *Stalin's Drive to the West 1938–1945: The Origins of the Cold War* (Stanford, CA: Stanford University Press, 1995).

Resis, A., 'The Churchill–Stalin Secret "Percentages" Agreement on the Balkans, Moscow, October 1944', *American Historical Review* vol. 83 no. 2 (1978).

Reynolds, D., Kimball, W., and Chubarian, A. (eds), *Allies at War: The Soviet, American and British Experience 1939–1945* (London: Macmillan, 1994).

Roberts, C., 'Planning for War: The Red Army and the Catastrophe of 1941' *Europe–Asia Studies* vol. 47 no. 8 (1995).

Roberts, G., *Stalin's Wars: from World War to Cold War, 1939–1953* (New Haven, CT: Yale University Press, 2008).

Rzheshevsky, O., *War and Diplomacy: The Making of the Grand Alliance: Documents from Stalin's Archives* (Amsterdam: Harwood Academic, 1996).

Uldricks, T., 'The Icebreaker Controversy: Did Stalin Plan to Attack Hitler?' *Slavic Review* vol. 58 no. 3 (1999).

Wegner, B. (ed.). *From Peace to War: Germany, Soviet Russia, and the World, 1939–1941* (Providence, RI: Berghahn, 1997).

Zhukov, G. K., *The Memoirs of Marshal Zhukov* (London: Cape, 1971).

6 The Soviet Union and the early Cold War, 1945–53

Following victory in the Great Patriotic War, the Soviet Union emerged as a powerful player on the international stage. Military might had been demonstrated, and in becoming part of the Grand Alliance the Soviets had engaged in discussion of the post-war world. After the defeat of Germany and Japan, however, the relationship between the three powers of the Grand Alliance was cooling, if not beginning to fragment. As time wore on, relations between the powers, especially between the United States and the Soviet Union, became increasingly strained and developed into the Cold War.

Soviet actions and perceptions account in part for this state of affairs, but they were not the only factors at play. American and British desires, and perceptions of Soviet intentions, also played a role. One of the major sticking points was that the Soviet Union appeared to create an empire in the territories that it had occupied in Eastern Europe and was seen to be engaged in the spread of communism around the world. The world was effectively divided into two camps, both in terms of the proclamations made by both sides, and also in the development of two global systems that were at loggerheads with one another.

This chapter addresses Soviet foreign policy thinking and actions in the last years of Stalin's rule, a period known in Soviet historiography as 'High Stalinism'. The Soviet extension of power into Eastern Europe, and attendant imperial style of behaviour, began in this period and deepened the rift between East and West. Also during Stalin's last years, the Soviets acquired the atomic bomb and became involved in the extension of communist power in Asia and a relationship with communist regimes in the region.

The beginning of the Cold War – early conflict and declarations

The Potsdam Conference had, on the face of it, secured the shape of the post-war world. The reality, however, was that difficult decisions had been deferred at the conference and the lack of a common aim of defeating Germany and Japan had been removed. This left the former allies in a position where they focused more on their own preoccupations and security concerns. This led to a situation in which Soviet and Western approaches to the post-war order were almost inevitably going to collide. For the Soviets, who distrusted their wartime allies and remained concerned about capitalist encirclement, cementing their own power and security was key.

The Cold War did not begin immediately the Second World War was over. There was some sustained cooperation between the former allies, not least through a series of meetings of foreign ministers, as had been agreed at Potsdam. The problem was that these yielded little in the way of results. In meetings between the autumn of 1945 and the summer of 1946 there was some agreement on the situation of some of the more minor states that had become allied with Nazi Germany, and peace treaties were agreed. The Council of Foreign Ministers, as it became known, failed, however, to address some of the problematic questions that had faced the allies at Potsdam – namely, the agreement of peace treaties with Germany and Austria – not least because they remained under Allied occupation. While it has been suggested that one of the reasons why the Council of Ambassadors failed to achieve settlement of these issues rested in a lack of willingness to address what where thorny and contentious issues, it is clear that there was unlikely to be much agreement between the powers, as the relationship between them steadily deteriorated through 1946 and into 1947.

The first expression of the developing Cold War came with Stalin's 'election speech', delivered on 9 February 1946. In this speech Stalin emphasized the fact that the Soviet Union had been victorious in war because of its strength, both economically and militarily. He also spoke of the Second World War as the result of the growth of capitalism, and declared that the capitalist world would soon collapse into war yet again. Certain figures in the United States read these statements as an aggressive intention to wage war, if not by force then at least by ideology. General Lucius Clay, Commanding Officer of American forces in Germany, warned that the Soviets might attempt to seize all of Germany by force. In the 'Long Telegram' sent on 22 February 1946, the American Diplomat George Kennan put forward the notion that there could be no *modus vivendi* found with the Soviets, that they were bent on expansion and that they were deeply suspicious of the West. He pointed to Soviet ideology as a driving factor in the Soviet world-view and in the intractability of the Soviets.

The United States was not the only power to respond to the Soviet challenge that had apparently been thrown down through the occupation of Eastern Europe and Stalin's speech. On 5 March 1946 Winston Churchill, speaking in Fulton, Missouri, gave his famous 'Iron Curtain' speech, in which he stated that Europe had become divided into two camps, with an Iron Curtain having descended between them and placed Eastern Europe firmly in the Soviet sphere. Appeasing Stalin would only make the situation worse, he argued, and what was needed was a concerted alliance against the Soviets in order to push back the extension of the Soviet grip over

Eastern Europe. The speech cemented the division between East and West, and further inflamed Soviet suspicions as to Western intentions, not least because in Soviet quarters Churchill's speech was seen to indicate British policy and to be an open appeal to the United States for cooperation against the Soviet Union.

While these speeches amounted to the proclamation of stances in relation to the developing post-war world order and indicated an ideological division between the two camps, real clashes were in fact occurring at this time. The initial clashes between the Soviets and their former allies had come in Soviet activity with regard to the Middle and Near East in the aftermath of the Second World War. The first focus of Soviet attention had been Turkey, where the Soviet Union sought bases in proximity to the Turkish Straits. Soviet security was doubtless a concern here, but there was an attendant aim of gaining a foothold in the Mediterranean and better access to the Balkans. As Soviet troops threatened the Turkish border, the United States responded by reinforcing its naval presence in the Eastern Mediterranean and by giving diplomatic support to the Turkish government. Soviet proposals were rejected, and Truman declared that his 'get tough' policy had worked in stemming Soviet advances.

In Iran, however, a more inflammatory conflict took place. The Soviets had agreed, along with the other Allies, at the Tehran Conference in 1943 that their forces would leave Iran after the war was concluded. The Soviets, however, had become involved with and developed the Tudeh Party (Communist Party) in northern Iran, and attempted to annexe the territory. This led to an appeal by Iran to the United Nations in January 1946 on the grounds that the Soviet Union was interfering in its sovereign affairs. More importantly, the Soviet presence in Iran was seen as a challenge to United States interests, specifically with regard to access to oil in the Middle East. The United States saw Soviet moves as aggressive and confrontational, and moved in an attempt to create anti-Soviet sentiment within the United Nations and to give clandestine support to the Iranian government in bringing the matter before the United Nations Security Council in March 1946. The Soviets, faced with the prospect of war, came to an agreement with Iran on 4 April that Soviet troops would be removed on condition that Iran and the Soviet Union would cooperate in the exploration of Iranian oil. This concession led to a Soviet withdrawal, but the Iranian government failed to ratify the agreement with the Soviets and, as a result, Soviet access to the Iranian oil fields was denied. The Soviets did not press the issue. Importantly, though, what this episode showed was that Stalin was prepared to concede influence over territory and resources in order to avoid direct confrontation with Britain and the United States.

The drawing of early battle lines and the success of strategies aimed at having the Soviets back down demonstrate that the beginnings of the policy of containment of the Soviet Union were in place and were enjoying some degree of success. With no *modus vivendi* to be found with the Soviet Union, containment of the spread of Soviet power and influence became the aim of United States foreign policy. That policy was to be further developed in 1947, with the announcement in March of the Truman Doctrine, which cemented the Cold War.

The genesis of the Truman Doctrine came with the British abandonment of Greece and Turkey. Greece had become embroiled in civil war, with communist forces fighting conservatives for control, and Turkey remained in a precarious position, despite Soviet withdrawal. That the Soviets were seen to be supporting the communists, while Britain and the United States had made military and economic attempts to support the Greek regime, fuelled the tension between East and West, and also led logically to the United States stepping into the breach once Britain announced withdrawal of its forces from Greece in February 1947. Truman announced the United States policy with respect to supporting Greece on 12 March 1947, in a speech that has become known as the Truman Doctrine. Despite the wider implications of the Truman Doctrine, the speech concerned the plan to support Greece and Turkey in resisting the advance of communism, pledging economic support and military assistance. Truman made plain the plan to resist the spread of communism, arguing that it was a poor economic situation that would lead to the development of communism and painting it as oppressive and authoritarian. The tone of the Truman Doctrine was distinctly anti-communist, and while it initially applied to the situation in Greece and Turkey, it soon became one of the guiding principles of United States foreign policy. With its articulation, the Cold War had definitively begun.

The Soviet response to the Truman Doctrine was immediate, and accused the United States of taking on the British mantle of supporting the *status quo* as a cloak for its own desire for expansion. Accusations in the Soviet press even went as far as to allege that the United States was attempting to use the United Nations as a facilitator of its own foreign policy. The division was only to become deeper, however, with the announcement of the European Recovery Plan, better known as the Marshall Plan, by Secretary of State George Marshall on 5 June 1947.

The Marshall Plan was the extension of the Truman Doctrine, not least in following the line that it was fragile economic situations in post-war Europe that would lead to communist domination. The aid was offered to all European states, including those in Eastern Europe and to the Soviet Union, but on terms that made it difficult for the Soviets to accept. The major issue was that acceptance of the plan required that the United States be able to inspect a state's economic data and impose American-style business models. The Soviet Union was unlikely to accept, given these proposals, and on 29 June 1947 made plain its refusal.

In the midst of a conference in Paris, Molotov stormily denounced the Marshall Plan, arguing that it was designed to extend American control and undermine the sovereignty of states. Andrei Vyshinksii, in front of the

United Nations, pushed the line that the Truman Doctrine and the Marshall Plan trampled on the principles of self-determination and non-interference. This vitriol was perhaps unsurprising, given that the terms were hardly designed to lead to Soviet acceptance. More problematic for the West was that the Soviets' rebuttal of the Marshall Plan also saw them insisting that none of the states within the Soviet sphere could accept the proposal either – both Poland and Czechoslovakia, who had indicated initially that they would like to participate in the Plan, returned the message that they could not, for fear of angering the Soviet Union.

The Soviets also responded with a counter-plan to the Marshall Plan in the form of the so-called Molotov Plan of July 1947 and with the formation of the Cominform (Communist Information Bureau). The former was the precursor to the January 1949 COMECON (Council for Economic Cooperation), and suggested that a speedy *ad hoc* response to the Marshall Plan was being concocted. The plan reflected the Marshall Plan in that it aimed to strengthen post-war economies and came with a degree of control from the Soviet Union. The plan had a centralized agency under Moscow's control, although it had a semblance of democracy, member states being able to discuss trade affairs, but not obliged to engage in discussion of matters that did not concern them. Even so, it cemented the role of Moscow in Eastern European economies, resulted in a swift rise in Soviet trade, and ensured that Eastern Europe was economically dependent on the Soviet Union and impervious to Western capitalism.

The formation of the Cominform extended the political control of the Soviet Union over Eastern European Communist parties as well as including those of France and Italy. To some extent it was the Comintern reborn, although had a much smaller number of parties as members and was headquartered in Belgrade, rather than in Moscow. Its First Congress was held in September 1947 at Sklarska Poreba in Poland, where Andrei Zhdanov gave a speech in which he articulated the Soviet vision that the world had become divided into two camps, capitalist and socialist, which, while they were capable of coexisting and cooperating, would inevitably clash if the Western powers pushed a line of isolating the Soviet Union while at the same time attempting to extend control that interfered with the sovereignty of states. This forcefully stated line of Soviet foreign policy, known as the 'two camps thesis', embodied the thrust of Soviet foreign policy in the developing Cold War and effectively entrenched the conflict between the Soviet Union and the United States in the early years following the end of the Second World War.

Empire building: the spread of Soviet domination in Eastern Europe

With the battle lines clearly drawn by the end of 1947, and both the Soviet Union and the United States making clear that they could see no way that the two powers could avoid conflict, the Soviets set about consolidating their power in Eastern Europe. The aims of pursuing this were to ensure security against a reinvigorated West Germany, to repel a potential invasion of the Soviet Union by the Western powers, to exploit Eastern European economies in order to gain reparations for Soviet reconstruction, and to ensure that the Soviet Union had control over Eastern Europe and its pro-Soviet governments. In this light, it was domination and control that became most important, and a Soviet imperialism can be seen to have emerged in the approach to Eastern Europe during this period. Particularly striking in the project for gaining and asserting control were the communist takeover in Czechoslovakia, the Soviet blockade of Berlin and the expulsion of Tito's Yugoslavia from the Communist bloc.

The Soviet strategy for the domination of Eastern Europe, which the Hungarian Communist leader Matyas Rakosi referred to as 'salami-slice tactics', was played out in 1948. The process began with a *bona fide* coalition between non-Communist and Communist parties, which were then twisted into forced coalitions with Communist dominance, the post of Minister of the Interior being reserved for a Communist, such that the non-Communists could be pushed out of the coalition. The next stage involved a purge of non-Communists from these coalitions, either through branding the non-Communists as Nazi collaborators or, on occasion, through deploying force. The final stage was the conduct of a purge of the all-Communist leadership in order to root out any individuals seen as potential non-adherents to the line pushed by Moscow.

Specifically, in Czechoslovakia the coalition government began to be over-taken by the Communists in early 1948. The trigger for this was the action of the Communist Minister of the Interior, who made moves to have the Czech police dominated by Communist officers, leading to the resignation of the majority of non-Communist government ministers. Those resistant to the Communist takeover were pushed out, the Foreign Minister, Jan Masaryk, falling to his death from a window in March 1948. The Soviets then applied further pressure to Czechoslovakia, forcing the President, Eduard Benes, to resign. A Communist 'coup' had taken place, which cemented Soviet power over Eastern Europe, and shocked the West.

The reality was, however, that this was simply the most extreme form of Soviet domination in Eastern Europe. Poland had undergone a similar process, with the Communists being elected as the only option in 1947, and Bulgaria had experienced a rigged election in 1946 that ended the monarchy and brought a Communist government to power in late 1947. Romania suffered the same fate as its Balkan neighbour, and became the People's Republic of Romania in March 1948. Hungary had shown more resistance to the penetration of Communist politics, with Communists consistently performing poorly in elections until Ferenc Nagy, the premier, took a trip abroad in 1947. In his absence, the Communists altered the electoral process to favour themselves, and in August 1947 they gained enough ground within the coalition that they were able to take power by the end of the year.

Yugoslavia presented a more problematic case for the Soviets, not least because an indigenous Communist movement had gained control before the Soviets took Belgrade in late 1944. Control had been gained by partisans under the leadership of the Communist Josip Broz Tito, who had defeated forces loyal to the Yugoslav monarchy in exile in London and established a provisional government. While the British, Americans and Soviets tried to protect the monarchy, the Communists dominated the cabinet formed in March 1945 and, through the use of terror and intimidation forced out non-Communists and created a position in which free elections could not take place. In November 1945 the Yugoslav Constituent Assembly declared that Yugoslavia had become a People's Republic, and the 1946 Constitution bore the hallmarks of Stalin's 1936 Constitution of the Soviet Union. Despite its Communist power and its apparent closeness to the Soviets, in June 1948, the Soviets expelled Yugoslavia from the Cominform.

This move surprised Western observers, who believed that, of all the states in Eastern Europe, Yugoslavia was the most closely aligned with the Soviet Union. The problem, it seemed, stemmed from the fact that Tito was seen as being too independent, and the Yugoslavs were in fact somewhat resistant to the extension of Soviet hegemony within their borders over the economy, the state and the Communist Party. The Soviets argued that it was they, not the Partisans who had liberated Yugoslavia in 1944, which further inflamed resentment of the Soviet Union. Tito clearly presented a challenge to Soviet domination, which was fast becoming imperialistic, and some questioned whether Stalin's intentions were to annexe Eastern European states so as to form part of the Soviet Union, and so had to be dealt with.

Stalin began his turn against Tito in February 1948, summoning the Yugoslav and Bulgarian leadership to Moscow for a meeting, which Tito refused to attend on the grounds of ill health. Stalin was enraged, and unleashed a torrent of anger, turning particularly fiercely on the Bulgarian leader, Georgi Dimitrov, for apparently forging an agreement between Bulgaria and Yugoslavia without obtaining permission from Moscow. From this point onwards, Stalin turned fiercely on Yugoslavia, and Tito in particular. Issuing a series of rebuttals and making attempts to smear Tito, the Soviets eventually pushed the Cominform to expel the 'Tito-clique' in June 1948, seemingly in the hope that Tito would lose control over Yugoslavia. Despite Soviet desires, Tito retained control, and Yugoslavia slipped from the Soviet Union's sphere, despite remaining Communist.

The Yugoslav case showed Moscow that despite, having control in Eastern Europe by the spring of 1948, it still faced dissent, or what its believed was dissent, within the territory it dominated. Moscow's response was to attempt to assert its dominance and to remove those who were seen as a threat to Soviet power. Beyond Tito, the Soviets rooted out others whom they saw as problematic and carried out a series of repressive moves against the leaderships of Eastern European states, including execution, imprisonment and expulsion from the Communist Party, and the use of show trials. In 1949 the 'Polish Tito', Władysław Gomułka, the leader of the Polish Workers' Party, was removed from office. What then followed was a procession of show trials that claimed the lives of Laszlo Rajik in Hungary and Traicho Kostov in Bulgaria in 1952, and of Vladimir Clementis in Czechoslovakia and Lucretiu Patrascanu in Romania in 1954. In addition to these, approximately a quarter of other officials and Communist Party members suffered in the process of purging the Eastern European parties of those who were not seen as completely loyal to Moscow.

At the same time as they launched repressive measures, the Soviets also introduced a system designed to tie Eastern European states to the Soviet Union, which consistently put the Soviets in the primacy. A series of agreements between the Soviet Union and its satellites gave the Soviets the means to extract economic gains, and to assert control through sending military advisers, diplomats and troops. Linked to this was the export of a single, monolithic Soviet model for government and economic structures and practices, which was expressly designed to ensure that Moscow controlled an Eastern bloc and was able to Sovietize it, making it a part of a Soviet Empire.

Control of Eastern Europe was also a factor in the Soviet blockading of Berlin in 1948. In early 1948 an agreement was reached to unify the Western zones of occupation in Germany, with the announcement that a Federal Government would be established in West Germany. In the context of a worsening relationship between the Soviet Union and the West, the Soviets viewed this as an attempt to create a power base in Germany that would become militarized. Further adding to the problem was that when the Soviets had refused to give details to the allies of the reparations they were extracting from East Germany, the Allies had stopped sending industrial machinery and equipment. In June 1948 a new currency for West Germany was announced, aimed at preventing the Soviets from being able to disrupt the economic rebuilding of the Western sector. When it was suggested that it be implemented in West Berlin, the Soviets moved to blockade the city, which, although it was under joint occupation, lay within the Soviet-controlled zone of East Germany. This move exploited the fact that although Berlin was under joint control, the land routes into the city were controlled by the Soviets. Initially, on 24 June 1948, the Soviets demanded to be able to inspect goods and passengers entering West Berlin by rail. When they were refused, they stopped all traffic from entering by either road or rail from West Berlin. The Soviets made clear their demands – that they wished to see the cessation of the creation of a West German state, which they believed posed a serious threat to their interests in East Germany and within Eastern Europe. The West refused to meet these demands, however, and the United States undertook the airlifting of foodstuffs and materials into West Berlin in order to circumvent the blockade. The Berlin Airlift, coupled to a Western blockade of East Germany, led the Soviets to concede, in secret negotiations, that the Western powers would not agree to their demands. The result was the establishment of two states: the Federal Republic of Germany in the West and the German Democratic Republic in the East. Berlin remained divided between East and West, and the tension remained.

Despite Soviet failure to prevent the formation of the West German state, and certain concerns about individuals or groups who threatened Soviet dominance within the Eastern bloc, the Soviet Union had embarked in 1948 on a programme designed to extend its control over Eastern Europe. In its doing so, the division between East and West became cemented, although Stalin did question the hard-line stance that Zhdanov had set out. However, Zhdanov's death in late July 1948, after a violent disagreement with Stalin, did not lead to any apparent change of direction in Soviet policy towards Eastern Europe, not least because the Western powers increased their pressure for the containment of Soviet power and moved to extend their military presence and cooperation in Europe and the Near East through the establishment of military bases and the formation of NATO in 1949. The lines were firm, and in 1949 there seemed little chance of their moving.

Beyond Europe: the Soviet Union and the Far East, 1949–53

With Soviet power consolidated over Eastern Europe, and the United States' policy of containment preventing its spread, the Soviets found their attention drawn to the situation in the Far East. The year 1949 saw Chinese Communists under Mao Zedong achieve victory over the Kuomintang under Chiang Kai-shek, after a civil war that had been fought since 1946, despite United States attempts at preventing it. Even so, Stalin was somewhat ambivalent to Mao, despite their both being Communists, and appears to have had a preference for a China in which neither the Communists nor the Nationalists held the dominant position. Even after Communist victory in Manchuria in 1948, the Soviet press still paid scant attention to the situation in China, and in early 1949 the Soviets advised Mao to pursue a settlement with the Nationalists for the partition of China between them. Mao ignored Soviet advice, and the Communists went on to be victorious over the Kuomintang in October 1949. With the emergence of the new People's Republic of China, the Soviets turned about and gave recognition to the new regime, both diplomatically and on the front page of *Pravda*. Even so, the Soviets took similar steps in relation to the Chinese Communists as they had done in Eastern Europe and attempted to bend them to their will and ensure their loyalty and subordination to Moscow.

While China would never become fully subordinate to the Soviet Union, the two powers did have common ground and entered into agreements with each other with regard to economic and military affairs. These agreements were concluded in February 1950 with a Sino-Soviet Treaty, which followed several months of discussion that had begun when Mao travelled to Moscow to that end in December 1949. Within the treaty was a mutual assistance pact in which the two states agreed to support one another in the event of an attack by Japan or one of Japan's allies, by which was meant the United States. The Soviet Union received guarantees of its interests in Manchuria and Outer Mongolia, in return for which it granted $300 million of aid to the Chinese. The lack of Soviet generosity was apparent here, and, despite the Chinese Foreign Minister Zhou Enlai's remarking that the conclusion of the treaty ensured that the United States' attempt to drive a wedge between the Soviet Union and China had failed, it was clear that the Soviet Union had a somewhat cool relationship with the Chinese. Part of the reason for this lay in the fact that the Soviets had not been the victors in the conflict that led to the establishment of Communism in China. Just as in Yugoslavia under Tito, the indigenous Chinese Communists had established their regime on their own, and offered a challenge to Moscow's predominance in the region.

The Soviets had other interests in the Far East. Following the defeat of Japan, Korea had been divided, with a Communist government established in the North, and there was also significant Communist influence over Ho Chih Minh's regime in Vietnam. As with the Chinese, Stalin showed a marked ambivalence to these regimes, and little interest in supporting their development, even in the face of declining colonial control by Western powers in the region. The rise of Communist China, however, was perceived as a threat to Moscow's dominance in South-east Asia, and in 1950 events came to a head with the outbreak of the Korean War.

Korea had been occupied by Soviet troops in the North, and American troops in the South, until both states withdrew in 1949. Even so, the Soviet influence over the North Korean Army remained, along with Soviet equipment and supplies. With their much larger forces, the North Koreans under dictator Kim Il-Sung launched an attack on the South on 25 June 1950, expecting a swift victory. The move was not, it seems, ordered by Stalin, but he gave his consent to the North Koreans' invasion. His reasons for allowing the move lay in preventing the spread of United States or Japanese bases in South-east Asia and in ensuring that the Chinese did not gain the upper hand in the spread of Communism in the region.

The immediate response from United States President Truman to the outbreak of war in Korea was to request that the United Nations Security Council be convened to discuss action. Truman, criticized for the 'loss' of China to the Communists, was keen to prevent the further spread of communism in the Far East, and pushed for intervention via the United Nations. The Soviet Union had boycotted the United Nations as a result of its refusal to admit the People's Republic of China after 1949 and, as a result, was unable to veto the United Nations resolution demanding the withdrawal of North Korean forces from the South and calling for aid to be given to South Korea by United Nations member states. Despite Truman's informing Stalin on 27 June 1950 that United States aims were limited to the restoration of a Korea divided between North and South, the Soviets fiercely criticized the United States for intervening in a civil war in a sovereign state and made accusations concerning American-backed South Korean aggression towards the North. Even so, the Soviets could not prevent intervention by United Nations forces.

Neither, though, were the Soviets prepared to become involved in assisting North Korea. Again, their ambivalence towards Communists in the region was apparent, but it was also clear that the Soviets were not prepared to risk the potential of a 'hot' war with the United States. Here, a marked contrast to the approach in Eastern Europe can be seen, not least because it appears that after 1949 the tensions between East and West were becoming increasingly entrenched through the extension of militarization on both sides and the developing nuclear arms race, following the Soviet acquisition of the atomic bomb in 1949. In avoiding armed conflict with the United States, the Soviets left North Korea to military conflict with United Nations forces, and allowed the spread of Chinese influence rather than their own in Korea.

The North Koreans enjoyed early success in the conflict, pushing along the length of the Korean peninsula to Pusan, but were then swiftly repelled by United Nations forces, which intervened in October 1950. The North Koreans, pushed back into their own territory, looked set to suffer wholesale defeat, at which point Chinese forces were sent to aid the North Koreans and United Nations forces were pushed back to the South. With Chinese intervention, the conflict reached a standoff along the previous dividing line of the 38th Parallel. With this stalemate, peace talks began in July 1951, and continued into 1953.

The Korean War, far from being a swift victory for Communism in Asia that would bring strength for the Soviet Union, in fact served to weaken Soviet power on a global scale. Unwilling to risk war with the United States, Stalin left military intervention in Korea to the Chinese, meaning that it was China rather than the Soviet Union that developed power in the region. Additionally, the Korean War led to a sizeable increase in United States military strength, as first Truman, and then Eisenhower, sought to prevent the 'domino effect' of the spread of Communist power in the Far East. With the bolstering of American might through the militarization and rearmament of West Germany, the Soviet Union was in a position in which it faced widespread challenges to its power around the world.

Conclusion

The Cold War did not develop through Soviet actions alone, and its origins can be seen in tensions that existed well before the declarations of 1946–47 by Stalin, Truman and Churchill. Nonetheless, what is apparent is that both the Western powers and the Soviets viewed the world as divided into two camps following the Second World War, and they saw those camps as entirely incompatible with one another. What began to evolve was a situation in which the Soviets responded to a perceived challenge from the West by ensuring that they held tightly in their grip those Eastern European states that they had occupied during the latter stages of the Second World War. The means to do this was a systematic process of installing friendly Communist governments, removing opposing factions and ensuring that opposition could not develop. They were successful in cementing their power by these means across Eastern Europe, effectively building a Soviet Empire in the Eastern bloc. One state escaped this process: Yugoslavia, which had a Communist movement that had not been installed by the Soviets and took a different path to the rest of Eastern Europe, but also did not forge links with the West that challenged the stability of Soviet power in Eastern Europe.

The Soviets also became interested in the extension of Communism in the Far East, but seem to have been less keenly concerned about countering Western challenges. While Japan was a concern for the Soviets, the latter lacked either the means or the commitment that they had in Eastern Europe for the aggressive extension of their own power. The ambivalence shown towards the Chinese Communists, particularly Mao, and the failure to subjugate the People's Republic of China to the Soviet Union meant that the Soviets struggled to gain a position in the Far East that mirrored the one they had achieved in Eastern Europe. In part, the reasons for this lay in unwillingness to risk a war with the United States, particularly with the development of a resurgent West Germany towards the end of the 1940s. While not abandoning the Far East, the Soviets did not develop power in the region as successfully as they had done elsewhere.

Even so, Soviet forays into Eastern Europe and the Far East drove a response from the United States that increased the extent to which the Soviet Union, and particularly Stalin, felt threatened and encircled. The United States' development of the containment of Soviet power, which became militarized, challenged Soviet dominance around the world, and while it may not have rolled back the Soviet Empire, it certainly served to limit it and to restrict Soviet foreign policy behaviour. In 1952, having been blocked to the West and South, and conceding ground to the Chinese in the Far East, at the Nineteenth Party Congress Stalin announced a commitment to a more defensive foreign policy line. This approach called for the removal of aggressive confrontation and attempts to spread Soviet power and influence, instead focusing on exploiting tensions in the capitalist world. Stalin was insistent that the capitalist world was on a collision course towards renewed war, with the United States as a belligerent, which would lead to the peaceful takeover of the world by socialism. While this was a step back, it was not a new line in Soviet foreign policy, but it marked a significant departure from the confrontational stance of the late 1940s and the forceful spread of Communism in Eastern Europe. In a return a more isolationist foreign policy of coexistence, Stalin's policy echoed Lenin's of thirty years earlier and laid the foundations for what would follow under his successor, Nikita Khrushchev. Even under coexistence, however, the intensity of the Cold War waned little.

Further reading

Aronsen, L., and Kitchen, M., *The Origins of the Cold War in Comparative Perspective: American, British and Canadian Relations with the Soviet Union, 1941–48* (London: Macmillan, 1988).

Djilas, M., *Conversations with Stalin* (New York: Harcourt Brace, 1962).

Garson, R. A., 'American Foreign Policy and the Limits of Power: Eastern Europe 1946–50', *Journal of Contemporary History* vol. 21 no. 3 (1980).

Gori, F., and Pons, S. (eds), *The Soviet Union and Europe in the Cold War, 1943–53* (Basingstoke: Palgrave, 1996).

Haslam, Jonathan, 'Russian Archival Revelations and Our Understanding of the Cold War', *Diplomatic History* vol. 21 no. 2 (1997).

Levine, A. J., *The Soviet Union, the Communist Movement, and the World: Prelude to the Cold War, 1917–1941* (New York: Praeger, 1990).

Mastny, V., *The Cold War and Soviet Insecurity: The Stalin Years* (Oxford: Oxford University Press, 1996).

Nogee, J. L., *Soviet Foreign Policy since World War II* (New York: Pergamon, 1981).

Roberts, G., *Stalin's Wars: from World War to Cold War, 1939–1953* (New Haven, CT: Yale University Press, 2008).

Roberts, G., *The Soviet Union in World Politics: Coexistence, Revolution and Cold War, 1945–1991* (Oxford: Routledge, 1999).

Tucker, R., 'The Cold War in Stalin's Time: What the New Sources Reveal', *Diplomatic History* vol. 21 no. 2 (1997).

Ulam, A., *Expansion and Coexistence: Soviet Foreign Policy, 1917–1973* (New York: Holt, Rinehart and Winston, 1974).

Walker, J. S., '"No More Cold War": American Foreign Policy and the 1948 Soviet Peace Offensive', *Diplomatic History* vol. 5 no. 1(1981).

Westad, O., Holtsmark, I., and Neumann, I. (eds), *The Soviet Union in Eastern Europe: 1945–89* (Basingstoke: Macmillan, 1994).

Zubok, V. M., and Pleshakov, K., *Inside the Kremlin's Cold War: From Stalin to Khrushchev* (Cambridge: Harvard University Press, 1996).

Stalin died in March 1953, and had no clear successor. A power vacuum opened, with several individuals vying for power – significantly Nikita Khrushchev, Georgii Malenkov, Vyacheslav Molotov and Lavrentii Beria. A fairly bitter power struggle ensued, during which time an attempt was made to present a sense of unity to the rest of the world, not always with great success. The death of Stalin not only left instability within the Soviet Union, but also led to the questioning of Soviet power within the Soviet Empire of Eastern Europe, and some calls for independence from the Soviet Union. Additionally, the leaders locked in their power struggle adopted policies, both domestic and foreign, that were far less aggressive or repressive than Stalin's.

As the power struggle unfolded, Nikita Khrushchev eventually emerged as the dominant figure. Under Khrushchev, a process of destalinization was embarked upon, both at home and abroad, which brought challenges and was strictly limited. Within it, Khrushchev developed a foreign policy of peaceful coexistence with the capitalist world. This policy had its origins in the defensive stance adopted by Stalin in 1953 and that had been preserved through the years during which the leaders vied for power after his death, but it did not always see the Soviet Union avoiding conflict either within its own sphere of influence or in the wider world.

In the aftermath of Stalin's death, the Soviets were met with serious challenges to their power in Eastern Europe, with uprisings in East Germany in 1953 and Hungary in 1956. The repressive aspect of the Stalin era was apparent in the response to these challenges, even though the approach was slightly more moderate. At the same time, as the result of a series of challenges that it faced though, the Soviet Union was forced to shift its approach to what had become a *de facto* Empire in Eastern Europe, and to make concessions.

The power struggle after Stalin's death and Soviet foreign policy, 1953–56

Stalin was initially replaced with a joint leadership, led by Georgii Malenkov as premier and leader of the Communist Party of the Soviet Union.

The other members of the group were Lavrentii Beria, the head of the Political Police, Vyacheslav Molotov, the Foreign Minister and Nikita Khrushchev, who fairly swiftly took over the Party leadership. The system was not entirely stable and the population was told not to panic, despite the disarray that ensued as the leadership battled over who would become dominant. Malenkov retained the most senior position, and until 1955 seems to have been in the position of leader. Consistently, though, there was a pervasive aspect of the leadership attempting to break away from the brutal authoritarianism of the Stalin years. Beria disappeared first, not least because he was seen to represent the repressive aspects of the Stalin era, removed by the rest of the group in June and executed in December 1953. This was followed by a struggle for general popularity between Malenkov and Khrushchev, both of whom competed for the top Party position. Both tried to reach out to the population, calling for a relaxation of Stalinist repression – what they both termed a 'thaw' – both at home and abroad.

Khrushchev eventually won, and displaced Malenkov in February 1955, not least because he pushed the Party as dominant in the apparatus of state management. This not only side-lined Molotov and Malenkov, but also gained Khrushchev a great deal of support. His domestic policy pursuits garnered him much favourable publicity. In foreign policy, he showed a strong grasp of the turning-point of 1953 – Stalin was dead, and Truman had been replaced by Eisenhower. Khrushchev condemned Zhdanov's Two-Camp Doctrine, arguing that it had done great harm in the relationship between the Soviet Union and the capitalist world, and instead took the standpoint of Peaceful Coexistence. He made the point that although the capitalist and socialist systems were incompatible, they did not necessarily have to clash with one another.

Khrushchev's identification of a turning-point in 1953, with the death of Stalin, was borne out fairly soon after the event in terms of foreign policy, and put into practice Khrushchev's point about the lack of an inevitable clash. The Soviet Union had become isolated after first the aggressive policies of the late 1940s and then a shift to a defensive policy in 1952, but the new leaders swiftly made moves to reverse the situation. They sought to restore links that had been broken under Stalin, and offered the West a more conciliatory approach. A new, more moderate ambassador was sent to Beijing in March 1953. In April, a speech by Eisenhower was published in *Pravda*, devoid of the usual trappings of the tension between the United States and the Soviet Union. The Soviets also sought to repair the damaged relationship with Yugoslavia, stopping the anti-Tito invective in May 1953. Additionally, concessions were made to the West in order to reduce tensions, notably in the Soviets abandoning their pursuit of territory from Turkey and working with China towards concluding a peace in the Korean War. On this latter point, the Soviet initiative resulted in the conclusion of an armistice at the end of July 1953.

This change of attitude impressed Western leaders, although some more than others, and certainly showed that the Soviet Union was starting to emerge from its isolation. The British Prime Minister, Winston Churchill, called for the re-establishment of dialogue between the West and the Soviet Union under its new leadership, although the United States Secretary of State, John Foster Dulles, proposed the maintenance of containment and isolation of the Soviet Union. Dulles was of the opinion that, despite the apparent overtures of the Soviets to the West, they had not changed in their outlook and continued to view the world as divided into two opposing camps. Eisenhower took a less hard-line view, and accordingly a conference of foreign ministers was organized in Berlin in January 1954, heralding a return to discussion between the former wartime allies.

Despite the reopening of dialogue between the Soviet Union and the Western powers, little ground was gained and the relationship quickly faltered. When the conference of foreign ministers met, Molotov espoused the same hard-line policies that he had done under Stalin, while the battle over Germany continued to rage, although the Soviets appear to have believed that they might be able to achieve their aim of diminishing the threat they saw from West Germany. The Soviets proposed an independent German Republic established by West and East Germans. Once it was established, the Soviets proposed, there should be a free election, while the United States wanted the election be held first, believing that the Soviet Union was attempting to subjugate a unified Germany to its control, just as it had done with Eastern Europe in the late 1940s. Soviet hopes for a resolution of the German situation were further dashed when, in October 1954, West Germany was admitted into NATO.

The Soviet reaction to West Germany's becoming a part of NATO, and to its attendant permitted rearmament, was to pursue the formation of an opposing body. Moscow moved to conclude the Warsaw Pact with its Eastern European satellites, which was signed in May 1955. Clearly meant as a counter to Germany's becoming part of NATO, the conclusion of the Warsaw Pact served to reinforce the sense of a conflict between East and West, as well as strongly indicating Soviet intractability with respect to Germany. Although aggressive, the Pact formalized the military aspect of the agreements that Moscow had concluded with Eastern European states while extending its control in the late 1940s. Designed to have a twenty-year duration, the Warsaw Pact remained an entrenched aspect of Soviet foreign policy and the Cold War for far longer than this.

The concurrent Soviet evacuation of Austria mitigated to some degree the challenge that the Soviets had presented to the West in concluding the Warsaw Pact. This was a move clearly designed to show that the Soviet Union was not committed to the idea of a divided Europe, and it flew in the face of the Western view that the Soviet Union would never retreat; but it became abundantly clear that this was the only area in which the Soviet Union would ever make such a territorial concession voluntarily.

The Soviets, or rather Khrushchev, did show willingness to heal the relationship with Tito. In May 1955, Khrushchev visited Belgrade to mend the relationship between the Soviet Union and Yugoslavia. The groundwork for this had been done in 1954 with the Soviet and Comintern abandonment of the anti-Yugoslav line in public, and Tito had given indications during the year that Stalin's death heralded a new era in which the repressive policies of the Soviet Union were diminished, if not removed, and had intimated that a restoration of relations between the two states might be possible. Even so, Tito had some clear stipulations: Yugoslavia would not become subservient to the Soviet Union, nor abandon its links with the West, and, perhaps more importantly, he wanted a public apology from Khrushchev for Soviet conduct. The apology, made in June, sent out shock waves throughout the Eastern bloc. Khrushchev conceded that Stalin had been at fault, implying that Tito was in the right and giving legitimacy to the independent Communist stance that had been adopted in Yugoslavia. At the same time, there was marked sense that if the Yugoslav approach was legitimate, then the Soviet domination of Eastern Europe and the imposition of Soviet-style institutions lacked a degree of legitimacy. If not explicitly, then tacitly, Khrushchev acknowledged the right to the adoption of Titoism across the Soviet Empire. The implications of this were potentially shattering for Soviet hegemony over Eastern Europe, and for the Soviet relationship with the Chinese.

In the Far East, the Soviets were also able to repair the relationships that had suffered under Stalin. Not only were the Soviets involved in brokering peace in Korea, but also they were able to broker a ceasefire between France and the Vietminh in Indochina in early 1954. The agreement came following the French loss of Dienbienphu, and resulted in partition between a Communist North Vietnam and a non-Communist South Vietnam along the 17th Parallel. The Soviets saw this as a great triumph in securing territorial gains for Ho Chi Minh's Communists, and were of the belief that they had gained influence in the region as a result. That Ho Chih Minh had been trained in Moscow (as had been Tito) was also seen as giving weight to the development of Soviet influence in South-east Asia via North Vietnam.

The relationship with China was also partly restored, with a Soviet delegation travelling to Beijing in September 1954. The Chinese appeared open to Soviet advances, although it swiftly became apparent that the Soviets were in a relatively weak position with Mao, as they had been with Tito, and they made significant concessions of the Ports of Darien and Port Arthur and the Chinese Eastern Railway, all of which had been restored to Soviet control after the defeat of Japan in 1945. Despite, or perhaps because of, these territorial concessions, the Chinese and Soviets concluded an agreement whereby the Soviet Union was to aid the economic and military development of China in order to counter the development of United States power.

By the end of 1955, the Soviet Union had gone through a transitional phase following Stalin's death. That transition had been marked by a power struggle for the leadership of the Soviet Union, and also by a shift in the foreign policy approach that the Soviets took. A standpoint that focused on re-engagement, rather than isolation, emerged, and the new leadership, notably Malenkov and Khrushchev, showed that they were willing to make some concessions in relation to the hard-line stance of the Stalin era, particularly with regard to the Two-Camps Doctrine that Zhdanov had espoused in the late 1940s, and in their articulation of the notion of Peaceful Coexistence with the capitalist world. Even so, the Soviets conceded nothing of substance to the West, and indeed intensified the contested position of Germany with the conclusion of the Warsaw Pact in 1955. In the Far East, they did seem to make some headway, but were also keen to end war, lest the West should in fact prove to be victorious, or China make more ground. Within their Eastern European sphere, which had become a *de facto* Soviet Empire, they remained keen to keep their influence, but were less willing to resort to the repressive tactics of the Stalin era, and even willing to mend bridges that had been burnt during that time. In relaxing their policy, though, they gave rise to a questioning of Soviet power, and indeed of Soviet-style Communism. The opening of that opportunity for questioning Soviet dominance in Eastern Europe, and the moves made by Khrushchev after securing power in 1956, resulted in a crisis within the Soviet Empire.

The 'Secret Speech' and its implications

On 14 February 1956 Khrushchev, now the Soviet leader, spoke at the Twentieth Congress of the Communist Party of the Soviet Union in Moscow. He expressed the ideas of Peaceful Coexistence, giving a report on the development of the socialist world, while stressing that the Soviet Union had no intention of making moves to extend the reach of socialism to countries within the capitalist world. He also made plain that this idea had roots in Leninism, and so was politically justifiable, that war was not inevitable, and gave a run-down of the Soviet moves that had been designed to reduce the tension between the Soviet Union and the West.

A more profound statement was made after this, on 24 February 1956, when Khrushchev gave his 'Secret Speech' to a closed session of the Twentieth Party Congress. In this speech Khrushchev denounced Stalin and his actions, particularly his cult of personality, the purges and the excesses of Stalin's personal dictatorship. While not going so far as to invalidate Soviet rule, or the basis of Soviet economic development in the 1930s, Khrushchev launched a programme of destalinization across the Soviet Union and sent out signals that a liberalization of Soviet power over Eastern Europe might also be feasible. Despite the notion that this was a 'secret speech', Khrushchev was not able to keep the content secret. Copies leaked out across Eastern Europe as they were circulated to Communist parties, which called into question the very nature of the Soviet dominance and the way in which it had been achieved.

This led to further questioning of Soviet power in Eastern Europe, although, to a degree, the Soviets were prepared for this. Everything was blamed on Stalin. The falling-out between the Soviet Union and Yugoslavia was attributed to Stalin's desire for personal power, and the relationship between the two was improved, even if once again Tito declined to subjugate Yugoslavia to the Soviets. But even with the ability to turn the situation to their advantage, the Soviet Union faced challenges, not least because Khrushchev had all but admitted that the Soviet Empire of Eastern Europe was entirely illegitimate.

As if confirming this illegitimacy, the Cominform was dissolved in April 1956. While to some extent this move was to placate Tito, it had the effect of removing one of the mechanisms via which the Soviets had exerted influence over Eastern European Communist parties. In addition to the furore unleashed by the admission that national communism was legitimate, and by the 'secret speech', this move fanned the flames of a growing movement for reform in Eastern Europe. While he had not offered it explicitly, Khrushchev's moves were seen as heralding a shift, if not to a complete withdrawal of Soviet influence, to some form of federation of Eastern European Communist states that had autonomy, rather than being subjugated to the Soviet Union. This led to conflict within the Soviet sphere, and while the East German Workers' uprising in 1953 following Stalin's death had been swiftly dealt with, the challenge of 1956 was to be much greater.

The first flashpoint came in October 1956 in Poland, although the opposition had been building for some time before that. Anti-Soviet sentiment had been building through 1955 and 1956 following, the release of the purged Polish leader, Władysław Gomułka, in December 1954. Discussions centred on reform, although to some extent they resulted in crystallization between conservatives and younger Communists over whether Poland should purse a path of national communism. The death of the Polish leader, Bolesław Bierut, in March 1956 was seen as a potential slipping point for Poland to move away from the Soviet Union, but Khrushchev moved quickly to install Eduard Ochab – who, while conservative, was more lenient than his predecessor – in the vain hope that the tide of anti-Soviet sentiment in Poland might end. While a gradual liberalization did seem to be taking place, the workers' uprising in Poznan made it clear that Khrushchev's 'secret speech' and the manner in which it had been interpreted in Eastern Europe threatened not only to destabilize Poland, but to set off a cascade of revolt against Soviet power in Eastern Europe.

The Soviet response to the uprising in Poznan was to suppress it, using armed force, and then to argue that the West had attempted to exploit, if indeed it had not been responsible for, the situation in Poznan and that a strong, unified Communist position was needed, not just in Poland, but across Eastern Europe. This approach failed to work and unity did not appear in Poland, but rather, a division between reformist and Stalinist elements was becoming apparent. With a split becoming apparent, the reformist wave grew and demonstrations broke out across Poland in the summer and early autumn of 1956 which called for the Soviets to withdraw their troops and which had a distinctly anti-Soviet tone. The Soviets, however, did not quit Poland, and when the Eighth Plenum of the Polish Central Committee convened on 19 October 1956, with the express intention of forming a new Politburo, a Soviet delegation which included Khrushchev, Anastas Mikoyan, Molotov and Lazar Kaganovich forced themselves on the meeting at the same time as Soviet tanks advanced on Warsaw from their base in Wroclaw. The Soviets once again tried to deploy force to deal with the Polish situation.

However, the Soviets issued an order for the tanks to stop their advance when Gomułka, who had been co-opted into the Polish Central Committee, demanded that Khrushchev call them off before a violent conflict took place between Soviet forces and the population of Warsaw. Khrushchev, impressed by the unity of the Polish leadership, and swayed by the argument that the potential conflict could be extremely damaging to both Poland and the Soviet Union, withdrew not only the Soviet tanks, but also the Soviet delegation at the Plenum. A new Polish Politburo was formed with Gomułka as First Secretary and with the commander of Soviet forces in Poland, Konstantin Rokossovskii, excluded. Conflict with the Soviet Union was avoided, and a compromise reached because Poland's autonomy was recognized, even if that country did not entirely escape the Soviet sphere of influence. Poland remained a member of the Warsaw Pact but secured better trading relations with the Soviets, and Soviet-style policies were relaxed or abandoned. The 'Polish October', which was quickly defused, saw Gomułka following a line that had been identified as legitimate in the apology to Tito, a line whereby Poland achieved a degree of independence of the Soviet Union, even though it was not carried so far as to mirror the situation of Yugoslavia. Importantly, Gomułka, who was seen as a victim of Stalin and was, as a result, popular in Poland, retained a notable loyalty to the Soviet Union that Tito did not express. However, it is clear that the Soviets were keen to make concessions in Poland for the stake of stability, first and not least because the loss of Poland would further challenge Soviet legitimacy and enhance the position of the West's anti-Soviet campaign, but also in the hope that similar challenges would not spread elsewhere within Eastern Europe.

Soviet hopes were to be dashed by the uprising in Hungary that followed hot on the heels of the 'Polish October', in November 1956. Hungary differed from Poland and Yugoslavia in that it did not attempt to pursue either the line of greater autonomy within the Soviet sphere, or the position of Titoism. Instead, Hungary pushed for independence and the removal of Soviet power, as had happened in Austria, Hungary's neighbour to the west.

The challenge to Soviet power began in 1955, with Matyas Rakosi forcing the more moderate Imre Nagy from power. The return to power of Rakosi, a staunch Stalinist who had been Hungarian premier prior to June 1953, stimulated opposition and he was forced to make political concessions in 1955 in order to keep the Hungarian population pacified, although he continued to adopt a Stalinist policy line. Pressure on Rakosi mounted, and in July 1956 he was forced from power following a visit to Budapest by Mikoyan, and Moscow installed Erno Gero in his place. Gero pursued a line of reform but did not abandon the Stalinist elements of control via the army and secret police, and he failed to restore or maintain stability in the Hungarian situation. Events spiralled out of control, and by September 1956 reformists in Hungary were calling for ties with the Soviet Union to be broken and a declaration of Hungarian independence. In a last-ditch attempt to quell revolt, Nagy was restored as leader on 23 October 1956 as unrest broke out in Budapest.

Nagy, occupying the middle ground, had the support neither of reformists, nor of hard-line Communists and could not regain control. The Soviet response, yet again, was to use military means to attempt to restore order, tentatively at first and then with greater force. While Nagy concluded a ceasefire between Hungarian insurgents and the Soviet forces on 29 October, which led to the beginning of the withdrawal of Soviet troops, order was not restored and the Soviets articulated a legitimization of the use of armed force. The Soviets, or so they claimed, had deployed troops in order to assist an allied state in the restoration of order in a situation that the Hungarians could not manage alone. While this point was accurate, the Soviet Union also intervened in an attempt to repress an anti-Soviet nationalist movement that, if left unchecked, could spell disaster for Soviet power in Eastern Europe.

This last point was borne out in early November 1956, when Soviet forces were redeployed to Budapest. On 1 November, Nagy announced Hungary's intention to leave the Warsaw Pact and to become independent and neutral. The Soviet reaction was to move towards military re-intervention, although the move was made only after some deliberation in Moscow. On 4 November 1956 Soviet forces once again advanced against the Hungarian opposition, deploying 250,000 troops and 5,000 tanks. The Soviets swiftly defeated the Hungarian rebellion, ignoring calls from the United Nations to withdraw and again arguing that the West had been involved in inciting unrest. Nagy was deposed, and later tried and shot. The Soviets then followed up their victory over the Hungarian people with repressive measures that resulted in an estimated death toll of 25,000. Approximately 200,000 Hungarians fled to the West as Austria opened its borders. The Soviets, though, had regained control of Hungary and prevented it breaking away from the Soviet sphere.

The Soviet response to the Hungarian challenge made the point that there could be no toleration of any attempt to escape Soviet power. Neither, it seemed, could the Yugoslavian situation be allowed to be recreated. The 'Polish October' had shown that a degree of liberalization was acceptable, as long as a state remained loyal and subjugated to the Soviet Union, but this was as far as things could go. Abundantly clear, though, was that Soviet power in Eastern Europe stemmed from the use of military force as a means to ensure that states remained firmly within the grip of Soviet control, and that the Soviet leadership was prepared to use that force. Khrushchev, realizing this, and the fragility of such a means of enforcing Soviet rule, announced a programme of reform to build a 'socialist commonwealth' that had fewer of the facets of Soviet-style colonialism, especially in the economic arrangements between the Soviet Union and Eastern European states.

Reform did materialize, but it remained limited. The Hungarian regime under Janos Kadar made limited reforms that gave some degree of autonomy to Hungary, and Poland achieved an improved position within the Soviet Empire. Even so, the reaction to the events of 1956 was the extension of control via military power, repression and ensuring that any political moves were strictly limited. Across Eastern Europe, the Soviets created an atmosphere wherein there was no scope for another challenge in the face of extended Soviet military power. In short, while limited reforms could be countenanced, the Soviets held Eastern Europe in its grip by force.

The events of 1956 caused problems for Khrushchev. Khrushchev and his process of destalinization were blamed for causing the uprisings in Eastern Europe in late 1956, as he had signalled that concessions to undo Stalinist policy were possible, concessions that other members of the Soviet leadership were not prepared to countenance. Arguing that, through his policies, Khrushchev had unleashed a whirlwind of dissent, his political rivals attempted to oust him from power in early 1957. They failed, as Khrushchev maintained a narrow majority within the Central Committee of the Communist Party of the Soviet Union, but clearly his power had been rocked by the events that had unfolded in Eastern Europe during 1956 and by the fact that he had been portrayed as the culprit in encouraging protest against Soviet power and was therefore responsible for the repression that followed.

At the same time, however, the West had not pushed its strategy of rolling back Communism when the opportunity had presented itself in 1956, and had stood by as Hungary suffered the fierce reprisals of a Soviet Union that would not let it out of the Soviet grasp. The West's failure to act in support of Hungary, despite all of the proclamations made by Dulles to that end, meant that the Soviets were able to discredit the Western powers and decry them as unreliable and self-interested. That to an extent the stand-off was the product of the developing nuclear arms race did not escape notice, and it was becoming apparent that while the Soviets were not prepared to risk hot war with the United States, the converse position was also true.

The Soviet Union, the Suez crisis and relations with the Arab world

One of the reasons why the Soviets were able to act with such military force in Hungary was that the Western powers were distracted at the very moment that Moscow launched repressive measures against Hungary on 4 November 1956, by the outbreak of the Suez crisis. Suez not only pre-occupied the West, leaving Hungary to its fate, but also gave Khrushchev the opportunity to forge a stronger relationship with the Egyptian leader, Gamel Nasser, and through this to begin to develop a relationship with other Arab states, notably Syria.

The Soviets had already begun developing a more cordial relationship with Egypt after Stalin's death. While Stalin had criticized the Egyptian leadership's nationalist position in the fight against British and French colonialism, Khrushchev had attempted to draw Egypt into the Soviet sphere by encouraging the rejection of Egypt's ties to the European powers, hoping that this might weaken the cordon of containment that the United States had constructed along the frontiers of the Soviet Union and its empire. Western pressure on Egypt resulted in 1955 in a request from Nasser to the Soviet Union for military aid. This led to the conclusion of a proxy agreement between the Egyptians and the Soviets in the form of an Egyptian–Czechoslovak agreement for the provision of arms, and for aid in developing and modernizing the Egyptian economy. While the Czechs ostensibly were the providers of the aid, it was clear that they were a front for the Soviet Union, and the arrangement resulted in a significant improvement in the relationship between the Soviets and the Egyptians, as well as creating a position of Egyptian dependence on the Soviet Union, even if Nasser did not become subservient to his benefactors.

With an improved state of affairs, the Soviets supported the Egyptian moves against the British and United States refusals in July 1956 to provide funding for the construction of the Aswan Dam on the River Nile. Seen as vital to the development of Egypt, the nationalization of the Suez Canal Company was announced by Nasser, threatening British and French inter-ests. The Soviet Foreign Minister, Dmitrii Shepilov, signalled Soviet backing for the Egyptian move to nationalize the Canal, arguing that it was within Egypt's rights to do so and giving a sharp warning to Britain, France and the United States that reacting with force could lead to the spread of conflict in the Middle East and beyond.

The British and French attempted to address the Egyptian challenge over Suez by convening a conference of Canal users in London. Finding this an ineffective avenue for achieving a resolution of the situation, they then moved the discussion to the United Nations Security Council. It was in the midst of these negotiations that Israel launched a surprise attack on Egypt on 29 October 1956. The conflict developed further when, on 5 November, Britain and France joined Israel and launched an invasion of Egypt across the Suez Canal. The Soviets quickly made moves to turn the situation to their advantage – not least because the events in Suez drew attention away from Soviet aggression against Hungary – decrying Israeli and Anglo-French actions as a violation of Egyptian rights to self-determination. The Soviets demanded that the United Nations Security Council impose a ceasefire and indicated their preparedness to use military force to restore order in the Middle East. Promising the destruction of Israel, and missile attacks on London and Paris if the conflict were not halted, the Soviets gained an enormous upsurge of support within the Arab world. Britain and France backed down, but the Soviets were to find that they steadily lost favour with Egypt because they were viewed as having held back somewhat, out of fear of reprisals from the United States.

Conclusion

Stalin's death was a watershed for Soviet policy, in both domestic and foreign contexts. A clear realization that policy under Stalin had been flawed and that any leadership following his death would need to distance itself from the worst excesses of Stalinist repression and imperialism, as well as a shift to collective leadership, characterized the power struggle that followed after 1953, although it swiftly became apparent on the international stage that the Soviets were prepared to make only limited concessions, and that there were certain reforms that were unacceptable. The hopes of Eastern European states and of the watching world were buoyed up by what they saw in early concessions and in the moves to acknowledge the legitimacy of national communism, but were then dashed as the Soviet Union enforced its imperial control over Eastern Europe when its dominance was challenged in Poland and Hungary during the latter part of 1956.

Despite the fallout of 1956, and its ramifications for Khrushchev's leadership and the fate of Eastern Europe, Soviet foreign policy did enjoy some success in the period after Stalin's death and during the years of wrangling for power within the collective leadership. The Soviet Union became involved in the brokering of peace in Korea and was able to improve its relationship with China and Yugoslavia, which served to lessen tension between the Soviet Union and the West to some degree. These gains, however, not only came at the price of admitting that Stalin had been overzealous in his desires to extend monolithic Soviet control over the socialist world, and accordingly wrong to deny the legitimacy of national communist movements, but also in fact called into question the legitimacy of the extension of Soviet power beyond its borders.

In the push for control of Eastern Europe, and especially in the manner in which the Soviets responded to the formation of West Germany, the Cold War deepened. The conclusion of the Warsaw Pact split East from West, and the fact that it had been predicated by the German situation was clear. By 1956, although the Soviets had ensured that their power within the empire they controlled in Eastern Europe was firm, the means to ensure this had been, and would remain, the ability and willingness of the Soviets to employ military force to maintain their position, and Soviet rejection of concessions to the West. Importantly, however, the deployment of military force remained limited to the Soviets' sphere of influence, demonstrating Soviet unwillingness to move to a position of hot war with the United States or to risk nuclear war. Soviet actions, despite the early indications of liberalization, ultimately served to heighten Cold War tension in the years immediately following Stalin's death, and to cement the division between the capitalist and socialist worlds.

Further reading

Bialer, S., *Stalin's Successors: Leadership, Stability, and Change in the Soviet Union* (Cambridge: Cambridge University Press, 1980).

Dallin, A., *Soviet Foreign Policy after Stalin* (Philadelphia: Lippincott, 1961).

Ilic, M., and Smith, J. (eds), *Soviet State and Society under Nikita Khrushchev* (New York: Routledge, 2009).

Kemp-Welch, T., 'Khrushchev's "Secret Speech" and Polish Politics: The Spring of 1956', *Europe–Asia Studies* vol. 48 no. 2 (1996).

Khrushchev, S., Gleason, A., and Taubman, W. (eds), *Nikita Khrushchev* (New Haven, CT: Yale University Press, 2000).

Larres, K., and Osgood, K. (eds), *The Cold War after Stalin's Death: A Missed Opportunity for Peace?* (Lanham, MD: Rowman and Littlefield, 2006).

Medvedev, R., and Medvedev, Z., *Khrushchev: The Years in Power* (Oxford: Oxford University Press, 1977).

Nation, R. C., *Black Earth, Red Star: A History of Soviet Foreign Policy* (Ithaca, NY: Cornell University Press, 1992).

Nogee, J. L., *Soviet Foreign Policy since World War II* (New York: Pergamon, 1981).

Roberts, G., *The Soviet Union in World Politics: Coexistence, Revolution and Cold War, 1945–1991* (Oxford: Routledge, 1999).

Talbott, S. (ed.), *Khrushchev Remembers* (Boston: Little, Brown, 1970).

Taubman, W., *Khrushchev: The Man and His Era* (New York: Norton, 2003).

Ulam, A., *Expansion and Coexistence: Soviet Foreign Policy, 1917–1973* (New York: Holt, Rinehart and Winston, 1974).

Westad, O., Holtsmark, I., and Neumann, I. (eds), *The Soviet Union in Eastern Europe: 1945–89* (Basingstoke: Macmillan, 1994).

Zubok, V., and Pleshakov, K., *Inside the Kremlin's Cold War: From Stalin to Khrushchev* (Cambridge, MA: Harvard University Press, 1996).

8 Peaceful coexistence and confrontation
Soviet foreign policy, 1957–64

While 1956 was marked by a series of crises for the Soviets, both within their sphere of influence and beyond, that appeared to have been dealt with, their legacies endured. While the challenges to Soviet power were dealt with by Khrushchev by means of force, these moves served to weaken his position within Soviet politics somewhat. Although he was able to survive the political challenge from his rivals in 1957, and to neutralize a potential future threat from them, by scattering them to the winds, Khrushchev was forced to retreat and to reconsolidate his position. In doing so, he drove a foreign policy line that, while it emphasized the notion of peaceful coexistence with the capitalist world, served to ensure that a firm division between East and West became more deeply entrenched. And while he was able to achieve recognition of the Soviet Union as the predominant socialist power in the world, he also created discord in the relationship between the Soviet Union and those Communist states, which while friendly, were not subjugated to the Soviet Union, namely Yugoslavia and China.

While the Soviet Union's preparedness to use force to maintain its position with regard to its Eastern European satellite states was clearly one aspect of Khrushchev's position, he also made moves to compete with the West and to attempt to strengthen the Soviet Union and its Empire. To this end, in his foreign policy Khrushchev continued to espouse the notion of Peaceful Coexistence with the West, although it manifested itself in a somewhat modified form that was aimed more at an enforced coexistence, with a clear division between East and West, than it was at easing tension with the Western powers. Indeed, in the period between cementing his leadership and his fall from power in 1964, Khrushchev's policies and behaviour led to a heightening of tension with the West.

In this vein, the Khrushchev era became marked by a series of rifts within the Communist world – with Yugoslavia and China – and by confrontational stand-offs with the United States over Germany and Cuba, at the same time as the United States began to engage in a war against Communist elements in Vietnam. While these never escalated to the point of direct confrontation between the Soviet Union and the United States, nor into military clashes within the socialist world, the era was nonetheless tense at times. Khrushchev's confrontational stance, and the concessions that he had to make in order to avoid a catastrophe, ultimately saw him ousted from power in 1964. Of particular note here was the Cuban Missile Crisis of 1962, which seriously eroded Khrushchev's credibility as Soviet leader.

Discord within the socialist world: Yugoslavia and China 1957–64

One of the challenges that Khrushchev failed to deal with successfully was that of regimes that, while socialist, or indeed Communist, were not under Soviet control and had no desire to be. In the late 1950s and early 1960s, despite early signs of cordial relations between the Soviets, Chinese and Yugoslavians, the Soviets were to find that the respective paths of communism could not be prevented from diverging. Yugoslavia and China both desired different things, not least with regard to their relationship with the Soviet Union and with the West. Under Khrushchev, a deteriorating relationship with other states within the communist camp but outside of Soviet dominion began to develop and take hold. While the Soviet relationship with Yugoslavia took the character of an open dispute, the situation with China by the early 1960s was one of outright division and competition. Both disputes, though, displayed an important characteristic of both Khrushchev and Soviet policy towards the Communist bloc – unwillingness to compromise and a desire to maintain Soviet superiority within the socialist world.

Thus it was that a second dispute with Tito began in the late 1950s. Despite his having apparently mended the relationship between the Soviet Union and Yugoslavia through his apology to Tito in 1955, Khrushchev again fell out with Tito in 1957–58. The root of the problem between the Soviet and Yugoslav regimes was the issue of alignment, and that Tito was not willing to subjugate Yugoslavia to the Soviet Union under any circumstances or to reject Yugoslavia's ties with the West. Khrushchev, who viewed the world as divided between East and West, was unable to come to an accommodation with Tito's desire for a neutral position between East and West.

The split followed on from an apparently amicable beginning. In the summer of 1957 the relationship between the Soviets and the Yugoslavs seemed to be improving as Tito and Khrushchev made pronouncements that they did not differ on most of their views and desired the relationship between the two states to develop into a deeper cooperation. In August 1957 Khrushchev and Tito met in Bucharest and reached an agreement that Yugoslavia would support Soviet foreign policy in Europe and the Middle East. Tito secured a somewhat limited acknowledgement of Yugoslavia's independence from Soviet power. The meeting was concluded with Tito accepting the invitation to a conference of Communist parties to be held in Moscow in November 1957.

It was in the build-up to the November 1957 conference that it became apparent that, despite what seemed to have been agreed in August between Khrushchev and Tito, the Soviet world-view remained unchanged. Draft resolutions circulated in advance of the conference made it plain that the Soviets continued to view the world as divided between East and West, and that the division remained one of incompatibility one with another. While this was perhaps unsurprising, given the line that the Soviets had pursued prior to this point, the implication was that Moscow was denying the Yugoslav claim to non-alignment with either bloc. There was, as far as the Soviets were concerned, no middle ground.

The situation escalated as the conference approached. The Soviets denounced what they viewed as revisionist policy in Yugoslavia, angering Tito to the point that he refused to attend the conference himself, instead sending Aleksandr Ranković and Edvard Kardelj (Tito's most senior colleagues within the Yugoslav leadership) as the Yugoslav representatives. When they arrived in Moscow for the conference, the Yugoslav delegates were to find that Soviet desires went significantly further than the draft resolutions had detailed, with a line of Soviet domination over Yugoslavia being pushed and Mao calling for recognition of Soviet hegemony over the Communist world. The Yugoslav delegates, unwilling to accept the Soviet demands of Yugoslavia's subordination to Moscow, refused to sign the final conference agreement. This defiance enraged the Soviets, but Yugoslavia's voice was alone and unsupported by other Communist leaders. Yugoslavia was, at this stage, the outsider.

Tito's position moved swiftly further away from the Soviet Union and he asserted the Yugoslav desire to remain socialist, but aligned to neither the Soviet Union nor any other power. In March 1958 the draft programme for the Yugoslav Communist Party's Seventh Congress set out a fierce anti-Soviet position. The emergence and development of the Cold War was blamed on both the Soviet Union and the United States, the implication being that Soviet inflexibility had deepened the conflict between East and West, even if it was not solely to blame. A call was made for the recognition both of the independence of states and that there were national roads towards Communism rather than achieving it only through the imposition of a monolithic model and strict centralized controls. It was, however, the denunciation of Soviet deviance from Marxism–Leninism that most enraged the Soviet leadership, who clung to the position that their version of the ideology was the only correct route to full-blown Communism.

The Soviets raised their objections to Tito, arguing that his position placed too much emphasis on the ills of the Stalinist past, which Khrushchev had denounced in 1956. Tito accordingly modified his line somewhat, but not to the extent that the Soviets were placated. Such was the Soviets' view of Tito's actions and proclamations that they announced a boycott of the Yugoslav Communist Party Congress in April 1958 and demanded that all other Communist parties under Moscow's influence adhere to it. The Yugoslav response was to fiercely criticize Soviet actions at the Congress, although the leadership worked to forestall a complete break with the Soviet Union.

With tensions running high, the Chinese accused Tito, and what was now identified as Titoism, of working to fragment international Communism and sow discord. Echoing Mao's calls for the recognition of Soviet hegemony in November 1957, an article published in the Chinese newspaper *Jen Min Jim Pao* on 5 May 1958 was reprinted by *Pravda* the following day with strong endorsement from the Soviet leadership, and was then followed by a tirade of articles decrying Titoism as revisionist and both non-Marxist and anti-Leninist. Still, the Yugoslavs stood in defiance to Chinese and Soviet accusations of deviance from the true path of Communism, and the situation worsened when, on 3 June 1958, Khrushchev denounced Tito and stated that Yugoslavia was not a socialist state. Tito's rebuttal of Khrushchev accused him of deliberately engineering the situation and of manipulating the Chinese, with the intention of subjugating Yugoslavia to Soviet power. Others chimed in against Yugoslavia, notably the Polish leader, Gomułka, and the Yugoslavs found themselves ousted from the Communist camp.

The Soviet Union and Yugoslavia had decidedly broken with each other in the summer of 1958, but it was clear that the threat of Soviet invasion or intervention that had characterized the split between them a decade earlier did not form a part of Khrushchev's approach to foreign policy. Tito pursued his agenda on non-alignment with either East or West, building relationships with other non-aligned states, working to restore the Yugoslav relationship with the West and maintaining a civil, if not friendly, relationship with the Soviet Union.

The dispute between Yugoslavia and the Soviet Union had been born out of resistance to a Soviet desire for dominance over the Communist world, resistance from a state that had taken a national path to communism without Soviet imposition. Khrushchev was to find, not long after falling out with Tito, that another state that had taken a similar path would also disagree with Soviet desires for hegemony over the Communist world. So it was that, in 1960, long-standing tensions between the Chinese and the Soviets burst out into a public and open conflict that would lead to the development of a complete rift between them by 1963.

The relationship between Communist China under Mao and the Soviet Union had never been particularly solid. From the point that China became Communist in 1949, and the meetings held between Stalin and Mao in 1949 and 1950, it was clear that China was not going to fall under domination from Moscow and that the Sino-Soviet relationship was quite different to the Soviet relationship with the Communist states of Eastern Europe. With the onset and development of the Korean War, it was clear that China, not the Soviet Union, was the dominant Communist state in South-east Asia and that to some extent the Soviet Union had ceded that position to the Chinese.

Even so, Mao was a committed Marxist and had adhered to a Stalinist line. When Khrushchev criticized Stalin in his speech at the Twentieth Party Congress in 1956, Mao espoused a negative view of Soviet revisionism and the departure from the Stalinist line. At the November 1957 conference of Communist parties in Moscow, where Mao insisted on the recognition of Soviet hegemony over the Communist world, Khrushchev noted that Mao sounded very much like Stalin. His call for Soviet hegemony was, it seems, made very much in a Stalinist mould.

By November 1957 the Sino-Soviet relationship was rocky, but far from hostile. Much of the tension centred on whether the Soviets would help the Chinese in the development of nuclear weapons, possibly even giving China an atomic bomb. In October 1957, hoping to keep the Chinese satisfied in the build-up to the Communist Party's conference in Moscow in November, Khrushchev agreed to assist the Chinese in creating a nuclear capability and the relationship between the two states improved significantly. The air of Sino-Soviet friendship contributed in no small part, it would seem, to Mao's calls for recognition of Soviet hegemony in 1957 and the Chinese attack on Titoism in 1958.

Khrushchev, though, increasingly pushed the Chinese away after the middle of 1958. Mao took an ultra-left stance in both foreign and domestic policy at the time, which meant that Khrushchev's efforts to improve the Soviet relationship with the United States were viewed negatively, and even as a potential threat, by the Chinese. When the Chinese threatened to launch an attack on Taiwan and other Chinese offshore islands, almost precipitating a military confrontation with the United States in 1958, the Soviets refused to offer military aid if a conflict should break out. It was clear that the Soviet Union and the Chinese had never been on the same path, and by 1959 their paths were rapidly diverging in terms of both domestic and foreign policies. The promise of assistance in the development of nuclear arms had eased the tension between the two powers, but as differences arose through 1958 and into 1959, in June 1959 Khrushchev saw fit to nullify his agreement to render the aid that the Chinese desired, and accordingly the relationship worsened rapidly.

An absolute split did not occur until 1963, but from mid-1959 onwards the division between the Soviet Union and China was severe. While both claimed to follow Marxist–Leninist principles, the ideology and revolutionary trajectory of the two states differed increasingly. The Soviets had pinned their revolution of the development of an industrial working class, while the Chinese sought to politicize an agrarian peasantry. Mao had been quietly subservient to Stalin, but after the latter's death became increasingly concerned to promote himself as the supreme Communist leader in the world, and a competition for dominance within the global Communist movement developed rapidly at the end of the 1950s. As Khrushchev tried to placate the West, Mao accused him of revisionism and moved to promote revolution in Asia and Africa and spread Chinese influence globally.

By August 1959, both the Soviet Union and China expected a breach in relations with each another. The differences in ideology and policy had, it seems, become too great for the leadership of the two states to overcome and they were battling for global dominance and for influence within revolutionary states around the world. With the promise of nuclear arms off the table, the Chinese found little reason to pander to the Soviets, and fierce criticisms and abuse were levelled both at Soviet advisers aiding Chinese industrial development and at Khrushchev's policy line. By the end of 1959, the Soviets had recalled their advisers from China and expelled Chinese students from the Soviet Union.

Even so, in early 1960 the United States remained unaware of the depth of the division in Sino-Soviet relations. Problems had been apparent, as had divergent policy lines, but it was only in May 1960 that Mao made the dispute publicly visible, and much more violently contentious. An article published in *Red Flag* in April 1960, and written by Mao, denounced Khrushchev as a revisionist and fiercely criticized his attempts to achieve peaceful coexistence with the capitalist world. In June, Khrushchev fired back while attending the Romanian Communist Party Congress, where he clashed with the pro-Chinese Albanian delegation and the Chinese delegate, in addition to distributing written attacks on the Chinese leadership in which he made accusations of Chinese nationalism, adventurism and desires for nuclear war.

Khrushchev then moved to ease the tension within the Communist world, calling a World Communist Congress in Moscow to which delegates from eighty-one Communist parties came. On the face of things, the disagreements were patched up – peaceful coexistence with the West was defended and Titoism was denounced as a deviation from the direction of the international Communist movement. Underneath the veneer, however, Khrushchev wrangled with the Chinese delegate over criticisms of Mao and Khrushchev's positions in relation to the capitalist powers. There was even a suggestion that Khrushchev favoured Nehru's India over China. None of this, though, was particularly threatening to the Sino-Soviet relationship in mid-to-late 1960, and the accusations that had been thrown back and forth ceased for a time.

The situation then worsened again in 1961, with events coming to a head around the Twenty-second Congress of the Communist Party of the Soviet Union in October. From late 1960 and through 1961, the Soviets had placed pressure on Albania to return to the Soviet camp and abandon the Chinese. When the Congress opened in October 1961, the Albanians refused to attend and to submit to Soviet power, and the Albanian leader, Enver Hoxha, denounced Khrushchev while praising Stalin. Khrushchev was incensed, and launched fierce attacks on Albania and Hoxha during the Congress, before breaking off Soviet–Albanian relations in December 1961. This led to a shift in the Sino-Soviet relationship to one of denunciation by proxy throughout 1962 – the Soviets criticized Albania when they meant

China, while the Chinese directed their assault at Yugoslavia when they meant the Soviet Union. By 1963, the Chinese had moved to open attacks on Khrushchev's foreign and domestic policies, and in July 1963 they created a territorial dispute based on claims that the Russian Empire had appropriated Chinese territory during the nineteenth century. This last blow caused Sino-Soviet relations to unravel completely.

The break between the Soviet Union and China reverberated within the Communist world. As had happened before, with the Soviet recognition of the legitimacy of the national path to Communism, through the 1955 apology to Tito, now the rupture in Sino-Soviet relations and the fact that it presented two divergent Communist powers to the world gave rise to a renewal of nationalist sentiment within Soviet-controlled Eastern Europe, and Soviet power faltered somewhat. Khrushchev did not lose control over the Soviet empire, but his efforts to hold it together were met with increased challenges following the division of the Communist camp into those who looked to Beijing and those who looked to Moscow.

From peaceful coexistence with the West to crisis, 1957–62

While Khrushchev was dogged by disputes within the Communist world in the late 1950s and into the 1960s, he maintained the stance of peaceful coexistence with the West that he had espoused since Stalin's death. This is not to say that he necessarily sought cordial relations with capitalist powers, but rather that he sought to avoid armed confrontation, nuclear war and the development of West German militarism towards the acquisition of nuclear armaments. To that end, he adopted a policy of not conceding much politically to the West, particularly to the United States, and of making gains where he could while not provoking an attack on the Soviet Union or its satellites in Eastern Europe.

The Soviet Union, in 1957, was in something of a position of strength in relation to the United States. Since 1950 the Soviet economy had developed at a greater rate than had that of the United States, and Khrushchev bragged that the Soviet Union would soon overtake American productivity and was no longer threatened by being in a weaker economic position, and indeed was poised to become the world's dominant economic power. Further, on 4 October 1957 the Soviets had launched the first man-made satellite into space, *Sputnik*, which caused great consternation in the United States, bolstered Soviet prestige and began the space race between the Soviet Union and the United States, with the Soviets having scored the first goal. By 1958 Khrushchev believed he was in a position to make a bold move towards the West.

This move was the issuing of an ultimatum, on 27 November 1958, to the Western powers to remove their troops from West Berlin within six months. Precipitating a second Berlin crisis, a decade after the first, Khrushchev was pushing for Berlin becoming a 'free city' to which the West would have to negotiate access from East Germany. United States Secretary of State John Foster Dulles rejected the ultimatum, with agreement from NATO, threatening military action should the West be prevented from maintaining access to Berlin. Unflinchingly, in March 1959 Khrushchev drew up a draft treaty that proposed the creation of an independent Germany. Although the timing was short of the expiration of Khrushchev's ultimatum of the previous November, the draft treaty sent a strong message to the Western powers that Khrushchev was serious in his intent, and the upshot was that he held the upper hand in negotiations. Britain, still reeling from the Suez crisis, seemed to be particularly concerned by Khrushchev's moves, and Harold Macmillan, the British Prime Minister, travelled to Moscow to meet with Khrushchev. In Moscow, Macmillan made a string of concessions aimed at having Khrushchev abandon his ultimatum. Even so, the matter remained unresolved and Khrushchev appeared to believe that he could press his advantage further, presenting grand demands over Germany to a conference of foreign ministers which threatened to bring negotiations to an end. The deadlock was broken by American delegates extending an invitation for Khrushchev to visit the United States in late 1959, which he duly accepted.

The crisis, however, was far from over, even if it was temporarily relaxed. Khrushchev remained vociferous on Soviet strength in relation to the capitalist powers, and was further buoyed up by his feeling that he had won the upper hand in East–West relations over his pressing of the Berlin issue. His invitation to the United States, he believed, signalled a major coup in negotiating with the West and was recognition of the status of the Soviet Union as a power in American eyes. It was in a mood of friendly relations that Khrushchev travelled to the United States in September 1959, even if matters remained somewhat tense between the two powers.

Khrushchev had not only scored a major coup in being invited to the United States, and in being the first Soviet leader ever to visit it, he was also regarded positively by the American population during his visit. Travelling with his wife, and briefed beforehand by Anastas Mikoyan on potential business links, Khrushchev came across as friendly, inquiring and keen to be frank and open with his hosts. These qualities seemed to strike a chord with the Americans, and by the time he sat down to meet with President Dwight Eisenhower the world was buzzing with the 'spirit of Camp David'. The two heads of state met in an air of friendliness, and Eisenhower made clear to Khrushchev that only if provocation were extreme would the United States countenance the outbreak of war. Khrushchev was convinced to make concessions to the United States with regard to his position on Germany and Berlin, the ultimatum having not been enforced, and the basis for a possible development of *détente* appeared to have been laid. The two leaders did not agree on all matters. Most notably, Khrushchev refused to agree to Eisenhower's 'Open Skies' proposal for aerial surveillance by each state of the other's territory, which in reality was an attempt by Eisenhower to agree on parity with what he was aware was already a Soviet capability. He conceded that Khrushchev's refusal was neither surprising nor a blow to the relationship between the United States and the Soviet Union at the time. A further meeting in Geneva was set for the spring of 1960.

When Khrushchev returned to the Soviet Union, it was clear that he was of the opinion that the Soviet–American relationship was on the brink of becoming increasingly friendly. He had been impressed by what he saw in the United States, not least when he travelled to Iowa to see American farming methods and to discuss crops, and would later use the examples that he saw in the development of Soviet agricultural policy – not with outstanding success. Khrushchev's overestimation of the success of his bridge-building with Eisenhower appeared as a major weakness through the early part of 1960. While he had reported to the Supreme Soviet in January 1960 that a new era of Soviet–American cooperation was on the horizon – much to the consternation of the Chinese, who viewed such a development as weak and revisionist – by April the situation was looking considerably less favourable as tensions continued over the status of Germany. Khrushchev made a series of proclamations that, in the absence of any agreement on Soviet proposals over Germany, the Soviets would conclude a treaty with East Germany that would end Western access to West Berlin. On 20 April 1960 the United States, which still refused to recognize East Germany, made plain its commitment to supporting West Germany and maintaining access to West Berlin. Khrushchev viewed this as a threat to use force and a reversal of the principles he that believed had underlain his meeting with Eisenhower the previous autumn.

Worse was to come in the relationship between the Soviets and Americans. Immediately prior to a summit meeting in Paris, the Soviets shot down an American U-2 spy plane over Soviet territory on 5 May 1960. The United States Department of State initially claimed that the aircraft had been pursuing meteorological research, but Khrushchev was able to refute this by the production of surveillance film and evidence that the pilot, Francis Gary Powers, who was alive but in Soviet custody, had been interrogated. Eisenhower, somewhat gracefully, conceded the reality of American surveillance flights over the Soviet Union, and took responsibility for all such activity since 1956. Khrushchev wasted no effort in taking the Americans to task and publicly exposing what he portrayed as American duplicity. When Eisenhower refused to offer an apology for United States actions, Khrushchev called for the Geneva summit to be cancelled and withdrew his invitation to Eisenhower to visit the Soviet Union later in the year. While Khrushchev felt that he had little choice but to take a stern line with the United States over the incident, the collapse of the Geneva summit, continued discord over Germany and the U-2 crisis caused the chance for rapprochement between the United States and the Soviet Union slip away.

Despite this, Khrushchev returned to the United States for a visit in the autumn of 1960. Far from making the favourable impression that he had made one year before, however, he achieved little, and indeed made moves that weakened his position. He addressed the United Nations General Assembly, calling for a change in the structure of the United Nations. Khrushchev proposed that the Secretary General be replaced by a commission composed of three representatives, one to represent each of the socialist, capitalist and non-aligned states. That Khrushchev was locked in a battle with Dag Hammarskjöld, the then Secretary General, did not escape notice, and Khrushchev found little support for his proposal. Rather than take the defeat with grace, however, Khrushchev made matters worse when he banged his shoe on the table during a speech by the British Prime Minster, Harold Macmillan, bringing derision upon himself and leaving others within the Soviet leadership acutely embarrassed at their Premier's behaviour.

The relationship between the United States and the Soviet Union was again becoming increasingly difficult and Khrushchev weakened his own position in late 1960 as a result of his actions in New York. Conflict with the Chinese was developing and there were serious problems in the Soviet economy that were viewed as a result of Khrushchev's mismanagement. Khrushchev sought a way to both score a blow against the United States and salvage his position within the socialist world. The opportunity that he seized upon came with the election of a young and inexperienced United States President in November 1960, John Fitzgerald Kennedy and the rise of Communist power in Cuba following the successful overthrow of Batista's regime and the victory of Fidel Castro. Cuba, it seemed, was to be Khrushchev's ticket to salvation. In reality, it was to become one of the major sources of his downfall.

The Soviets had done nothing to encourage or to bring about the Cuban Revolution, but when it became apparent that Castro was a committed Marxist and was keen to lean towards Moscow rather than Beijing, Soviet interest increased. Cuba provided an opportunity for a direct challenge to the United States – it was very close to the United States and, importantly, under the Monroe Doctrine, fell into the United States' sphere of special interest. The Soviets and Cubans became increasingly friendly after the cancelling of the Geneva summit and, as Soviet–American relations deteriorated, so Soviet–Cuban relations improved. In return for political allegiance and the opportunity to drive a thorn into the United States side, the Soviets bought Cuban sugar and provided arms, technology and advisers to Cuba. As Soviet involvement with Cuba increased, Khrushchev informed the United States that the Soviets could now pose a military threat to American soil and that the Soviet Union was prepared to lend military assistance to the Cubans against American military actions. Cuba, accordingly, became a major point of contention in Soviet–American relations.

The issue of Cuba, and its place in the Soviet–American relationship, became worse in early 1961. Kennedy, keen to be seen to be tough on the Communist world as a new president, gave his assent to a CIA plan approved under the Eisenhower administration. It was apparent that

Kennedy was not entirely at ease with what he agreed to, and the CIA would later accuse him of being less than entirely committed to the action that was taken. What was launched, though, was an invasion of Cuba via the Bay of Pigs using Cuban exiles with CIA support. Crucially, Kennedy had refused air support for the invasion, and the exiles were swiftly and comprehensively defeated, not least because Soviet intelligence was aware of the plans and had informed Castro. The Bay of Pigs was labelled a fiasco in the United States, not least because it failed, but also because it highlighted the breadth of Cuban support for Castro's Communist regime, particularly among the Cuban middle classes. Castro, and Khrushchev by proxy, claimed a great triumph for the Communist world against the forces of capitalism and were spurred to take more adventurous action. Yet again, as in 1957–58, Khrushchev felt that he had gained the upper hand in dealings with the United States.

It was with this sense of Soviet supremacy that Khrushchev met with Kennedy in Vienna in June 1961. In what promised to be a replacement for the cancelled Geneva summit of the year before, discussion was entered into on the position of Germany. Khrushchev reiterated Soviet demands, but Kennedy remained largely consistent with the position that Eisenhower had adopted on the issue, although he seemed to be more interested in the development of peaceful coexistence with the Soviet Union than his predecessor had been. Nothing was agreed, but a basis for dialogue was clearly established that would become vital to the conduct of negotiations between the two men.

Despite this air of friendliness and mutual respect, it was plain that Khrushchev saw Kennedy as young and inexperienced and took the opportunity to attempt to frighten him into making concessions over Germany. Khrushchev made threats that the Soviets would conclude a treaty with East Germany in December 1961 if an agreement over Germany had not been reached by that point. This move, rather than prompting a basis for settlement, resulted in an increase in tension between the Soviets and the Americans, and General Lucius Clay, a veteran of the 1948 Berlin crisis, was dispatched to Berlin by Kennedy to coordinate resistance to the ultimatum Khrushchev had issued. The Soviets accordingly stepped up their military presence in East Berlin. In the summer of 1961 tension was running high in Berlin and people were flooding from East to West as the situation worsened.

The Soviets found a solution to the German problem in August 1961, albeit one of force and partition. The shift of population from East to West Berlin was seen as a challenge to the East German regime, and so the East Germans erected a wall, almost overnight, with Soviet support. With an Iron Curtain built of concrete, rather than just figurative, East and West Berlin were divided. Soviet and American tanks became involved in a stand-off, but no shots were fired. Nonetheless, a division was made that would remain until 1989, ensuring that tension over Germany would persist, but now a physical as well as an ideological barrier existed between the Soviet Union and the West. Khrushchev, it was apparent, was prepared to force the issue of Germany earlier than had been outlined in his ultimatum.

For a brief time, Khrushchev seemed to hold a bargaining chip in the discussion over Germany. In October 1961 Andrei Gromyko, the Soviet Foreign Minister, indicated that the West was keen to resolve the German situation. Khrushchev, showing his concern over the development of West German nuclear capabilities, and also presenting a snub to China, pushed for the development of nuclear-free zones in Germany and the Far East as a possible basis for a Soviet–American settlement of the German question and even a potential alliance. These moves, or at the very least the perception that they were being made, deepened the tensions between the Soviets and the Chinese, not least because Zhou Enlai, the Chinese Premier, had denounced the United States as the chief enemy of peace. Soviet moves towards the United States were not viewed favourably by Beijing, and while Khrushchev seemed to gain some ground in relations with the Americans, the trade-off was a deterioration in Sino-Soviet relations.

Khrushchev's moves in late 1961 and early 1962 were not only, then, concerned with building a relationship with the United States, but also aimed at restricting the rise of Chinese nuclear capabilities and preventing the challenge that he continued to see in West Germany. Soviet intentions to control the proliferation of nuclear arms seemed to be genuine, not least because they was born out of a fear that China or West Germany would present a much greater threat to Soviet security if they became nuclear powers. Despite this, the Soviets were unable to convince the United States on the matter of nuclear disarmament during the Geneva summit between Kennedy and Khrushchev in July 1962, although Soviet action later in the year would result in the beginnings of an agreement.

That action was the installation of Soviet nuclear missiles in Cuba. Khrushchev appears to have decided on this course during the summer of 1962, even as he met with Kennedy and attempted to secure an agreement on arms control, but his decision stemmed from a long-standing desire to protect Cuba from a potential invasion by the United States. An added dimension was that placing nuclear missiles in Cuba would bring the Soviets back into contention with the United States, pose a threat to American soil that had not before been possible and potentially work as a means of leverage with the United States over both Germany and nuclear arms control. It would also, Khrushchev hoped, offer some redress to the problems he faced at home as economic and political decisions went awry.

The Soviet Union began shipping large quantities of equipment, and sending technicians to train the Cubans, in August and September 1962. The United States noticed the step-up in Soviet shipping to Cuba and Kennedy warned on 4 September that there would be serious repercussions if the Soviets were supplying nuclear missiles to the Cubans. An American over-flight on 14 October 1962 identified that the Soviets had shipped medium-range and intermediate-range missiles to Cuba and were building no fewer than forty launching pads for them. Importantly, the work had not been completed, but if had it been, then most of the east coast of the United States, including Washington DC and New York, would have been within the strike capability of the missiles. Mobile launchers were identified, which the United States were concerned would deliver missiles to the United States in advance of the completion of other launch sites. A crisis began over the Soviet installation of nuclear missiles in Cuba.

The United States leadership, seriously concerned at this Soviet move, began to debate a course of action in the face of what they saw as Soviet aggression. The 'hawks', Dean Acheson, Maxwell Taylor and the Joint Chiefs of Staff, recommended immediate air strikes against the missile sites, with the intention of neutralizing them at any cost. George Ball, the Undersecretary of State, argued persuasively for the installation of a naval blockade that would prevent further material entering Cuba and dissuade the Soviets from a confrontational stance. Robert MacNamara, the Secretary of Defence, supported this line, but argued that the use of an air strike could still be resorted to should naval action fail to resolve the situation. This latter line was the one that President Kennedy decided to adopt, rather than risk war with the Soviets from the outset. As the crisis unfolded, Khrushchev's gamble that the United States would avoid war, particularly nuclear war, seemed to pay off, even if it ended with Soviet capitulation and retreat.

The Cuban missile crisis developed when Kennedy announced the American discovery of Soviet nuclear missiles in Cuba on 22 October 1962 and declared a naval blockade. The initial Soviet reaction was one of defiance, but within twenty-four hours Khrushchev had decided to follow a path of caution and negotiation with Kennedy. The two began an exchange of telegrams that led to a compromise and resolution of the crisis over the course of the next few days, although at times the lengthy delays between transmission, receipt and response escalated the tensions of the situation. By 26 October Khrushchev had agreed to the removal of Soviet missiles from Cuba in exchange for an American pledge not to launch an invasion against Castro's regime. He went further in a subsequent telegram, requesting that the United States also remove its Jupiter missiles from Turkey in a reciprocal move. The terms were agreed and the crisis came to an end. The world had stepped back from the brink of nuclear aggression.

Khrushchev's agreement to back down in the Cuban missile crisis, while it averted war between the Soviet Union and the United States, ended what was for him a catastrophic policy venture. While he tried to claim a victory in receiving an agreement from the United States not to attack Cuba or interfere in its sovereign affairs, he had damaged his political credibility beyond salvation. The United States was aware of this and portrayed the outcome as a victory for itself, and Khrushchev appeared weak and adventurist and had yet again failed in a policy gamble. For Khrushchev, already beset by domestic failure, the disastrous foreign policy approach of installing missiles in Cuba and then being seen to capitulate to the United States was embarrassing, and heralded the beginning of his diminishing power within the Soviet Union.

Fallout: the implications of the Cuban missile crisis and the end of Khrushchev

After the Cuban missile crisis, with his authority severely badly damaged, Khrushchev attempted to limp on as leader of the Soviet Union. He was beset on all sides, both from within the Soviet Union and without, and Soviet prestige on the global stage had been severely dented. Soviet relations with China, already problematic in late 1962, worsened, and at the same time the Soviets' grip over their Eastern European satellite states slipped somewhat. Khrushchev, and by implication the Soviet Union, lacked the confidence of the socialist world as a result of the way in which the Cuban missile crisis had unfolded, and even at home Khrushchev's policies were reversed or stopped within the Politburo, in an attempt to avoid a further disaster.

Khrushchev tried to defend his position over Cuba and the events of 1962, arguing that he had made the move in order to protect a socialist ally in the face of American aggression. The missiles, he claimed, had been purely for the defence of Cuba and the intention had been to use them as a basis for bargaining with the United States on contentious foreign policy issues. While he may have believed this, not everybody did so, but he was able to regain sufficient credibility that he can be seen to have made a partial political recovery by mid-1963. With a worsening situation over China, Khrushchev made renewed approaches to the West in the summer of 1963 and was able to conclude the Limited Test Ban Treaty with the United States and Great Britain on 25 July 1963, which prohibited the testing of nuclear devices within the atmosphere, in space or under water (but not underground). Clearly a product of the world's having come so close to nuclear war during the Cuban missile crisis, the conclusion of the treaty was portrayed as a major success of Khrushchev's Cuban venture, as was the installation of a hotline between Moscow and Washington in mid-1963 in order to allow for the prevention of future catastrophes in American–Soviet relations. These gains further bolstered Khrushchev's ailing position, but still he had not regained a position of strength.

One of his problems was that every move he made towards the United States produced more conflict with the Chinese, not least in the personal relationship between Khrushchev and Mao. Following the split between the Soviet Union and China in 1963, the animosity increased, with Khrushchev portraying Mao as Stalinist and Mao criticizing Soviet imperialism and adventurism. While this had implications for the Soviet hold over Eastern

Europe, which the Soviet Union effectively held as an empire, the situation worsened in the light of Mao's argument in August 1964 that the Soviet Union maintained imperial holdings in the Far East. Mao even went so far as to make a claim for large swaths of Soviet Siberia as Chinese territory and to demand that the Soviet Union restore the Kurile Islands to Japan. Khrushchev chose not to inflame the tension with China, and kept his response to Mao restrained. Nonetheless, when the Italian Communist Palmiro Togliatti left a deathbed 'testament' that indicted Khrushchev as severely lacking in prestige outside of the Soviet Union, it was clear that Khrushchev could no longer remain in power.

Within the Soviet Union Khrushchev was hardly faring any better. Others within the leadership viewed Khrushchev's time in office as having left a trail of disastrous domestic and foreign policies. He was also losing the support of the Soviet population as economic growth and rises in standards of living began to tail off. Disaster on the agricultural front, partly caused by climatic conditions but equally the result of misguided policy, worsened the economic situation and further alienated Khrushchev's support base. The biggest problem for Khrushchev, however, was that he had lost the support of the upper levels of the Party. Backed by the KGB, Khrushchev's colleagues within the Politburo moved to remove him from power in the middle of October 1964.

Conclusion

The end of the Khrushchev era was the result of a string of failures and embarrassments, particularly after 1959. One should be wary of discrediting him entirely – the early phase of his time as Secretary General of the Communist Party of the Soviet Union did see some gains on both the domestic and foreign policy fronts. His problems, however, were his propensity to gamble and an unwillingness to find accommodation within the socialist bloc with powers that were unwilling to subjugate themselves to Moscow. On the whole, his policies can be characterized as moderate, but with some sharp and fairly disastrous outbursts. As his policies failed, or were attacked, he lost support and the Soviet grip on Eastern Europe began to falter. His immediate successors, keen not to repeat the mistakes of the Khrushchev era, would take a markedly more aggressive line in their early dealings with the Soviet bloc and with the United States.

Further reading

Abel, E., *The Missiles of October: The Story of the Cuban Missile Crisis 1962* (Philadelphia: Lippincott, 1966).

Edmonds, R., *Soviet Foreign Policy, 1962–1973* (Oxford: Oxford University Press, 1977).

Fursenko, A., and Naftali, T., *'One Hell of a Gamble': Khrushchev, Castro, and Kennedy, 1958–1964* (New York: W.W. Norton, 1997).

Greiner, B., 'The Cuban Missile Crisis Reconsidered: The Soviet view – an Interview with Sergo Mikoyan', *Diplomatic History* vol. 14 no. 2 (1990).

Harrison, M., and Barber, J., (eds), *The Soviet Defence Industry Complex from Stalin to Khrushchev* (Basingstoke: Macmillan, 2000).

Ilic, M., and Smith, J. (eds), *Soviet State and Society under Nikita Khrushchev* (New York: Routledge, 2009).

Khrushchev, S., 'Defence Sufficiency and the Military–Political Conception of Nikita Khrushchev', in T. G. Otte and C. Pagedas (eds), *Personalities, War and Diplomacy* (London: Cass, 1997).

Khrushchev, S., Gleason, A., and Taubman, W. (eds), *Nikita Khrushchev* (New Haven: Yale University Press, 2000).

Medvedev, R., and Medvedev, Z., *Khrushchev: The Years in Power* (Oxford: Oxford University Press, 1977).

Nation, R. C., *Black Earth, Red Star: A History of Soviet Foreign Policy* (Ithaca, NY: Cornell University Press, 1992).

Talbott, S. (ed.), *Khrushchev Remembers* (Boston: Little, Brown, 1970).

Taubman, W., *Khrushchev: The Man and His Era* (New York: Norton, 2003).

Ulam, A., *Expansion and Coexistence: Soviet Foreign Policy, 1917–1973* (New York: Holt, Rinehart and Winston, 1974).

White, M., 'New Scholarship on the Cuban Missile Crisis', *Diplomatic History* vol. 26 no. 1 (2002).

Zubok, Vladislav M., and Konstantin Pleshakov, *Inside the Kremlin's Cold War: From Stalin to Khrushchev* (Cambridge, MA: Harvard University Press, 1996).

9 The Brezhnev era

With Khrushchev's departure from office in October 1964, the Soviet Union once again entered into collective leadership under Leonid Brezhnev as General Secretary of the Communist Party of the Soviet Union and Alexei Kosygin as the Premier. In contrast to Khrushchev's rash gambling, the pair seemed to be much more cautious and, indeed, to embody a more technocratic approach of making the system work. In many ways, the Brezhnev and Kosygin partnership was much more introspective in its early years, not least in reaction to the disasters into which Khrushchev had led the Soviets on the international stage.

Brezhnev gradually became the dominant partner and *de facto* leader of the Soviet Union. As time went on, Brezhnev found that there was still much to be dealt with in terms of foreign policy and in competition with the West. His time in office was marked by an initial reversal of many of Khrushchev's policy positions and a return to policies that harked back to the Stalin era. Restalinization became a reality under Brezhnev, with repression and control within the Soviet Union and its Eastern European satellites. The economy improved before 1973, but then began to decline and stagnate, not least as a result of heavy expenditure on defence and armaments. Brezhnev's foreign policy was marked by an initially difficult relationship with China, the United States and the Eastern bloc. While repression was used to deal with an early challenge in 1968 from Czechoslovakia, Brezhnev was able to achieve rapprochement with China and a period of more cordial relations with the United States, known as *détente*. In the first decade of Brezhnev's rule his foreign policy appeared to be successful, not least as it was set against the United States' entrenchment in the quagmire of the Vietnam War. During the 1970s the relationships with the United States and with China seemed to be largely repaired and arms limitation talks began in earnest. By the end of the 1970s, however, much of the ground gained in improving relations with the outside world, or at least holding back the tide of resistance in Eastern Europe, was undone by a series of Soviet military interventions in Africa, and then by the Soviet invasion of Afghanistan. By the time Brezhnev died in office, the Cold War had been reignited and the United States and Soviet Union had amassed such large quantities of nuclear weaponry that the world existed in a state of nuclear stand-off.

Reaction, retreat, restalinization

The Brezhnev era can be viewed to some extent as one of reaction to, and retreat from, aspects of Khrushchev's domestic and foreign policies, particularly in its early years. Khrushchev was blamed for the poor performance of the Soviet economy and the declining rate of improvement in living standards. The 'thaw' was also seen to have opened up a sphere in which dissent was growing, and which Brezhnev and Kosygin saw as challenging to the domestic stability of the Soviet Union. On the foreign policy stage, the rift with China, unrest within the Eastern bloc, the adventurism of Soviet policy in the third world and a less than cordial relationship with the United States were all seen as problems that needed to be addressed. In the approach to these foreign policy challenges, however, there was marked shift from the explosive and decisive character of the Khrushchev years. Soviet diplomacy adopted a focus of gentle and quiet coexistence with the capitalist world, and lacked a drive to push revolution outside the Soviet Union, for fear that it would upset relations with the West, as had been the case under Khrushchev.

Within the Soviet Union the process of restalinization began with the reintroduction of tighter controls over the Soviet state and society. Once again, state management became heavily repressive of dissenting voices and restricted opinions that could be voiced. This approach was not limited to the Soviet Union, and Brezhnev extended similar measures to the Eastern bloc in order to limit growing challenges to Soviet rule within the empire that had developed during the late 1950s and early 1960s. Khrushchev had not effectively dealt with these and Brezhnev saw them as having been exacerbated by the foreign policy blunders made by his predecessor.

Even so, Brezhnev struggled to halt the development of Eastern European nationalism. A major factor in this was the continued wrangling with the Chinese, which allowed for states to see the development of national communism without domination by the Soviet Union as a legitimate path. This has been a problem for Khrushchev, and was one that Brezhnev was never able to defuse, but that he did find the means to check. In the initial period after Brezhnev came to power, there was some growth of national communist states within the Eastern bloc. In 1965 Romania, which had aligned with China and had established a good relationship with the West, was recognized as independent of the Soviet Union. Romania remained an ally of the Soviet Union, but its constitution made it clear that it would only become involved in armed conflict should it choose to do so. Confirming that Romania had slipped from Soviet control, in May 1966 the Romanian leader, Nicolai Ceausescu, issued a denunciation of both the Soviet Union and the United States for causing militaristic division as a result of the creation of two hostile military organizations, and called for a change to the Warsaw Treaty Organization in order to reduce Soviet domination over the military affairs of the communist world. This was seen to pose a fierce challenge to Soviet hegemony over Eastern Europe, should it be taken up elsewhere, as was the development of Romanian diplomacy with West Germany. Even so, because Ceausescu ruled Romania with similarly tight controls to the Soviet Union, the Soviets were tolerant of Romanian independence.

Part of the reason for allowing Romania to follow its own path was a Soviet desire to weaken the grip of the United States over Western Europe, and in particular West Germany. In contrast to Khrushchev's approach of confrontation in dealing with the German question, Brezhnev capitalized on the facts that the United States was becoming increasingly involved in war in Vietnam and that in January 1965 the new West German leadership under Willy Brandt signalled a desire to heal the division between East and West Germany to some extent. Brandt outlined a policy towards East Germany, *Ostpolitik*, which called for the development of economic and cultural relations between East and West Germany. The Soviets responded favourably to the development of West German policy under Brandt, albeit cautiously and with a keen desire to ensure that Soviet authority and dominance in East Germany and the rest of Eastern Europe were not undermined. *Ostpolitik*, it seemed, offered both opportunities and threats.

The Soviet response to *Ostpolitik* was developed via the organization of a European security conference under Adam Rapacki, the Polish Foreign Minister, in April 1967. The conference resolved that European security rested upon the maintenance of the *status quo* of territorial division, in particular the division of East and West Germany. The message was clear, that territorial revision and the issue of sovereignty were not areas that the Soviets were prepared to discuss with the West in the late 1960s, and that Soviet control was still very much something that Brezhnev desired to maintain. Similarly, a focus on keeping West Germany from possessing nuclear weapons was articulated, much as it had been under Khrushchev, and the Soviet Union's policy remained one of ensuring that no threat could be posed to its sphere of influence in Eastern Europe. With these lines clearly laid out, however, the Soviets and West Germans became involved in talks in 1967 and the beginning of 1968, and would eventually come to an accord in the early 1970s. Brezhnev moved to reduce the friction over Germany, but was nonetheless not prepared to relax Soviet control over the Eastern bloc.

At the same time as the relationship with West Germany was developing in the mid to late 1960s, problems with China were deepening and Soviet relations with the United States worsened. In part, this stemmed from the Vietnam War and Soviet policy towards it. The United States had become increasingly involved in the conflict in Indo-China during the 1950s, but in 1964, under President Lyndon Johnson, United States military involvement in Vietnam was escalated in support of the South Vietnamese regime under Ngo Dinh Diem in fighting the Communist North Vietnamese. As the American fight against the spread of Communism in the Far East deepened, so relations between the Soviet Union and the United States became accordingly beset with difficulties, not least because the Soviets were seen to be supporting North Vietnam in the war against the South. It was the nature of Soviet support to North Vietnam that was part of the increasing tension with the Chinese, as the Soviets were criticized for a lack of commitment to North Vietnam, as was borne out by the extension of fairly limited levels of Soviet support while China offered much more. The situation would get worse between both powers before improving.

The deterioration of Sino-Soviet relations gathered pace in the mid-1960s, not least because an argument raged over the direction of policy towards Vietnam and the two states vied for influence with the North Vietnamese Communists. Brezhnev did attempt to negotiate with China in 1964 and 1965, but every move he made was repulsed. When it became apparent in 1965 that China was developing its own nuclear capabilities and building intercontinental ballistic missiles (ICBMs), China went from being a power with whom the Soviets had broken and could not restore cordial relations to one that posed a potential threat to Soviet security. The Soviets' response was to increase their military presence on the border between the Soviet Union and China and to station forces within Mongolia. China accordingly perceived a Soviet threat to its security as a result of the increase of a Soviet military presence on its frontier, even going so far as to see the Soviets rather than the Americans as their chief enemy.

Tensions between China and the Soviet Union deepened during 1966 as Mao launched his Cultural Revolution and denounced the Soviet leadership as revisionist and non-Marxist. The Cultural Revolution attacked the orthodox Marxist–Leninist line, which only made the ideological conflict between China and the Soviets worse and led to Brezhnev's viewing Mao's policy in part as an attempt to undermine Soviet authority within the Communist world, and as the development of intense nationalism and adventurism.

With an ideological conflict and a competition for influence raging, the Sino-Soviet relationship turned into a border dispute along the length of the 400-mile Sino-Soviet border. While Mao had made claims in the past that the Soviet Union encompassed territory that had been taken from China by the Russian Empire, in the late 1960s the situation turned into one of sporadic armed conflict, as well as political proclamations. Violent clashes between Soviet and Chinese troops took place throughout 1968 and 1969, with a particularly intense series of skirmishes on the Ussuri River in March 1969, leading to an increase in Soviet troop levels along the frontier. By 1969 the sizeable Soviet military presence pushed the Chinese into negotiations with the Soviets at the same time as the two powers seemed to be on the brink of war with one another. This climate lasted into 1970, but the clashes tailed off in 1969. The situation remained tense through the

1970s and both powers maintained strong military forces along the border, but the prospect of war between the Soviet Union and China faded. Not least among the reasons for this was that the Soviets had proved at the end of the 1960s that they meant to defend their interests with powerful military force.

Czechoslovakia 1968: the Prague Spring and the Brezhnev Doctrine

It was with force that the Soviets responded to the rise of discontent within the Eastern bloc in the summer of 1968, when Soviet troops put down an uprising in Czechoslovakia. The Soviet grip over Eastern Europe had begun to falter in the 1950s and early 1960s, and Romanian independence and poor Sino-Soviet relations had further weakened the legitimacy of Communist rule and Soviet domination in the Eastern bloc. Within Czechoslovakia the Communist Party under Anton Novotny was losing popularity from the early 1960s onwards as the economic situation worsened, and in November 1967 students in Prague took to the streets in demonstration against the regime. The protests were violently broken up by the Czech police, but it was becoming apparent that the situation in Czechoslovakia was somewhat volatile. A division emerged within Czech politics, with Slovak communists rejecting orders from the centre and allying with reformist Czech elements. At a Central Committee plenum in January 1968 Novotny was removed as First Secretary of the Party and replaced by Alexander Dubček. Brezhnev believed that Dubček was pro-Soviet and that his appointment would stem the tide of unrest within Czechoslovakia. He was to be proved wrong.

Dubček embarked upon a series of reforms in the spring of 1968. He was, he claimed, attempting to create 'socialism with a human face' and to bring the Communist Party back to a position of popularity as a result. While keen to keep Czechoslovakia tied to the Soviet Union and to maintain the Communist Party's control over Czech society, Dubček embarked upon a programme of liberalization. Centralized control over the economy, with the exception of industry, was relaxed or removed, censorship of the media was done away with, Czech citizens were permitted to travel abroad and a diplomatic relationship was established with West Germany. The pace of change in Czechoslovakia in the spring of 1968 was unsettling, though, for the Soviets.

The Soviets, and indeed others within the Eastern bloc, including Poland's Gomułka and East Germany's Walter Ulbricht, feared that Dubček had unleashed a programme of liberalization that he could neither control within Czechoslovakia, nor prevent from spreading to other states within Eastern Europe, with a risk that Communist rule might be undermined. Fears also abounded that Czechoslovakia might develop a foreign policy independently of the rest of the Eastern bloc, and the prospect of full rapprochement with West Germany posed the greatest cause for concern. After April 1968, Czech foreign policy grew increasingly worrying to the Soviets and to other Communist bloc leaders, and a course of action to deal with the growing problem began to be discussed.

While Brezhnev did not launch an immediate assault on Czechoslovakia, he began amassing Soviet and Warsaw Pact troops on the Czech borders during the spring and early summer of 1968. By June a sizeable military presence was in place along the Czech borders. Hard-line Communist leaders argued in favour of military intervention to end a counter-revolutionary situation, while Brezhnev weighed the options for dealing with the situation. One of the chief concerns was what reaction to a Soviet invasion would come from the Czech army and from the United States. By the end of July 1968, it had become clear that the Czech army would not offer armed resistance to a military intervention and the United States would offer no response either, not least because Johnson hoped to organize a summit to discuss arms limitation with Kosygin, and the American involvement in Vietnam was problematic. Brezhnev was confident that he could embark on the course of military intervention to restore order to Czechoslovakia.

A final meeting of the Czech leadership with the Soviet Politburo at the end of July did nothing to dissuade the Soviets from intervening in Czechoslovakia, although it was clear that there remained some apprehension within the Soviet leadership. By mid-August 1968, however, the Soviet leadership had come to the opinion that there was no other course of action than to intervene militarily in Czechoslovakia using Soviet and Warsaw Pact forces. The Soviets believed that the Czech situation posed a threat to Soviet security in the Eastern bloc, not least because rumours were abounding in August 1968 of an impending coup backed by West Germany, and on the night of 16–17 August they passed a resolution to invade. Three days later, on 20 August, the final plan for invasion was agreed.

The Soviet invasion of Czechoslovakia was sizeable, swift and met with no armed opposition. As Soviet and Warsaw Pact troops swept across Czechoslovakia, however, they found few Czechs who supported the move. Some likened the Soviet invasion to the Nazi occupation during the Second World War. It was clear that the Soviet move was deeply unpopular within Czechoslovakia, and this resonated around the world. Some within the Soviet Union even commented on the brutal Soviet intervention and the damage that it was perceived to have done to Soviet relations with Czechoslovakia and the Eastern bloc. Even so, the invasion had the result of restoring order to Czechoslovakia, and after Dubček was replaced by Gustav Husak, who was staunchly loyal to the Soviets, there were no further challenges to Soviet dominion over Czechoslovakia until the ousting of the Communist Party in 1989.

The Soviet intervention in Czechoslovakia had wider ramifications. Liberalization in other Eastern bloc states was stopped, and ties to the Soviet Union were reinforced. The show of force clearly frightened other

Communist states in Eastern Europe, with Yugoslavia and Romania concerned that they too might be invaded, and saw hard-line repressive policies introduced to stop the potential threat that another reformist state might pose. While the intervention can be seen to have delivered the restoration of control that the Soviets desired, it also exposed the reality of the ends to which the Soviets would go in order to maintain their dominance within Eastern Europe. The Soviet Union had shown the world that it would contravene international law and intervene in a sovereign state in the pursuit of its own interests and to keep communist regimes in place. The Brezhnev Doctrine, which emerged in the wake of the Soviet action in 1968, articulated the notion that problems within the socialist world were to be addressed by the rest of the socialist world in the interests of the preservation of the socialist regime. This, although after the fact, gave a veneer of legitimacy to the Soviet invasion of Czechoslovakia, but also provided a pretext for further similar actions in support of troubled Communist regimes around the world. The Soviet Union had bared its teeth very publicly, and made it very clear that it would lash out in a similar fashion to other challenges to its authority.

Healing the wounds of the Cold War: *détente* with the United States and attempted rapprochement with China

After the Soviet intervention in Czechoslovakia in 1968, the Soviet Union enjoyed a tense relationship with the United States, but it was not long before the wounds of the past began to be healed and the two powers moved towards a situation of *détente*. Key in the development of this situation was that the Soviet Union, by the end of the 1960s, had caught up with the United States in nuclear arms possession and had achieved parity. This, coupled to the fact that neither power seemed to have an intention to use nuclear weapons as anything other than a deterrent, led to a situation where the Soviets and the United States focused more on maintaining the balance of power than on antagonizing one another. The battle over ideology largely decreased, as did competition for global influence. A situation of peaceful coexistence encompassed Soviet–American relations in the early 1970s.

What had in part brought about the change of position was massive Soviet defence spending under Brezhnev in the second half of the 1960s. Increasing the size of both conventional forces and nuclear armaments, Brezhnev had brought the Soviet Union into nuclear parity with the United States. Further, the Soviets had larger land forces than the West and were a strong naval and air power by 1968. The Soviet invasion of Czechoslovakia had, to some extent, made apparent the strength of the Soviet military, and it was clear at the end of the 1960s that the United States and the Soviet Union were well balanced in terms of the forces they could deploy. With the Soviet catch-up, the United States did not pose a threat to the Soviet Union as it had in the past, and so the relationship changed. As a backdrop to this the rift between the Soviet Union and China intensified. The increase in Soviet strength that led to the Soviets seeking better relations with the United States and the West at the end of the 1960s and into the 1970s was seen in Beijing to pose a threat.

The development of a formal Soviet relationship with West Germany in 1970 went a long way to defusing tensions between East and West. While the Soviet leadership had been concerned that Brandt's *Ostpolitik* was a potential threat to the stability of East Germany and other Eastern European states, on 12 August 1970 the Soviet Union and West Germany concluded the Treaty of Moscow. Effectively, the treaty was an agreement for peace in Europe between East and West. Both parties rejected the use of force in the conduct of relations with one another. It was agreed to respect the boundaries of Eastern Europe, in particular the Polish borders and the division of East and West Germany, although West Germany retained a right to reunification at some point in the future. The treaty was followed by a similar agreement between Poland and West Germany in December 1970. Although West Germany took two years to ratify the treaties, because of opposition within the German parliament to the agreement over the division of Germany, friendly relations between the Soviet Union, the Eastern bloc and West Germany had been achieved by 1972. The Soviets gained security, and the world was impressed at the change in Soviet behaviour towards the West.

The Soviet agreement with West Germany in 1970 boosted Soviet relations with the United States, which were already improving after 1969 with the development of arms limitation talks. The Soviets had decided to pursue an agreement on arms control with the United States in 1968, as they could not afford to continue competing with the Americans, and talks started in Helsinki in November 1969. With the Soviet achievement of nuclear parity with the United States and the development of Soviet and American missile defence systems, both powers seemed keen to reach an agreement on arms limitation.

The Strategic Arms Limitation Talks (SALT) begun in 1969 led to the conclusion of the SALT I treaty in 1972, and were instrumental in furthering *détente* between the Soviet Union and the United States. The talks were incredibly complex and drawn out, not least because the nuclear stockpiles of the two powers were so sizeable, and took into account the developments in nuclear technology in terms of the development of first-strike capabilities and missile defence systems. However, the stakes in concluding an agreement were very high, and the treaty was of great significance, heralding the beginning of a process of further arms control agreements.

The Soviet Union seemed to be more interested in SALT than was the United States. Its initial interest was piqued partly as a result of the Soviets' realization that, while the missile gap with the United States may have been closed, continuing to compete in the development of arms was not affordable. Further to this, the Soviets came to the realization that while parity in arms could be achieved and maintained, the balance could be tipped in favour of one power if it developed an effective missile defence system – an undertaking that would be much more costly than building more arms and one in which, again, the Soviets could not afford to compete with the United States. There was also a non-economic issue that lent weight to the Soviet desire for arms limitation and for *détente* with the United States, in the form of the Soviet relationship with China.

The Chinese, at the same time as the Soviets were moving towards *détente* with the United States, were also looking to improve their relationship with the Americans. The view of SALT from China was of its being a move to ensure American and Soviet monopolies over nuclear arms, which thereby posed a threat to China. China, still at loggerheads with the Soviet Union and seeing it as the main source of threat, turned to the United States. Secretary of State Henry Kissinger visited Beijing in July 1971, and on his return to the United States announced that President Richard Nixon had been invited to visit China in 1972 with the intention of re-igniting Sino-American relations on a friendly basis. As a result of this, China ceased to be isolated by the United States and was allowed membership of the United Nations. The Soviets were alarmed by this move, not least because China's acquisition of nuclear arms posed a threat to the Soviet Union, and Brezhnev moved quickly to extend an invitation to Nixon to visit Moscow.

SALT I was concluded as a major step in the process of *détente* between the Soviet Union and the United States and heralded an era of friendship between the two states. The Soviets emerged slightly on top in terms of missile numbers and in its military presence in Europe. The agreement on arms led to superpower cooperation in the early 1970s and even allowed for the United States to broker an improved Sino-Soviet relationship through triangular diplomacy. Nixon used the SALT talks as a means of leverage with the Soviet Union to help extricate the United States from the Vietnam War in 1972, making the case that no agreement could be reached while the war continued. The Soviets, accordingly, assisted in forging a truce in Vietnam, as they were much more interested in *détente* with the West than in continuing to support North Vietnam. The year 1972 apparently marked the beginning of a concrete footing for improved Soviet–American relations, even if Soviet ideological rhetoric continued to voice a somewhat ambivalent stance towards the capitalist world.

Détente led to early signs of mutual assistance when the Soviet Union imported American grain to deal with food shortages caused by a disastrous harvest in 1972. Beyond this, the Nixon administration extended credits and further trade with the Soviet Union between 1972 and 1975. For its part, the Soviet Union assisted with achieving a peace settlement in the Vietnam War, which allowed the United States to exit from the conflict in January 1973 with the Paris Peace Accords. Beyond this, however, the benefits of the relationship began to falter as Nixon became embroiled in the Watergate scandal and those who disagreed with Nixon's line made the path of American–Soviet relations more problematic, with trading relations lapsing in 1975.

Détente, while improving relations between the United States and the Soviet Union, functioned as a means of both mutual exchange and leverage. There were almost always conditions to be met such that something could be achieved. While this is not necessarily unusual in the conduct of international relations, the United States had a clear concept of 'linkage' within the *détente* process that was articulated by Kissinger. The Soviets, the Americans believed, could be persuaded to relax their involvement in Africa, the Middle East and South America, and their attempts to support revolutionary regimes outside of the Soviet sphere. This linkage, however, did not work well in practice, as it seems that Brezhnev never took the United States particularly seriously, not least as he suspected it would not confront the Soviets over their involvement around the globe. Soviet influence developed on the global stage during the early stages of the *détente* process, rather than declining.

With Nixon resigning in 1974 and Brezhnev suffering a stroke in early 1975, the *détente* process began to falter. The zenith of *détente* was achieved on 1 August 1975 with the conclusion of the Helsinki Accords, bearing the signatures of thirty-three European leaders and the leaders of the Soviet Union, the United States and Canada, recognizing the *status quo* of European borders and establishing a basis for mutual economic exchange between East and West, and giving hope for a subsequent agreement on arms control and the improvement of civil rights. The Helsinki Accords, however, were not held to by the Soviets, who continued to intervene in other states' affairs under the auspices of the Brezhnev Doctrine, and to repress the Soviet population, leading to condemnation from the United States President Jimmy Carter in the late 1970s.

Nonetheless, in 1976 Brezhnev was riding high on his success in achieving *détente* with the United States. China, however, remained a problem and the Soviets had still not re-established friendly relations with Beijing, despite Kissinger and Nixon's attempts at 'triangular diplomacy'. In September 1976 Mao died, presenting the Soviets with an opportunity to heal the wounds of the past with the Chinese. However, long-term tension between the Soviets and the Chinese led to the new Chinese leader Den Xiao-Ping refusing a resumption of normal relations with the Soviet Union and concluding a treaty with Japan in 1978 that denounced Soviet hegemony. Nonetheless, the tension between the two states declined to some extent, because the Soviets no longer viewed China as a military threat following the rapid increase of Soviet defence capabilities under Brezhnev.

From a position of stability in 1975, the Soviet Union made moves to extend its global influence at a time of declining economic growth and to capitalize on the rise of revolutionary regimes within the third world. Brezhnev continued to increase Soviet defence spending in order to accomplish the spread of Soviet power, and aided in the establishment of new regimes. In this way, the Soviets became involved in the former Portuguese holdings in southern Africa from 1974 onwards, beginning with Angola, and extending their reach into Somalia, Ethiopia and Mozambique. These moves not only caused difficulties for the *détente* process with the United States, but also led to disquiet within the Arab world as to the nature of Soviet intentions. Egypt's Anwar Sadat cancelled the Egyptian–Soviet treaty in March 1976 and made moves towards establishing better relations with the United States, and in 1977 made an opening towards a settlement between Egypt and Israel.

While *détente* was clearly in decline in the late 1970s, it was not dead in the water. With the impending expiration of SALT I in October 1977, Jimmy Carter sought to bring the Soviets back to the table for another round of negotiations on arms limitation. In March 1977, Secretary of State Cyrus Vance visited Moscow with proposals for talks, which the Soviets found unsatisfactory. The nub of this was the development in nuclear technology, in particular the United States' development of cruise missiles. After a brief tussle, however, the Soviets and the United States met to discuss SALT II in May 1977. The Soviets were in part motivated by a desire to ensure that the United States would not provide nuclear weapons to other countries, China being their chief area of concern, and by a desire to limit the American scope for military involvement in Europe. The talks stalled, although some resolutions were made in late 1977 in talks between United States officials and the Soviet Foreign Minister, Andrei Gromyko. They agreed to respect the agreements of SALT I, even though the treaty had expired, and to continue talking.

In 1978 the discussion of arms control became more contentious after the American development of the neutron bomb, which did not pose the longer-term effects of radiation. The Soviets countered by developing missiles that could strike into Europe. Even so, by the end of 1978 SALT II was ready to be signed, and United States President Carter's announcement of a potential American–Chinese rapprochement in early 1979 put enough pressure on Brezhnev that the treaty was concluded in May 1979 in Geneva. The agreement allowed for a rough nuclear parity, with decreases in arms to be made after 1981. The United States Senate, however, never ratified the treaty because the Soviet invasion of Afghanistan derailed the already ailing *détente* process completely.

The Soviet invasion of Afghanistan, 1979

In December 1979 the Soviet Union launched an invasion of Afghanistan in order to prevent a precarious Communist regime from collapsing. The Soviets had assisted in the establishment of the regime in 1977 with

Mohammed Tamaki and Hafizullah Amin as its leaders. The pace of change, and the alienation it caused, seriously unsettled Afghanistan and by 1978 a civil war between Muslim groups and the Communists was beginning. The Soviets blamed Amin for the unrest, and by September 1979 had decided to replace him with Tamaki. They were outmanoeuvred, however, when Amin dispensed with Tamaki later in the month. Unrest continued to grow in Afghanistan, as did the level of Soviet troop involvement, with more than 4,500 Soviet troops in Afghanistan as 'advisers' and Soviet air strikes against rebel positions. The Soviets were being drawn into a civil war – and Afghanistan became the Soviet Union's Vietnam for the next decade.

With a burgeoning conflict in Afghanistan, Brezhnev organized a military intervention to prop up the Communist regime. The Brezhnev Doctrine legitimized the move, which bore a striking resemblance to the invasion of Czechoslovakia in 1968. Soviet forces moved into Afghanistan on 24 December 1979. On 27 December an attack was launched on the presidential palace, killing Amin. Over the course of the next few weeks the Soviets gained control over the Afghan capital, Kabul, and outlying towns, and by the end of January 1980 they had 50,000 troops on the ground in Afghanistan. Military action had been swift and decisive, and the Soviets had installed a new leader in the form of Babrak Kamal, but they were to find that international reactions to the Soviet invasion were unfavourable and that they would become mired in a conflict that would drag on throughout the 1980s.

Carter was incensed at the Soviet action, and called on Brezhnev to withdraw Soviet forces from Afghanistan. Making clear that any attempt to gain control of the Persian Gulf would be met with severe repercussions, including military force, Carter imposed economic sanctions on the Soviet Union, withdrew SALT II from consideration by the United States Senate and installed missiles in Europe. The United States also boycotted the 1980 Olympic Games in Moscow. When the United Nations called for the removal of foreign troops from Afghanistan, the Soviets declined to act. As far as they were concerned, Afghanistan fell within their sphere of influence and they were acting to support a Communist regime against its enemies.

A bitter war raged, not least because Kamal was deeply unpopular with the Afghan population. Muslim rebels, the *Mujahidin*, fought back hard and achieved territorial dominance in what they called a holy war fought against godless Communists, leading to a Soviet escalation of troops to 115,000 by 1984. Soviet military actions were colossal, with carpet bombing and scorched-earth tactics being deployed against the Afghan rebels and driving out three million refugees into neighbouring states, primarily Pakistan, by 1985. However, fighting an insurgent war in difficult terrain, the Soviets struggled to achieve control over Afghanistan. The rebels increased their effectiveness in countering Soviet forces and the United States and Great Britain secretly provided them with armaments and training. The Soviets were stuck, able neither to gain the control they desired over Afghanistan, nor to abandon the Kamal regime to collapse.

The Cold War re-ignited

The Soviet invasion of Afghanistan brought about the beginning of a re-ignition of the Cold War. This deepened with the election of Ronald Reagan as United States President in 1980. He was vehemently anti-Soviet and criticized Carter as having made a series of moves to appease the Soviet Union rather than to control its imperialist desires. Under the Reagan administration, United States military spending increased, driving the Soviets and Americans into deeper arms competition. As tensions increased, the Soviet economy was stagnated, not least as a result of Brezhnev's enormous military expenditure, but Soviet power was also beginning to be questioned within the Eastern bloc and further afield.

While the quagmire of Afghanistan dragged on, Communism was being increasingly strongly opposed in Poland following the rise of the Solidarity movement in 1980. A trade union movement, it had crystalized around strikes during the summer of 1980 that were triggered by rising food prices, becoming a legal entity in October 1980. Its membership peaked at nearly ten million in 1981, prompting the Soviets to consider military intervention in order to preserve the Polish regime. Unlike Czechoslovakia in 1968, however, it was clear that any such action would meet with opposition from the Polish military. The Polish situation remained turbulent throughout 1981 and the Soviets attempted to deal with it by installing General Wojciech Jaruzelski as a dictator and authorizing his declaration of martial law in December 1981 to prevent a coup, rather than by launching a military intervention. The effect was to force the Solidarity movement to function underground until 1983, and to avert a Soviet invasion to stabilize Poland. Even so, the situation led to a deepening of Soviet–American tension and the imposition of further economic sanctions on the Soviet Union by the Reagan administration.

It now seemed likely that the Soviet Union and the United States would see accommodation between them slipping away, and Brezhnev's health was failing, along with his grip on power. In March 1982 Brezhnev suffered a second severe stoke, which left him hospitalized for some weeks, during which time the head of the KGB, Yuri Andropov, built support sufficient to take over as Soviet leader. By May 1982 Andropov was effectively in charge, although Brezhnev survived until 10 November 1982. Andropov breathed new life into Soviet foreign policy, although the changes were more in the way in which relations were conducted than in their substance. He was able to improve Sino-Soviet relations by assuaging Chinese fears somewhat, but the relationship still remained somewhat fraught. The ace up Andropov's sleeve, however, stemmed from his former position as the head of the KGB. He was very well informed about the United States, and relied heavily on the bargaining position of a reduction in Soviet arms to the levels of American missiles and NATO forces in Europe signalling a desire to decrease confrontation with the United States. He was in place, however, for only about a year before his health began to fail, in September 1983, and was able to achieve relatively little in changing Soviet foreign policy.

It was September 1983 that was to see a sudden crisis in any attempt to develop friendly relations between the Soviet Union and the West, when a Korean civilian airliner, KAL-007, was shot down over Soviet airspace while en route to Japan from the United States. All 269 passengers and crew were killed. Moscow initially denied the event, before claiming that a Soviet aircraft had shot down an aircraft suspected of being an American spy plane. It would take nearly a month for Andropov to issue a statement, and even then this failed to placate foreign opinion of the Soviet Union as a malevolent power that acted as it wished, with no regard for international law.

Andropov died in February 1984 and was replaced by Konstantin Chernenko, who held to a Leninist line but clung to power for such a brief period before his death in 1985 that little of significance changed in Soviet relations with the outside world. The last two Soviet leaders before Gorbachev came to power were unable to escape the legacy of the Brezhnev era and the deepening tensions with the United States.

Conclusion

The Brezhnev era was one of steady gains in foreign policy that then became undermined by Soviet attempts to extend influence through repression and military power, at the expense of preserving cordial relationships. It was apparent early on that a reversal of Khrushchev's liberalization and adventurism was key to Brezhnev's policy at home and abroad, and the fierce reaction to the Czech situation in 1968 demonstrated this fact very publicly. That an easing of tensions with the West was achieved in the early 1970s is significant, and the *détente* process would be picked up again in the late 1980s. Even so, by 1985 the Soviet Union had slid back into a renewed Cold War, was locked in a costly arms race with the United States, was beleaguered in Afghanistan and was facing unrest within the Soviet Union and Eastern Europe as its economy and foreign policy stagnated.

Further reading

Boyle, P. G., *American–Soviet Relations: From the Russian Revolution to the Fall of Communism* (London: Routledge, 1993).

Brezhnev, L., *Peace, Détente and Soviet–American Relations* (New York: Harcourt Brace, 1979).

Bundy, W., *A Tangled Web: The Making of Foreign Policy in the Nixon Presidency* (London: I. B. Tauris, 1998).

Cohen, W. I., *The Cambridge History of American Foreign Relations Vol. IV: America in the Age of Soviet Power* (Cambridge: Cambridge University Press, 1993).

Deutscher, I., *Russia, China, and the West* (London: Oxford University Press, 1970).

Edmonds, R., *Soviet Foreign Policy, 1962–1973: The Paradox of Super Power* (Oxford: Oxford University Press, 1975).

Edmonds, R., *Soviet Foreign Policy: The Brezhnev Years* (Oxford: Oxford University Press, 1983).

Garthoff, R., *Détente and Confrontation: American–Soviet Relations from Nixon to Reagan* (2nd edn, Washington, DC: Brookings Institution, 1994).

Gelman, H., *The Brezhnev Politburo and the Decline of Détente* (Ithaca, NY: Cornell University Press, 1984).

Hammond, P., *Cold War and Détente: the American Foreign Policy Process since 1945* (New York: Harcourt Brace, 1975).

Heller, A., and Feher, F., *From Yalta to Glasnost: The Dismantling of Stalin's Empire* (Oxford: Blackwell, 1991).

Hersh, S., *Kissinger: The Price of Power* (London: Faber, 1983).

Holloway, D., *The Soviet Union and the Arms Race* (New Haven: Yale University Press, 1983).

Hyman, A., *Afghanistan under Soviet Domination 1964–1991* (2nd edn, Basingstoke: Macmillan, 1992).

Kissinger, H., *The White House Years* (Boston, MA: Little, Brown, 1979).

Klass, R. (ed.), *Afghanistan: The Great Game Revisited* (London: Freedom House, 1987).

Landau, D., *Kissinger: the uses of power* (Boston, MA: Houghton Mifflin, 1972).

MacCauley, M. (ed.), *The Soviet Union after Brezhnev* (London: Heinemann, 1983).

Melanson, R., *American Foreign Policy since the Vietnam War: The Search for Consensus from Richard Nixon to George W. Bush* (Armonk, NY: M. E. Sharpe, 2005).

Nation, R. C., *Black Earth, Red Star: A History of Soviet Foreign Policy* (Ithaca, NY: Cornell University Press, 1992).

Olivier, R., *The Lessons of the Soviet–Afghan War* (Oxford: Brassey's, 1991).

Pipes, R., *US–Soviet Relations in the Era of Détente: tragedy of errors* (Boulder, CO: Westview Press, 1981).

Roberts, G., *The Soviet Union in World Politics: Coexistence, Revolution, and Cold War, 1945–1991* (New York: Routledge, 1999).

Saikal, A., and Maley, W., *The Soviet Withdrawal from Afghanistan* (Cambridge: Cambridge University Press, 1989).

Ulam, A., *Dangerous Relations: The Soviet Union in World Politics, 1970–1982* (Oxford: Oxford University Press, 1982).

10 Gorbachev and the end of the Soviet Union

Mikhail Sergeyevich Gorbachev became First Secretary of the Communist Party of the Soviet Union in March 1985. He was significantly younger than his predecessors, and indeed than other candidates for the office. He was seen as both a man untarnished by the Stalinist past and one who might initiate reforms to remedy the myriad problems that faced the Soviet Union in the mid-1980s. Nobody seemed to appreciate, not least Gorbachev himself, quite how deep those problems were, with a stagnated and declining economy, widespread corruption, antipathy towards ideology, growing nationalities tensions within the Soviet Union and a decline in Soviet influence in Eastern Europe. Similarly, no one expected that Gorbachev's reforms would be as far ranging as they proved to be, nor that by 1991 the Soviet Union would collapse.

Gorbachev escalated reform, and lost control as he unleashed forces that he had not foreseen. In domestic policy he ushered in economic reform, then turned to reform of the political system, while at the same time mobilizing civil society in his support. His twin policies of *Perestroika* (restructuring) and *Glasnost'* (openness) developed at home, but had an international dimension in the way that Gorbachev approached the outside world and allowed greater contact between the Soviet population and the rest of the world. However, his reforms undermined Soviet power both domestically and internationally and ultimately led to its destruction, and, arguably, to the end of the Cold War as a result.

Gorbachev's new thinking

Gorbachev ushered in a era of what he termed 'New Thinking' in Soviet politics, although it was clear from the outset that he was committed to Leninism and to the maintenance of the Communist Party's primacy in Soviet life. In his first months in power he moved to remove corrupt officials and the 'gerontocracy' who held sway over the Soviet Union, replacing them with younger allies more sympathetic to reform. Most significantly, he moved the Foreign Minister Andrei Gromyko into the office of President, and replacing him in the office of Foreign Minister with Eduard

Shevardnadze, an old and close friend. The Moscow Party chief, Viktor Grishin, was replaced by Boris Yeltsin.

Gorbachev's new thinking encompassed bringing the Soviet system out of what he termed stagnation and decline. The path that he saw was one of economic development and liberalization, but this was linked to foreign policy, as Gorbachev realized the need for the Soviet Union to avoid inter-national tension as much as possible in order to be able carry through his domestic reforms. In this, Gorbachev's aims bore a striking resemblance to the development of Soviet normalization with the world during the 1920s and the motivation for the initiation of the New Economic Policy. Reform began with *perestroika*, initiating piecemeal economic policy attempts that were aimed at acceleration (*uskorenie*) and the development of limited-scale capitalism. When these reforms failed to achieve the results that Gorbachev had hoped for, he turned to the policy of *glasnost'* in, the hope that this would garner support from the population.

Glasnost' opened discussion of the Soviet past, particularly the Stalin era, and involved stark criticism of Stalinist policy and rehabilitation of his political opponents. This had profound implications. It included criticism of Stalinist foreign policy during the 1930s as having contributed to the outbreak of the Second World War; the rehabilitation of Bukharin (a major exponent of NEP, which appeared as the model for Gorbachev's own reform); the portrayal of Khrushchev's destalinization in a positive light; and sharp criticism of Brezhnev's domestic and foreign policies. Civil society was allowed to develop, previously banned cultural works were permitted and a forum was opened up for limited dissent and criticism of the system.

In what Gorbachev believed to be a position of strength, he embarked on political reform. Ultimately he would reshape Soviet politics to be more democratic, and would be steadily pushed into the spreading of similar policy into Eastern Europe. However, what emerged through *glasnost'* and *perestroika* were fundamental challenges to the legitimacy of the Communist Party of the Soviet Union both at home and abroad. Part of this stemmed from the fact that Gorbachev's economic reforms did not yield the improvements that the Soviet Union needed or that its population and leadership expected, coupled to a greater level of transparency in Soviet society. Amongst the reasons for this were conservative opposition to Gorbachev's programme of reform and a lack of enthusiasm among the population, and a growing tension arising from the desire of Soviet nation-alities to assert their independence from Moscow's control. Ultimately, matters would spiral out of control, but nonetheless, Gorbachev was not entirely unsuccessful in the pursuit of reform.

Reform and foreign policy

In foreign policy a marked change can be seen under Gorbachev. With the replacement of Gromyko by Shevardnadze, Gorbachev was able to break with a Foreign Minister who had held office since the Khrushchev era and who had been seen as uncreative and awkward. He repudiated nuclear confrontation as a means to conduct foreign affairs and stressed security as a mutual concern, pushing a radically different line to Brezhnev's. He espoused the idea of peaceful coexistence, moved away from confrontation, and signalled a retreat from the arms race and the development of economic ties with the outside world. While these shifts in policy impressed the West, they also had the effect of undermining the legitimacy of Soviet power and ideology.

Importantly, Gorbachev was convinced that domestic reform could be carried through only if there was a radical change in the direction and conduct of Soviet foreign policy. The diplomatic corps was re-energized as competent individuals were appointed to positions and given increased scope to conduct negotiations, and a high staff turnover was evident within the Foreign Ministry, including almost all of the ambassadors in key strategic postings. A new Foreign Minister was installed, in the person of Edvard Shevardnadze.

Gorbachev's ability to make a significant change in Soviet foreign policy was facilitated by Shevardnadze. Sharing Gorbachev's vision of a need for stable relations between the Soviet Union and the outside world, the new Foreign Minister set about building a relationship with Western politicians and diplomats that his predecessor, Gromyko, had not enjoyed. From the outset, he developed a good relationship with the American Secretary of State, George Schultz, and with West German politicians, making it clear that it was friendship rather than confrontation that the Soviet Union, and Shevardnadze personally, wanted. A new era of Soviet foreign policy was ushered in. The notion of confrontation was pushed aside as an abnormal relationship that the Soviet Union no longer wanted, and there was increased openness to outsiders and accountability to and scrutiny from the Soviet population. The change was profound, on the one hand making for a greatly improved relationship with the West, while on the other hand diminishing the Soviet Union's ability to stand in a position of strength on the world stage.

The challenge of Eastern Europe

When Gorbachev came to power, significant challenges to Soviet power in Eastern Europe were already bubbling beneath the surface, and had in some instances they had broken through before 1985. What had been evident in the 1950s and 1960s, and was again expressed at the beginning of the 1980s, resurfaced in the late 1980s as Gorbachev's reforms within the Soviet Union developed. Moscow was at first alarmed and cautious when a wave of democratization broke over Eastern Europe after 1988, but resolved to let it develop. Shevardnadze adopted the 'Sinatra Doctrine' (they did it their way) on the basis that the preservation of the Soviet Union possibly depended on letting go of the Eastern European empire.

When Gorbachev came to power the Soviet grip over Eastern Europe was deeply problematic, with widespread resentment and dissent being held in check by repressive policies as the economic situation worsened. Across much of Eastern Europe the economic position was worse than that of the Soviet Union in the mid-1980s and COMECON was seen as a means by which the Soviet Union beggared the economies of its satellites, and engendered much resentment. In addition, the Warsaw Pact was in a state of decay, not least because the East European leadership feared that their allegiance to Brezhnev-era policy would damn them in the eyes of Gorbachev. Eastern Europe was a powder keg waiting to explode.

Gorbachev was initially keen to maintain stability within the Eastern bloc. He was at first keen to reinvigorate COMECON and the Warsaw Pact in an attempt to alleviate pressure in Eastern Europe, in much the same way as he was attempting to do so within the Soviet Union. Eastern Europe became a foreign ground for *perestroika* as Gorbachev urged reforms similar to those he was attempting to pursue at home. He was careful not to officially open up within the Eastern bloc the questioning of the system he had brought about via *glasnost'*, showing his awareness of the resentment of Soviet domination in Eastern Europe during the preceding forty years. Nonetheless, the changes he ushered in would lead to the end of Soviet domination in Eastern Europe at the end of the 1980s, and Gorbachev seemed to be rather naïve about the situation until it was too late.

Between 1987 and 1989, the leadership in the East European states remained unbending and loyal to the Soviet Union, even as crisis loomed. As Gorbachev encountered the challenges that his reforms had allowed to open up within the Soviet Union, he became less able to address problems in the Eastern bloc, and in June 1989 he signalled the Soviet Union's abandonment of the Brezhnev Doctrine and indicated that force would not be deployed to prevent the collapse of socialist regimes. The year 1989 became a significant one for the demise of Soviet control in Eastern Europe. Partially free elections were held in Poland in June, Erich Honecker fell in October, the Velvet Revolution took place in Czechoslovakia in November and the end of the Ceausescu regime in Romania came in December. By the end of 1989 the Berlin Wall had been broken down and the Soviets had lost Eastern Europe.

This collapse in Eastern Europe appeared to have been largely unconsidered by Gorbachev, who had believed that limited liberalization in Eastern Europe would galvanize support for his reforms in the Soviet Union. It had a profound impact on the Soviet Union, not least because it represented a rejection of Soviet rule that spilled over into tensions within the national republics of the Soviet Union, in particular in the Baltic States and the Caucasus. With Soviet inaction in Eastern Europe, particularly the absence of military intervention in East Germany, it came as something of a shock when Gorbachev deployed armed force against republics that attempted to break away during 1990.

The most problematic issue in the demise of Soviet control over Eastern Europe lay in Germany. While a new Polish regime announced its continued adherence to the Warsaw Pact, on the condition that Soviet–Polish relations were conducted on an equal footing and an assurance that the Soviets would not attempt to interfere in Polish affairs, East Germany was different. The collapse of the Berlin Wall in the latter part of 1989 had removed a physical barrier, but West German Chancellor Helmut Kohl had proposed the reunification of Germany. Kohl had initially proposed this in December 1989, as the Wall fell, and the Soviets had made the case that European security rested on Germany's not becoming a unified state. By February 1990, however, Gorbachev consented to German unification, having conceded that he was powerless to prevent it. In this, Gorbachev faced criticism that he had allowed Eastern Europe to escape, and it became starkly apparent that Soviet power was dwindling and the Warsaw Pact and COMECON were disintegrating.

The Warsaw Pact lost significance as Gorbachev abandoned the use of force as a means to preserve Eastern Europe and allowed German reunification. COMECON effectively collapsed in January 1990. Nonetheless, Eastern European states still had a need for the Soviet Union and its ability to provide them with raw materials and fuel, although a Soviet proposal to move to hard currency prices in 1991 led to objections from what were now, in effect, client states. There was also the issue of the Soviet troops stationed within Eastern Europe, particularly the 380,000 Soviet troops in East Germany, and, with German unification, the position of Germany within alliances became a subject of contention.

In early 1990 the Soviets had argued that a reunified Germany should remain neutral and not become a militarized power. When, on 18 May 1990, East and West Germany concluded an agreement on economic union it seemed that the Soviets were prepared for the new Germany to become part of NATO. It quickly became apparent that this was not the position that the Soviets held, but when an offer was made to the Soviet Union to honour all of East Germany's economic obligations in exchange for Germany's membership of NATO in July 1990 Gorbachev accepted and promised to remove Soviet forces from East Germany by 1994. By the middle of 1990 Gorbachev had agreed to a situation that his predecessors had tried to avoid since 1945 – a unified Germany allied to the United States.

The significance of the Eastern European revolutions of 1989 was clear. Soviet power had shown itself to lack legitimacy, and the decision not to use force exposed the nature of Soviet domination since the Second World War. The Soviet Union had also shown itself prepared to let go of its Eastern European empire.

'A man to do business with': working with the West

The changes in the Soviet approach to Eastern Europe and the reformist drive within the Soviet Union greatly impressed the West, and opened up the possibility for developing friendly relations. The period after 1985 marked a sea change in Soviet foreign policy and in outside perceptions of the Soviet threat. The Soviet Union ceased to be a power that the United States saw as the greatest threat to American security in terms of nuclear arms and in challenge posed to United States interests by pro-Soviet regimes outside of the Soviet Union. It seemed, in 1985, that there was no scope for progress, not least because Reagan's anti-Soviet policies stood in the way of progress on arms negotiations and the United States was rapidly increasing armaments and spewing out an aggressive rhetoric that labelled the Soviet Union as the 'evil empire'.

Shortly after coming to power, in April 1985, Gorbachev signalled in *Pravda* a desire to change the situation of super-power confrontation. Following this, in July 1985, the Soviet Union and the United States announced that their leaders would meet at Geneva later in the year. When Reagan and Gorbachev met for three days in November 1985 they conducted lengthy talks which led to the issuing of a joint statement that indicated that American–Soviet relations looked set to improve. Gorbachev and Reagan appeared to have struck a friendship, although the continued Unites States desire to maintain the 'Star Wars' missile defence system remained a stumbling block. Following the talks, it was the Soviet Union that moved first in announcing an intention to cut its nuclear capacity in half, as long as agreement could be reached on a ban on an offensive capability in space. Beyond this, in January 1986 Gorbachev echoed the Soviet disbarment proposals of the late 1920s when he proposed complete nuclear disarmament on a global scale by 2000, which was to begin with an absolute reduction of nuclear arms by 50 per cent within five to eight years and pushing for a mechanism of independent oversight of the disarmament process. The Soviets, not the Americans, were the instigators of the drive to change relations between the two powers as Gorbachev projected the principles of *perestroika* and *glasnost'* onto the world stage in a push to reduce arms expenditure and create a climate of openness.

The United States responded favourably, but still the initiative lay with the Soviet Union. In September 1986 Gorbachev called a summit with Reagan in Reykjavik. When they met in October, Reagan and Gorbachev very nearly agreed on mutual disarmament by the end of the twentieth century. Still, however, Reagan refused to compromise on the 'Star Wars' programme, the abandonment of which was a key condition, from Gorbachev's perspective, for concluding an agreement. Following the summit, Reagan became embroiled in the Iran–Contra Affair, in which the United States' sale of weapons to Iran and funding of the Nicaraguan Contras came to light. This not only stalled the talks between the Soviets and the Americans, but led Gorbachev to conclude that there might not be a possibility of reaching an agreement with the United States over arms limitation so long as the Reagan administration remained in power.

All, however, was not lost and American–Soviet relations began to pick up again shortly afterwards. During 1987, Reagan made a complete *volte face* in his approach to the Soviet Union's demands for an abandonment of 'Star Wars'. During a visit to the United States in September 1987, Shevardnadze indicated that the Soviet Union would be prepared to moderate its demands for the removal of missile defence systems in favour of their reduction, as long as other treaties with regard to arms limitation could be strengthened, in particular the Anti-Ballistic Missile Treaty (ABM). When Gorbachev and Reagan met in Washington in December 1987, the Intermediate Nuclear Forces Treaty (INF) was concluded, in which both parties pledged to give up medium- and short-range nuclear missiles. Gorbachev sold this to the world as the beginning of the end of the Cold War and that the road towards complete nuclear disarmament had been embarked upon.

Further summitry between Reagan and Gorbachev during 1988 did not lead to further agreements between the United States and the Soviet Union, but the friendship between the two men developed and the relationship between the two states became increasingly cordial. So profound was the progress between 1985 and 1988 in super-power relations that George Kennan, architect of the United States' containment policy, argued in favour of negotiating further nuclear and conventional arms reduction with the Soviet Union and putting the two powers on a footing of normal rather than adversarial relationship. Heeding Kennan's advice, President George Bush and Gorbachev met in an air of friendship in their December 1989 summit as Soviet power in Eastern Europe was withering away.

The demise of Soviet power in Eastern Europe also prompted a change in the Soviet approach to Western Europe and in the way that Western European leaders viewed the Soviet Union. In part this was born out of the fact that the Soviets were largely powerless to stop the Eastern European revolutions of 1989, but also from the fact that Gorbachev saw Europe as an artificially divided continent. The landmark agreement between the European Community (EC) and COMECON in June 1988 reflected this, as did a developing relationship with Germany's Helmut Kohl and Britain's Margaret Thatcher, the latter branding Gorbachev as 'a man to do business with'.

With the change in Soviet relations with the West cemented by the end of 1989, Gorbachev had changed the face of the Cold War, but had not ended it. During 1990 he struggled to conclude an agreement over German reunification as conservative reactionaries within the Soviet Union raised objections to a unified Germany being part of NATO. His foreign policy, along with his Foreign Minister, Shevardnadze, was criticized for ceding Soviet security in Eastern Europe and abandoning the Soviet Union's client states around the world. Becoming increasingly beleaguered over domestic policy, Gorbachev retreated to a more conservative position on both domestic and foreign policy in an attempt to shore up his position. This weakened the Soviet relationship with the West, although it did not derail it. Gorbachev and Bush met during the summer of 1990, concluding the START II treaty at the end of July. Shevardnadze and Secretary of State James Baker discussed American–Soviet cooperation following Saddam Hussein's invasion of Kuwait and the outbreak of the Gulf War in August 1990, despite Iraq formerly having been a Soviet ally. By the end of Gorbachev's time in power and the collapse of the Soviet Union, Soviet relations with the West were the most cordial they had ever been.

The end of the Soviet Union

While Gorbachev had gone to great lengths in easing super-power tension, by 1990 he faced severe criticism and challenges within the Soviet Union. Soviet power in Eastern Europe had collapsed at the end of 1989, bringing into question the validity of Soviet ideology, the role of the Communist Party in Soviet life and Gorbachev's policies. Gorbachev faced a conservative backlash to his reforms, which led to hard-liners pushing for a return to tighter controls within the Soviet Union. Warning of a conservative-led coup within the Party, Shevardnadze resigned as Foreign Minister in December 1990. In August 1991 that coup came, and by the end of the year the Soviet Union had collapsed.

The demise of Eastern Europe struck a chord in certain Soviet republics. Rising nationalities tensions which had bubbled beneath the surface for years broke through and republics began to call for secession from the Soviet Union, with five republics – Latvia, Lithuania, Estonia, Armenia and Georgia – announcing their independence by the end of 1990. Gorbachev, who had eschewed the use of force in Eastern Europe, was less cautious within the Soviet Union and an armed crackdown was made in early 1991 in an attempt to quell unrest, but it had the effect of eroding some of Gorbachev's support in the West. Gorbachev moderated to a gentler line and began the process of drafting a new All-Union Treaty that would allow republics to break away from the Soviet Union. Gorbachev had just completed the final draft of the treaty, when he was overthrown by a hard-liner conservative coup.

Gorbachev, having completed the draft treaty, visited his dacha in the Crimea, planning to return to Moscow for the signing of the treaty on 20 August 1991. The day before, on 19 August, a coup was launched by an eight-man Committee for the State of Emergency (GKChP), led by Vice-President Gennadii Ianaev. Gorbachev was placed under house arrest, his communications with the outside world were severed and the plotters announced that he was too unwell to continue in office. Speaking in a press conference on 19 August, the GKChP put forward the line that Gorbachev's reforms had led the Soviet Union into a state of decline from which it needed to be rescued. They appeared to have little by way of a plan, and neglected to arrest the Russian President, Boris Yeltsin. Yeltsin denounced the coup and began mustering support against the GKChP.

On 20 August, the GKChP announced a curfew and mobilized armed forces towards Moscow. As tanks entered the streets of the Soviet capital, Yeltsin received a telephone call from United States President Bush pledging support and stating his belief that the coup could be overturned. With Yeltsin garnering widespread support from the population, and the refusal of Soviet tanks to fire on the Russian parliament building, from where he was operating, the tide turned against the GKChP. Yeltsin called for Gorbachev's return, and on 21 August the Soviet leader came back to Moscow and the coup collapsed. The plotters were arrested, some of them committing suicide. However, Soviet power had all but collapsed, Gorbachev's authority had been lost and Yeltsin's authority was in the ascendancy.

With Yeltsin at the fore, the Communist Party was banned in Russia. Gorbachev's attempts to create a new All-Union Treaty in the summer of 1991 were undone by the coup and what followed. It was clear by September 1991 that the Soviet Union as a political entity had been fatally undermined, and Soviet republics gathered pace in their moves towards independence. On 18 October 1991 the Alma Ata Accords were ratified, effectively heralding the disintegration of the Soviet Union and the formation of the Commonwealth of Independent States (CIS). When Ukraine announced independence on 1 December 1991, the Soviet Union was moribund. On 25 December 1991 Gorbachev left office, and the Soviet Union ceased to exist on 31 December 1991.

The implications for Soviet foreign policy of the collapse of the Soviet Union in late 1991 were unclear. Following the August coup, and with republics declaring independence, there was uncertainty as to whether there could in fact be a Soviet foreign policy at all. Gorbachev initially appeared to believe that there could continue to be such a foreign policy directed from the centre – the Soviet Union might have changed, but the world had not. He was to find, however, that there was no real basis for the conduct of a continued Soviet foreign policy, not least because the end of the Soviet Union came so quickly after the coup.

The August coup severely undermined Soviet influence and authority beyond the Soviet Union. While Eastern Europe had already slipped from Soviet hands in 1989, all Soviet power vanished in the second half of 1991. With the very basis of Soviet authority removed, and with its ideology so fundamentally challenged, there was no basis for the Soviet Union to continue as a political entity, nor for it to continue to have an enduring influence. With the end of the Soviet Union, some argued that the Cold War had ended in a victory for the United States.

Conclusion

Gorbachev's time in power was brief, as a result of the Soviet collapse. His reforms set in motion a chain of events on the domestic stage that he was ultimately unable to control and that severely undermined his authority and provoked conservatives to turn against him. However, the domestic challenges did not function in a bubble and foreign policy had a profound effect on the fate of the Soviet Union. The loss of Soviet power in Eastern Europe and the reduction of armaments, while positive in the Soviet relationship with the outside world and contributing to a significant easing in tension between the super-powers, undermined the validity of Soviet power and led to criticism that Gorbachev had sacrificed too much. While they were not the sole cause, Gorbachev's foreign policy and his new thinking contributed to unrest within the Soviet Union and the sparking of the reactionary coup of August 1991. Liberalization at home and abroad appeared to seal the demise of the Soviet Union as a global power, while at the same time heralding the re-emergence of Russia as a player in international politics.

Further reading

Balzer, H., *Five Years that Shook the World: Gorbachev's Unfinished Revolution* (New York: Praeger, 1991).

Blacker, C., *Hostage to Revolution: Gorbachev and Soviet Security Policy, 1985–1991* (New York: Council on Foreign Relations Press, 1993).

Brown, Archie, *The Gorbachev Factor* (Oxford: Oxford University Press, 1996).

Brown, J., *Surge to Freedom: The End of Communist Rule in Eastern Europe* (Durham, NC: Duke University Press, 1991).

Brzezinski, Zbigniew, *The Grand Failure: The Birth and Death of Communism in the Twentieth Century* (New York: Scribner, 1989).

Davies, R. W., *Soviet History in the Gorbachev Revolution* (London: Macmillan, 1989).

Forsberg, T., 'Power, Interest and Trust: Explaining Gorbachev's Choices at the End of the Cold War', *Review of International Studies* vol. 25 no. 4 (1999).

Garthoff, R., *The Great Transition: American–Soviet Relations and the End of the Cold War* (Washington, DC: Brookings Institution, 1994).

Gorbachev, M., *Perestroika: New Thinking for our Country and the World* (London: Collins, 1987).

Harle, V. and Livonen, J. (eds), *Gorbachev and Europe* (London: Pinter, 1989).

Hough, J., *Russia and the West: Gorbachev and the Politics of Reform* (New York, 1988).

McGwire, M., *Perestroika and Soviet National Security* (Washington, DC: Brookings Institution, 1991).

Oberdorfer, D., *The Turn. How the Cold War Came to an End: The United States and the Soviet Union, 1983–1990* (London: Jonathan Cape, 1992).

Patman, R., 'Reagan, Gorbachev and the emergence of New Political Thinking', *Review of International Studies* vol. 25 no. 4 (1999).

Wettig, G., *Changes in Soviet Foreign Policy toward the West* (Boulder, CO: Westview Press, 1991).

11 Russian foreign policy in the last decade of the twentieth century

As the Soviet Union collapsed, so it waned on the international stage, to be replaced by its fifteen former republics, now independent entities. The largest of these, and the most dominant, was the Russian Federation. For foreign powers, Russia remained almost synonymous with the Soviet Union in terms of the conduct of foreign relations between the former Soviet Union and the rest of the world. The reality of the situation was somewhat more nuanced, but prime concerns after the Soviet collapse in 1991 were the situation of Soviet armed forces and armaments, the relationship of the former Soviet Union's member states with one another and with Moscow and the relationship of the former Soviet Union with the rest of the world.

For this study, the concern remains Russia, with Boris Yeltsin as its leader during the final years of the twentieth century. With Soviet power gone, and with his tremendous gain in status following the coup of August 1991, Yeltsin stood as the obvious candidate for the presidency as Russia entered a stage of transition in the early 1990s before once again becoming a major player in world affairs.

The Soviet Union after collapse

Before the Soviet Union ceased to exist at the end of the 1991, a Commonwealth of Independent States (CIS) had been formed in Minsk, on 8 December 1991. The decision was made by the presidents of the three Slavic republics – Russia, Ukraine and Belorussia – and was aimed at the creation of a series of coordinating bodies for the CIS economy, foreign relations and defence, while heralding a common economic space that utilized the rouble as its currency. Gorbachev initially opposed the establishment of the CIS on such a basis as illegal, but found that other states were keen to sign up to it as the Soviet Union dwindled in power. In late December the Alma Ata Accords were signed, bringing the Central Asian republics into the CIS, and by the time that Gorbachev resigned, on 25 December 1991, all but one of the Soviet republics had joined. Only Georgia stood outside.

On the face of it, the formation of the CIS was a positive move to ensure a peaceful transition from the Soviet Union to a new political entity, but it was most definitely intended as a mechanism for Russian foreign policy, as a means both for coordination and for asserting Russian dominance over the other members. The CIS replaced the Soviet Union in the 1992 Olympics in Barcelona, and to the rest of the world a seemingly united Commonwealth sought to find its way in the world. The reality, however, was that it was immediately apparent that Russia was the dominant state and that the CIS was wracked by disagreement from the outset. Tension flared quickly between Russia and Ukraine, with what Ukrainian President Leonid Kravchuk termed a 'civilized divorce' quickly becoming fraught by arguments over territorial boundaries and control of the military. Elsewhere, disputes between nationalities flared and turned into armed struggle, most significantly in Nagorno-Karabakh, Moldova and Tajikistan. In stark contrast, Belorussia signalled its desire to maintain close ties to Russia. The creation of the CIS had not, it seemed, created a basis for a smooth transition into a post-Soviet era.

Yeltsin found himself beset with challenges in Russia as he sought to consolidate his position. With Soviet rule swept aside, some parts of Russia objected to being incorporated into the Russian Federation and declared themselves to be independent. Most notable amongst these was Chechnya, which declared independence, sparking a violent conflict that dogged Yeltsin throughout his presidency. In terms of the administration in Moscow, Yeltsin also endured a problematic situation. Under the Soviet Union Russia had housed the All-Union institutions of the Soviet state and had lacked its own administration. With the end of the Soviet Union, therefore, Yeltsin was faced with the problem of dealing with the former Soviet apparatus and those who had served within it. Further compounding the problem was the fact that while Yeltsin had banned the Communist Party, he lacked a political party of his own. The Congress of People's Deputies, a Gorbachev-era democratic institution formed in 1990, was full of opponents of Yeltsin, and the new President was far from unchallenged.

With the future of Russia uncertain in 1992, questions raged as to what form of government would be created, how the transition from the Soviet economy would be handled and on what basis Russia would interact with both the former republics of the Soviet Union and the rest of the world. In politics Yeltsin sought the path of democracy, in economics he sought reform and in foreign policy he emphasized the independence of the former Soviet Republics. His reforms were not universally popular, but they did gain favour with the international community, not least because Yeltsin continued to wave the flag of democracy.

At home Yeltsin's support was less assured. In 1993 he sought to address the problem posed to him by the Congress of People's Deputies. An opposition movement led by the Speaker of the Duma, Ruslan Khasbulatov, and the Vice President, Alexander Rutskoi, challenged Yeltsin's authority in the middle of 1993. Yeltsin responded to what he viewed as the beginning of an attempted coup by dissolving the Congress of People's Deputies on 21 September 1991 and calling new elections to be held in December. Rutskoi denounced this move as a coup by Yeltsin and announced that he was assuming power. Yeltsin's supporters blockaded the Duma building, which acquired notoriety as the White House (*bely dom*), for thirteen days before opening fire on it and ordering an assault on 4 October 1993. Sweeping aside the last vestiges of Soviet power, Yeltsin issued a decree for the dissolution of regional soviets, elections to a bicameral legislature in December 1993 and the holding of a presidential election in June 1994. Yeltsin triumphed in late 1993 in setting Russia on a path towards democratic government, it seemed, and gained the support of the European Community and the United States for this move.

Part of the opposition to Yeltsin had come from his struggle to reform Russia's post-Soviet economy. He also met with deep challenges in economic affairs. Working with his Premier, Eugenia Gaidar, he attempted to introduce a market economy and a programme of economic liberalization, while hoping that the Russian economy would attract capital investment from the West. A central tenet of Gaidar's approach to the economy was 'shock treatment', which proved unpopular. With inflation running wild, Yeltsin was forced to remove Gaidar from office in December 1992. Gaidar returned, however, in October 1993 and revived Russia's move to a market economy. Yeltsin's decrees overturning the 1993 coup attempt were well received by foreign governments, and further economic liberalization was seen in a positive light in the West.

In foreign affairs Yeltsin faced challenges in the transition from the Soviet Union and the need to deal with a range of diverse states that had once been under Moscow's rule. While keen to assert Russian dominance, Yeltsin respected the fact that the former republics were now independent and part of a Commonwealth rather than a Union. Despite the suggestion from his adviser, Sergei Stankevich, to create a Ministry of Commonwealth Affairs, Yeltsin was adamant that the former republics of the Soviet Union were to be treated as independent states and chose to deal with Russia's closest neighbours (originally referred to as the near abroad until the term became problematic) via the Ministry of Foreign Affairs. Russia was conducting a foreign policy with the states of the former Soviet Union.

While Yeltsin recognized the independence of the former republics, there remained the matter that a large number of ethnic Russians were domiciled within them, and questions arose as to their status. Integration within the CIS became a dividing point, with Ukraine, Azerbaijan, Moldova and Turkmenistan all keen to separate from Russia, while Armenia, Belorussia, Kazakhstan, Kyrgyzstan, Tajikistan and Uzbekistan wanted continued ties to Russia. Russia, unsurprisingly, was in favour of the latter approach.

One of the starkest battles in the division of the CIS came early on, over military matters. Within the initial agreements for the Commonwealth had been union in military affairs, not least because accession to such an arrangement had been a means to ensuring that the Soviet armed forces would allow the dissolution of the Soviet Union. In face of the attempt to establish a common military policy and command, however, tension began to flare. In May 1992 the Tashkent Treaty was concluded, which promised mutual non-aggression, and assistance in the event of an external attack. Effectively a collective security arrangement, it became a point of contention, not least because Russia sought to maintain an armed force that was shared by the CIS. Ukraine, in particular, opposed the joint forces, instead desiring a national army, which had been agreed during the first CIS summit on 30 December 1991. Ukraine clung to this, and to its nuclear arsenal, concerned that a unified military would be dominated by Russia and that Russia could act as it desired. With no concrete agreement on military cooperation, on 7 May 1992 Russia created its own High Command. Russian claims to control over nuclear arms, and military intervention during 1992 in Armenia, Georgia, Moldova and Tajikistan, made clear that Russia would assert its military authority within the CIS, and the Ukrainian concerns were understandable.

With lack of agreement on a coordinated military policy within the former Soviet Union, nuclear arms control became a matter of dispute. Following the demise of the Soviet Union and the creation of the CIS, four new states were now nuclear powers – Russia, Belorussia, Kazakhstan and Ukraine – as they had nuclear armaments within their borders. Added to the expansion in the number of global nuclear powers was the fact that START had been concluded with the Soviet Union, not the CIS, and while Russia agreed to uphold the agreements on non-proliferation and disarmament, the other states needed persuading. In May 1992, United States Secretary of State James Baker met with the Foreign Ministers of all four CIS nuclear states in Lisbon, and on 23 May 1992 a protocol to the START I treaty, agreeing to non-proliferation, was concluded and agreements were made to return arms to Russia for dismantling. Beyond this, however, President Kravchuk faced strong opposition within Ukraine over the retention of nuclear arms. Yeltsin met with Kravchuk at Massandra, where he struck a deal to compensate Ukraine by annulling Ukrainian debt to Russia in exchange for a transfer of nuclear arms. This move, again, raised protest in Ukraine and Kravchuk did not follow through on the agreement. It was only in January 1994 that the situation was resolved, through the intervention of United States President Bill Clinton. Even so, the issue of military power and nuclear armaments demonstrated the antagonistic position of Russo-Ukrainian relations in the early years following the end of the Soviet Union, and signalled that the CIS did not necessarily enjoy a balanced or cordial state of relations.

Beyond military matters, much of the discord within the CIS in its early years stemmed from Russia's economic policies. While there were desires to create a mutual economic system, Yeltsin showed a tendency to decide unilaterally in economic matters, despite an agreement that any changes within the Russian economy required consultation with the other states of the CIS. Yeltsin was committed to radical reform of the Russian economy through employing 'shock therapy' after 1992. This entailed price controls and reissuing currency, which alienated economically and politically other states, chiefly Ukraine. With the dominant currency the Russian rouble, and with the means to print money held by Russia, rapid inflation resulted and states were forced to use hard currency. The situation worsened in July 1993, when Russia announced a currency reissue in an attempt to counter inflation. This meant that pre-1993 roubles were prohibited, and only Russian citizens and businesses, as well as foreign visitors, were able to exchange old bank notes for new. This forced the disintegration of the rouble as a unified currency and other states chose to issue their own bank notes, with the attendant result that an exchange mechanism was set in place. Even so, the result was to reinforce the use of hard currency in dealings with Russia. Despite these reforms, the idea of a single economic space persisted late into the 1990s, although in reality the notion was merely a veneer that covered deeper tensions.

A new direction in foreign policy?

With the end of the Soviet Union and the rise of a new Russia as part of the CIS, the shape of international society was fundamentally changed. In contrast to the bipolarity of the Cold War era, the world had become multipolar, and the confrontational stance of the United States and the Soviet Union was replaced by cooperation between the two states. This sea change in Russo-American relations stemmed in part from the fact that the two powers were no longer vying for dominance – the United States was clearly the dominant player on the world stage and Russia could not hope to recover the power of the Soviet Union in the short term. The world had changed, but the question was what direction Russian foreign policy would take in the new era.

Following the demise of the Soviet Union, with Russia's economy in a disastrous state and Yeltsin's desire for 'shock therapy', there was little choice but for Russia to seek assistance from outside and invite foreign capital investment. Opening up to the West economically also brought with it the benefit of support for Yeltsin, not least because his articulated desires for a democratic Russia and for arms control were looked upon favourably. When facing domestic challenges, Yeltsin was to find that he enjoyed the support of the United States, which was to prove invaluable in countering the challenges he faced in 1993. There was clearly a new line in Russian foreign policy, of openness to the West rather than confrontation, but it was born less out of ideology than out of necessity.

By 1993, Russian foreign policy had become focused on integration and being seen as a great power on the world stage, while it saw the former

Soviet republics as lying within the Russian sphere of interest. Russian foreign policy remained somewhat unassertive, not least in its reaction to NATO expansion and in response to the Bosnian war. With the appointment of Yevgenii Primakov as Foreign Minister in 1996, a doctrine of 'competitive pragmatism' emerged and Russia's position in China, the Middle East and the Far East was strengthened without giving ground to the West. Primakov was clear that Russia was an important player in the international community and a great power, and he sought to stabilize the CIS and strengthen Russia while opposing the proliferation of armaments.

The shifts in Russian foreign policy during the 1990s were concerned with stability and the maintenance of Russia's interests. Integration with the West was an important aspect of early Yeltsin-era foreign policy, and it was attempts to build a new relationship beyond the end of the Soviet Union that characterized much of the foreign policy of the first half of the decade. Reaction to what was viewed as an overly concessionary and weak foreign policy line towards the West appeared in the mid-1990s, not least because many of the hoped-for gains had not been achieved. As Russia reached the end of the twentieth century, new tensions with the West were rising, not least in relation to the expansion of NATO and the EU into Russia's sphere of interest.

Russia and Europe

With a foreign policy of openness to the West, yet tempered by concerns about the United States' assertion of its dominance, Russia found friends in Europe. At the time of the Soviet collapse, the Western European governments were keen on European integration and moving towards the creation of the European Union (EU). While not intending to include Russia within the EU, West European leaders showed themselves keen to have Russia as an ally, rather than in isolation. A series of friendships between Yeltsin and European heads of state emerged, and a sense of cooperation was in the air.

The first, and indeed keenest, friendship was with Germany. Indeed, Germany proved to be the strongest advocate of Russia's integration into Europe during the 1990s. Crucial to this was that the reunification of Germany and the withdrawal of Soviet troops had been agreed during the Gorbachev era, with the result that Germany became an early ally of the new Russia. When Chancellor Kohl visited Russia in December 1992 he and Yeltsin signed a series of agreements that gave Russia economic breathing space in its commitment to East German debts and assistance in the repatriation of Soviet troops from Germany. A spirit of cooperation was clearly instilled between the two states, with Kohl terming Russia Germany's main partner in the East. A lasting friendship was established between Kohl's Germany and Yeltsin's Russia, although not without its hiccups.

Encouraged by the cordiality of the Russo-German relationship, France also moved favourably towards Russia. In February 1994, while visiting Paris, Yeltsin concluded an agreement on joint military cooperation. Later in the year the French pushed the line of a Europe that should integrate Russia, not least as a means of countering a perceived NATO expansion led by United States-backed involvement in the conflict raging in former Yugoslavia. Franco-Russian trade increased sizeably after the mid-1990s, and a close personal friendship was established between Yeltsin and the French President Jacques Chirac.

Yeltsin turned also to Great Britain. Buoyed up by the estimation that Gorbachev had enjoyed in Margaret Thatcher's eyes, Yeltsin travelled to London in January 1992. Meeting with Prime Minister John Major, he made a favourable impression and Britain agreed to increase its economic aid to Russia. Later in the year, Yeltsin and Major concluded a bilateral treaty and a further economic agreement for trade between the two states. The treaty led to little, not least because Britain was ambivalent about supporting Russia with regard to the war in Chechnya, but by the end of the 1990s Anglo-Russian trade was significant.

While Russian friendship and trade were developing with individual states, Russia was also building a relationship with the European Union during the 1990s. The challenge that Russia faced here was in preventing the EU from becoming a proxy for NATO dominance in Europe, not least because fears abounded that the situation could be similar to the development of Western militarism that had occurred under the auspices of the Marshall Plan in the late 1940s and beyond. Yeltsin was keen to open Russia to the EU, and to EU investment. The path to achieving this, however, was far from the smooth economic arrangements that had been established with some of the EU member states. The initial basis of trade between Russia and the EU, initiated in the spring of 1992, saw the EU treating the Russian economy on a par with those of the developing world. Beyond this, in December 1993, Yeltsin attempted to broker a partnership agreement with the EU, but the sense of economic unevenness prevailed and proved to be an obstacle. That the same obstacle had not been laid in the path of the Eastern European states incensed Yeltsin, but in June 1994 he signed an agreement with the EU allowing the transfer of capital, but still with limitations on trade. Further talks were derailed by the Russian invasion of Chechnya, which the EU condemned, but in October 1996 an agreement between Russia and the EU was finally approved, although it did not come into effect until December 1997. The agreement lowered EU tariffs on Russian exports, but allowed Russia to maintain high tariffs on EU imports and was designed to bring Russia into the European market. Even so, it was not until 2002 that the EU recognized Russia as a market economy.

Russia and the United States

Russia's relationship with the United States was one of openness, and began with arms control and weapons reduction. Russia held to the arms limitation agreements that had been made in the Gorbachev era, but Yeltsin demonstrated a keenness for disarmament as a means of removing one of the chief strains on the economy. The moves went further than this, however, with new negotiations for START II beginning in late 1992. Russian proposals in the talks were for a dramatic decrease in numbers of warheads, to between 2,000 and 2,500, while the United States was keen on a higher ceiling. What was agreed in START II was a ban on Inter-Continental Ballistic Missiles (ICBMS) with multiple warheads, which meant that the bulk of the Russian nuclear arsenal would require dismantling.

START II was a startling acceptance of an uneven nuclear balance with the United States, and Russian policy thus reinforced the superiority of American power in the 1990s. Not all in Russia were happy with this arrangement at the time, and Yeltsin met with fierce opposition because the treaty seemed to herald the end of Russia as a super-power. A stumbling-block, however, lay in the non-ratification of START I by the former Soviet republics, with Ukraine proving to be particularly unwilling to give up its bargaining power in possessing nuclear arms. The upshot was a lengthy triangular process that involved Russia and the United States in persuading Ukraine to ratify START I. While it seemed in May 1992 that Ukraine would agree, the commitment was not honoured. Under United States President Bill Clinton efforts were resumed at a summit meeting in Moscow in January 1994, but still Ukraine remained intractable until late 1994.

It was in 1994 that a change occurred in Russia's approach to the rest of the world. Its politics, with a new parliament and constitution in place, shifted sharply to the right at the beginning of 1994, and foreign policy became much more concerned with the preservation of national interests than with making concessions to the West. Part of this shift centred on apportioning blame to Yeltsin for the demise of the Soviet Union and for failures in dealing with the challenges of the post-Soviet order. Failure to rectify the economic situation was an area in which Yeltsin faced a multitude of critics, and the role of Western economic advice and aid was called into question as being potentially designed to weaken Russia. The Russian population clearly did not see openness to the West as desirable, and indeed saw it as a potential threat. Some even blamed the United States' support for Yeltsin as having contributed to Russia's struggle with some of the challenges of the post-Soviet Era.

A resurgent super-power?

By the end of the twentieth century, and as Russia moved into the twenty-first century, its interests were coming into conflict with those of other states. In March 2000 a New Foreign Policy Concept was announced, which was adopted in June 2000. Integration remained a key aspect of Russian foreign policy, as did the notion that Russia was a great power, but the focus shifted to an attempt to promote Russia's economy and image on the international stage. Despite the new President Vladimir Putin's taking a personal role in this and making numerous state visits during his first two terms, the image or Russia and its economy struggled to gain ground. It was apparent that some of the problem lay in Russia's lacking the material means to effect the desired change. Despite this, Russia under Putin became increasingly self-assured, and by the time his second term in office ended in 2008, some were talking of a 'Second Cold War'.

With the notion of a rebirth of bipolar conflict on the global stage, questions arose regarding the extent to which Russia could be seen as a resurgent super-power. Russian rhetoric, while holding to cooperation in security and the non-proliferation of weapons of mass destruction, became increasingly self-assured. When, in 2006, Russian arms exports rose sharply, particularly to China and India, the United States expressed alarm. American support for revolutions in Ukraine (the Orange Revolution, November 2004–January 2005), Georgia (the Rose Revolution, November 2003) and Kyrgyzstan (the Tulip Revolution, February–March 2005) led to Russian concerns that the United States was prepared to support civil protest at the expense of Russian interests and that an attempt to re-establish containment of Russia was part of the United States' intention in this regard. Russia appeared to become increasingly antagonistic to the rest of the world, not least with a renewed focus on being self-sufficient and a sovereign state, at the same time as the United States sought to exert greater influence in the world. With Russia's strength in energy exports, and its threats to stop the supply of gas, Russia appeared to wield great power on the global stage. At much the same time, however, Russia appeared to be moving towards isolation, and to stand again as a major power with interests of its own that did not square with those of the West.

Conclusion

Russian foreign policy in the decade following the end of the Soviet Union can be characterized by the focus on integration with the West. While this was less successful than Yeltsin seems to have hoped, it can be seen as the continuation of a foreign policy that was being developed by Mikhail Gorbachev before the end of the Soviet Union. In this respect, Yeltsin-era foreign policy towards the West bore many of the hallmarks of Gorbachev's ideas. The significant change lay in the interaction between Russia and the former Soviet republics, and it was here that confusion between domestic and foreign policy lay. In the early years of the twenty-first century it is clear that Russia retains an interest in the former republics, yet the relationship between Moscow and the republics has not always been received positively, not least when Moscow has been seen to have attempted to exert too much influence in the affairs of sovereign states.

Beyond the 'near abroad' of the former Soviet republics, openness initially went hand in hand with integration as Russia worked to build a relationship with the West, not least in the hope that this would aid the development of the Russian economy through foreign investment. The gains in this regard were less extensive than the population had expected, and Yeltsin became fiercely criticized for his approach to policy in the early years following the Soviet collapse. A more nationalist line emerged in the mid-1990s, which stressed Russian interests while not opposing the West, and steadily evolved at the turn of the twenty-first century into an increased Russian assertiveness on the world stage and a burgeoning antagonistic relationship with the West.

In the early years of the twenty-first century Russia stands as a major power on the world stage. Its past has informed its current policy, and many of the challenges of previous eras have persisted or left their mark on contemporary Russia. Russia has, throughout the twentieth century and into the twenty-first, occupied a major position on the world stage, and it seems unlikely that its status in this regard will change in the near future. Quite what the onward trajectory of Russian foreign policy will be in the future remains to be seen, but by examining its past an appreciation of the present state of affairs may be formed.

Further reading

Dawisha, A., and Dawsisha, K. (eds), *The Making of Foreign Policy in Russia and the New States of Eurasia* (Armonk, NY: M.E. Sharpe, 1995).

Dawisha, K. (ed.), *The International Dimension of Post-Communist Transitions in Russia and the New States of Eurasia* (Armonk, NY: M.E. Sharpe, 1997).

Donaldson, Robert H.. and Nogee, Joseph L., *The Foreign Policy of Russia: Changing Systems, Enduring Interests* (Armonk, NY: M.E. Sharpe, 2005).

Ivanov, I., *The New Russian Diplomacy* (Washington, DC: Brookings Institution Press, 2002).

Leopold, R. (ed.), *Russian Foreign Policy in the 21st Century and the Shadow of the Past* (New York: Columbia University Press, 2007).

Petro, Nicolai N., and Rubinstein, Alvin Z., *Russian Foreign Policy: From Empire to Nation State* (New York: Longman, 1996).

Shishkov, Iu., 'The Commonwealth of Independent States: A Decade and a Half of Futile Efforts', *Problems of Economic Transition* vol. 50 no. 7 (2007).

Stent, A., *Russia and Germany Reborn: Unification, the Soviet Collapse, and the New Europe* (Princeton: Princeton University Press, 1999).

Wallander, C. (ed.), *The Sources of Russian Foreign Policy after the Cold War* (Boulder, CO: Westview Press, 1996).

Select bibliography

The following bibliography details works consulted in the preparation of this book that have not been included in the further reading sections at the end of each chapter. It is far from exhaustive, and has been organized with the intention that the reader may find further works for the pursuit of particular areas and topics.

General works on twentieth-century Russia

Andrle, Vladimir. *A Social History of Twentieth-Century Russia* (London: Edward Arnold, 1994).

Brown, Archie. *The Rise and Fall of Communism* (New York: Ecco, 2009).

Freeze, Gregory (ed.). *Russia: A History* (New York: Oxford University Press, 1997).

Furet, Francois. *The Passing of an Illusion: The Idea of Communism in the Twentieth Century* (Chicago: University of Chicago Press, 1999)

Gellately, Robert. *Lenin, Stalin, and Hitler: The Age of Social Catastrophe* (New York: Alfred A. Knopf, 2007).

Hoffmann, David, and Yanni Kotsonis (eds). *Russian Modernity: Politics, Knowledge, Practices* (London: Macmillan, 2000).

Hosking, Geoffrey. *The First Socialist Society: A History of the Soviet Union from Within* (Cambridge: Harvard University Press, 1992).

Kenez, Peter. *A History of the Soviet Union from the Beginning to the End* [2nd edition] (New York: Cambridge University Press, 2006).

Laqueur, Walter. *The Dream That Failed: Reflections on Soviet Union* (New York: Oxford University Press, 1994).

Lewin, Moshe. 'Russia/USSR in Historical Motion: An Essay in Interpretation', *Russian Review* 50, 3 (July 1991): 249–66.

—— *Russia–USSR–Russia: The Drive and Drift of a Superstate* (New York: Norton, 1995).

Malia, Martin. *The Soviet Tragedy: A History of Socialism in Russia, 1917–1991* (New York: Free Press, 1994).

Pipes, Richard. *Communism, the Vanished Specter* (New York: Oxford University Press, 1994).

Suny, Ronald Grigor. *The Soviet Experiment: Russia, the USSR, and the Successor States* (New York: Oxford University Press, 1998).

—— *The Structure of Soviet History: Essays and Documents* (New York and Oxford: Oxford University Press, 2003).

Suny, Ronald Grigor (ed.). *The Cambridge History of Russia* vol. 3 (Cambridge and New York: Cambridge University Press, 2006).

Trenin, Dmitri V. *Getting Russia Right* (Washington: Carnegie Endowment for International Peace, 2007).

Verdery, Katherine. *What Was Socialism and What Comes Next?* (Princeton: Princeton University Press, 1996).

Walicki, Andrzej. *Marxism and the Leap to the Kingdom of Freedom: The Rise and Fall of the Communist Utopia* (Stanford, Calif.: Stanford University Press, 1995).

Foreign policy

Adibekov, Grant M. *Kominform i poslevoennaia Evropa, 1947–1956* (Moscow: Rossiia molodaia, 1994).

Anderson, Richard D. Jr. *Public Politics in an Authoritarian State: Making Foreign Policy During the Brezhnev Years* (Ithaca, N.Y.: Cornell University Press, 1993).

Andrew, Christopher and Vasili Mitrokhin. *The Sword and the Shield: The Mitrokhin Archive and the Secret History of the KGB* (New York: Basic Books, 1999).

Borezki, Jerzy. *The Soviet–Polish Peace of 1921 and the Creation of Interwar Europe* (New Haven: Yale University Press, 2008).

Carr, E. H. *The Soviet Impact on the Western World* (New York: H. Fertig, 1973).

Checkel, Jeffrey T. *Ideas and International Political Change: Soviet/Russian Behavior and the End of the Cold War* (New Haven: Yale University Press, 1997).

Chen, Jian. *Mao's China and the Cold War* (Chapel Hill: University of North Carolina Press, 2001).

Chubar'ian, A. O. (ed.). *Stalin i kholodnaia voina* (Moscow: In-t vseobshchei istorii RAN, 1997).

Coeuré, Sophie. *La Grande Lueur a l'Est: Les Français et l'Union soviétique, 1917–1939* (Paris: Seuil, 1999).

Creuzberger, Stefan. *Die sowjetische Besatzungsmacht und das politische System der SBZ* (Weimar: Böhlau, 1996).

Dallin, Alexander. *The Soviet Union at the United Nations* (New York: Praeger, 1962).

Danilov, Aleksandr A., and Aleksandr V. Pyzhikov. *Rozhdenie sverkhderzhavy: SSSR v pervye poslevoennye gody* (Moscow: ROSSPEN, 2001).

Dullin, Sabine. *Men of Influence: Stalin's Diplomats in Europe, 1930–1939* (Edinburgh: Edinburgh University Press, 2008).

Egorova, N. I., and A. O. Chubar'ian (eds). *Stalinskoe desiatiletie kholodnoi voiny: fakty i gipotezy* (Moscow: Nauka, 1999).

Egorova, N. I., and Ilya V. Gaiduk. *Stalin i kholodnaia voina* (Moscow: Institut vseobshchei istorii RAN, 1998).

English, Robert D. *Russia and the Idea of the West: Gorbachev, Intellectuals, and the End of the Cold War* (New York: Columbia University Press, 2000).

Evangelista, Matthew. *Unarmed Forces. The Transnational Movement to End the Cold War* (Ithaca, N.Y.: Cornell University Press, 1999).

Gaiduk, Ilya V. *Confronting Vietnam: Soviet Policy toward the Indochina Conflict, 1954–1963* (Stanford, Calif.: Stanford University Press, 2003).

Goldgeier, James M. *Leadership Style and Soviet Foreign Policy* (Baltimore: Johns Hopkins University Press, 1994).

Goncharov, Sergei N., John W. Lewis, and Xue Litai. *Uncertain Partners: Stalin, Mao, and the Korean War* (Stanford, Calif.: Stanford University Press, 1993).

Gorodetsky, Gabriel. *Stafford Cripps' Mission to Moscow, 1940–42* (Cambridge: Cambridge University Press, 1984).

Granville, Johanna. *In the Line of Fire: The Soviet Crackdown on Hungary* (Pittsburgh: Center for Russian and East European Studies, University of Pittsburgh, 1998).

Györkei, Jeno and Miklós Horváth (eds). *Soviet Military Intervention in Hungary, 1956*, trans. Emma Roper-Evans (New York: Central European University Press, 1998).

Haslam, Jonathan. *Soviet Foreign Policy 1930–33: The Impact of the Depression* (London: Macmillan, 1983).

Hirsch, Francine. 'The Soviets at Nuremberg: International Law, Propaganda, and the Making of the Postwar Order', *American Historical Review* 113, 3 (June 2008), 701–30.

Hixson, Walter L. *Parting the Curtain: Propaganda, Culture and the Cold War, 1945–1961* (Basingstoke: Macmillan, 1997).

Hough, Jerry. *The Struggle for the Third World* (Washington: Brookings Institution Press, 1986).

Kornienko, Georgii M. *Kholodnaia Voina: svidetelstvo ee uchastnika* (Moscow: Mezhdunarodnye otnosheniia, 1994).

Kramer, Mark. 'New Evidence on Soviet Decision-Making and the 1956 Polish and Hungarian Crises', *Cold War International History Project Bulletin* 8–9 (1996/97): 358–84.

—— 'Jaruzelski, the Soviet Union, and the Imposition of Martial Law in Poland: New Light on the Mystery of December 1981', *Cold War International History Project Bulletin* 11 (Winter 1998): 5–16.

Kramer, Mark. 'The Early Post-Stalin Succession Struggle and Upheavals in East-Central Europe: Internal–External Linkages in Soviet Policy-Making', pts 1–3, *Journal of Cold War Studies* 1 (Winter 1999): 3–55; 2 (Spring 1999): 3–38; 3 (Fall 1999): 3–66.

Kulik, Boris T. *Sovetsko-Kitaiskii raskol: prichiny i posledstviia* (Moscow: Institut Dal'nego Vostoka RAN, 2000).

Lieven, D. C. B. *Russia and the Origins of the First World War* (New York: St Martin's Press, 1983).

Mastny, Vojtech. *Russia's Road to the Cold War: Diplomacy, Warfare, and the Politics of Communism, 1941–1945* (New York: Columbia University Press, 1979).

Mendelson, Sarah E. *Changing Course: Ideas, Politics, and the Soviet Withdrawal from Afghanistan* (Princeton: Princeton University Press, 1999).

Mlechin, Leonid. *MID: Ministerstvo Inostrannykh Del, romantiki i tsiniki* (Moscow: Tsentrpoligraf, 2001).

Naimark, Norman M. *The Russians in Germany: A History of the Soviet Zone of Occupation, 1945–1949* (Cambridge, Mass.: Belknap Press of Harvard University Press, 1995).

Naimark, Norman, and Leonid Gibianskii (eds). *The Establishment of Communist Regimes in Eastern Europe, 1944–1949* (Boulder: Westview Press, 1997).

Rieber, Alfred. 'Persistent Factors in Russian Foreign Policy', in Hugh Ragsdale (ed.), *Imperial Russian Foreign Policy* (Cambridge: Cambridge University Press, 1993), 315–59.

Rozman, Gilbert (ed.). *Japan and Russia: The Tortuous Path to Normalization, 1949–1999* (New York: St. Martin's Press, 2000).

Rubinstein, Alvin Z. *The Foreign Policy of the Soviet Union* (New York: Random House, 1972).

Samuelson, Lennart. *Plans for Stalin's War Machine: Tukhachevskii and Military-Economic Planning, 1925–1941* (New York: St. Martin's Press, 2000).

Service, Robert. *Comrades! A History of World Communism* (Cambridge: Harvard University Press, 2007).

Siniavskaia, Elena. *Frontovoe Pokolenie: Istoriko-psikhologicheskoe issledovanie* (Moscow: IRI-RAN, 1995).

Stites, Richard (ed.). *Culture and Entertainment in Wartime Russia* (Bloomington: Indiana University Press, 1995).

Suri, Jeremy. 'The Promise and Failure of "Developed Socialism": The Soviet "Thaw" and the Crucible of the Prague Spring, 1964–72', *Contemporary European History* 15, 2 (May 2006): 133–58.

Thomas, Daniel C. *The Helsinki Effect: International Norms, Human Rights, and the Demise of Communism* (Princeton, N.J.: Princeton University Press, 2001).

Thompson, J. M. *Russia, Bolshevism and the Versailles Peace* (Princeton: Princeton University Press, 1967).

Torkunov, A. V. *Zagadochnaia voina: koreiskii konflikt 1950–1953 godov* (Moscow: Rosspen, 2000).

Volokitina, Tatiana V. et al. *Moskva i vostochnaia Evropa. Stanovlenie politicheskikh rezhimov sovetskogo tipa (1949–1953). Ocherki istorii* (Moscow: Rosspen, 2002).

Westad, Odd. *The Global Cold War: Third World Interventions and the Making of Our Times* (Cambridge: Cambridge University Press, 2005).

——. *The Global Cold War* (Oxford: Oxford University Press, 2006)

Westad, Odd (ed.). *Brothers in Arms: The Rise and Fall of the Sino-Soviet Alliance, 1945–1963* (Stanford, Calif.: Stanford University Press, 1998).

Wheeler-Bennett, John W. *Brest-Litovsk: The Forgotten Peace, March 1918* (New York: Norton, 1971).

Zubok, Vladislav M. *A Failed Empire: The Soviet Union in the Cold War from Stalin to Gorbachev* (Chapel Hill: University of North Carolina Press, 2008).

Russia before 1917

Ascher, Abraham. *The Revolution of 1905*, vol. I: *Russia in Disarray*, vol. II: *Authority Restored* (Stanford, Calif.: Stanford University Press, 1988, 1992).

—— *P. A. Stolypin: The Search for Stability in Late Imperial Russia* (Stanford, Calif.: Stanford University Press, 2001).

Bonnell, Victoria. *Roots of Rebellion: Workers' Politics and Organizations in St. Petersburg and Moscow, 1900–1914* (Berkeley: University of California Press, 1983).

Bonnell, Victoria (ed.). *The Russian Worker: Life and Labor under the Tsarist Regime* (Berkeley and Los Angeles: University of California Press, 1983).

Brooks, Jeffrey. *When Russia Learned to Read: Literacy and Popular Literature, 1861–1917* (Princeton: Princeton University Press, 1985).

Clark, Katerina. *Petersburg, Crucible of Cultural Revolution* (Cambridge, Mass.: Harvard University Press, 1995)

Clowes, Edith, Samuel Kassow, and James West (eds). *Between Tsar and People: Educated Society and the Quest for Public Identity in Late Imperial Russia* (Princeton: Princeton University Press, 1991).

Engelstein, Laura. *The Keys to Happiness: Sex and the Search for Modernity in Fin-de-Siècle Russia* (Ithaca, N.Y.: Cornell University Press, 1992).

—— 'Combined Underdevelopment: Discipline and the Law in Imperial and Soviet Russia', *American Historical Review* 98, 2 (April 1993), 338–53.

—— 'The Dream of Civil Society in Tsarist Russia: Law, State, and Religion', in Nancy Bermeo and Philip Nord (eds), *Civil Society before Democracy: Lessons from Nineteenth-Century Europe* (Oxford: Rowman & Littlefield, 2000).

Evtuhov, Catherine. *The Cross and the Sickle: Sergei Bulgakov and the Fate of Russian Religious Philosophy, 1890–1920* (Ithaca, N.Y.: Cornell University Press, 1997).

Freeze, Gregory. 'The *Soslovie* (Estate) Paradigm and Russian Social History', *American Historical Review* 91, no.1 (February 1986), 11–36.

—— 'Counter-Reformation in Russian Orthodoxy: Popular Response to Religious Innovation, 1922–25', *Slavic Review* 54, 2 (Summer 1995): 305–39.

—— 'Subversive Piety: Religion and the Political Crisis in Late Imperial Russia', *Journal of Modern History* 68 (June 1996): 308–50.

—— '"The Problem of Political and Social Stability in Urban Russia on the Eve of War and Revolution" Revisited', *Slavic Review* 59, 4 (Winter 2000): 848–75.

Friedgut, Theodore. *Iuzovka in Revolution, 1869–1924*. 2 vols. (Princeton: Princeton University Press, 1989 and 1994).

Gatrell, Peter. *Government, Industry and Rearmament in Russia 1900–1914: The Last Argument of Tsarism* (Cambridge: Cambridge University Press, 1994).

Haimson, Leopold. 'The Problem of Social Stability in Urban Russia, 1905–17', pt. 1, *Slavic Review* 23/4 (Dec. 1964): 619–42; 24/1 (Mar. 1965): 1–20.

McDaniel, Tim. *Autocracy, Capitalism, and Revolution in Russia* (Berkeley: University of California Press, 1988).

Melancon, Michael. *The Socialist Revolutionaries and the Russian Anti-War Movement, 1914–1917* (Columbus: Ohio State University Press, 1990).

Mironov, Boris, with Ben Eklof. *The Social History of Imperial Russia, 1700–1917* (Boulder, Colo.:Westview Press, 2000).

Moon, David. *The Russian Peasantry, 1600–1930: The World the Peasants Made* (London: Longman, 1999).

Radkey, Oliver. *The Agrarian Foes of Bolshevism* (New York: Columbia University Press, 1958).

Read, Christopher. *Religion, Revolution and the Russian Intelligentsia, 1900–1912* (London, 1979).

Robinson, Geroid Tanquary. *Rural Russia under the Old Regime: A History of the Landlord-Peasant World and a Prologue to the Peasant Revolution of 1917* (Berkeley: University of California Press, 1972 [1932]).

Rogger, Hans. *Russia in the Age of Modernisation and Revolution, 1881–1917* (London: Longman, 1983).

Starr, S. Frederick. 'Tsarist Government: The Imperial Dimension', in Jeremy Azrael (ed.). *Soviet Nationality Policies and Practices* (New York, 1978): 3–31.

Steinberg, Mark. *Proletarian Imagination: Self, Modernity, and the Sacred in Russia, 1910–1925* (Ithaca, N.Y.: Cornell University Press, 2002).

Stites, Richard. *The Women's Liberation Movement in Russia* (Princeton: Princeton University Press, 1978).

Stites, Richard. *Russian Popular Culture* (Cambridge: Cambridge University Press, 1992).

Von Laue, T. H. *Sergei Witte and the Industrialization of Russia* (New York: Atheneum, 1969).

Walicki, Andrzej. *A History of Russian Thought. From the Enlightenment to Marxism* (Stanford: Stanford University Press, 1979).

Wortman, Richard. *Scenarios of Power: Myth and Ceremony in Russian Monarchy*, 2 vols. (Princeton: Princeton University Press, 1995–2000).

Yaney, George. *The Urge to Mobilize: Agrarian Reform in Russia 1861–1930* (Urbana: University of Illinois Press, 1982).

Zelnik, Reginald. 'Russian Workers and the Revolutionary Movement', *Journal of Social History* Vol. 6, No. 2 (Winter, 1972–73): 214–36

Russia during the First World War

Eley, Geoffrey. 'Remapping the Nation: War, Revolutionary Upheaval, and State Formation in Eastern Europe, 1914–23', *Ukrainian–Jewish Relations in Historical Perspective* (Edmonton: Canadian Institute of Ukrainian Studies Press, 1988), pp.205–46.

Engel, Barbara Alpern. 'Not by Bread Alone: Subsistence Riots in Russia during World War One', *Journal of Modern History* 69 (1997): 696–721.

Gatrell, Peter. *A Whole Empire Walking* (Bloomington: Indiana University Press, 1999).

—— *Russia's First World War: A Social and Economic History* (Harlow: Longman, 2005).

Holquist, Peter. *Making War, Forging Revolution: Russia's Continuum of Crisis, 1914–1921* (Cambridge, Mass.: Harvard University Press, 2002).

Jahn, Hubertus. *Patriotic Culture in Russia during World War I* (Ithaca, Cornell University Press: 1995).

Lih, Lars. *Bread and Authority in Russia, 1914–1921* (Berkeley: University of California, 1990).

Lohr, Eric. *Nationalizing the Russian Empire: The Campaign against Enemy Aliens during World War I* (Cambridge, Mass.: Harvard University Press, 2003).

Sanborn, Joshua A. *Drafting the Russian Nation: Military Conscription, Total War, and Mass Politics, 1905–1925* (DeKalb: Northern Illinois Press, 2003).

Sanborn, Joshua. 'Unsettling the Russian Empire: Violent Migrations and Social Disaster in Russia during World War I.' *Journal of Modern History* 77, 2 (June 2005): 290–324.

Siegelbaum, Lewis. *The Politics of Industrial Mobilization, 1914–1917: A Study of the War-Industries Committees* (New York: St. Martin's Press, 1983).

Stone, Norman. *The Eastern Front, 1914–1917* (London: Hodder and Stoughton, 1975; New York: Penguin, 1998).

Von Hagen, Mark. 'The Great War and the Mobilization of Ethnicity in the Russian Empire', in Barnett Rubin and Jack Snyder (eds). *Post-Soviet Political Order: Conflict and State-building* (New York: Routledge, 1998): 34–57.

Werth, Nicolas. 'Les déserteurs en Russie: Violence de guerre, violence révolutionnaire et violence paysanne (1916–21)', in *La Violence de guerre, 1914–1945: Approches comparées des deux conflits mondiaux* (eds). Stéphane Audoin-Rouzeau, Annette Becker, Christian Ingrao, and Henry Rousso (Paris: IHTP-CNRS, 2002).

—— 'La guerre de huit ans (1914–22)' in *Les sociétés en guerre, 1911–1946* (eds). Bruno Cabanes and Édouard Husson (Paris: Armand Colin, 2003).

—— 'Une guerre de huit ans: Le cataclysme politique et social d'un "second temps des troubles" (1914–22)', in *Les sociétés, la guerre, la paix, 1911–1946* (eds). Dominique Barjot *et al.* (Paris: Sedes, 2006).

Wildman, Alan. *The End of the Russian Imperial Army*, 2 vols. (Princeton: Princeton University Press, 1980, 1987).

The Russian Revolution

Acton, Edward, Vladimir Iu. Cherniaev, and William G. Rosenberg (eds). *Critical Companion to the Russian Revolution, 1914–1921* (London: Arnold, 1997).

Anweiler, Oskar. *The Soviets: The Russian Workers', Peasants' and Soldiers' Councils, 1905–21* (New York: Pantheon, 1974).

Brovkin, Vladimir. *The Mensheviks after October: Socialist Opposition and the Rise of Bolshevik Dictatorship* (Ithaca: Cornell University Press, 1987).

Browder, R. P., and A. F. Kerensky. *The Russian Provisional Government*, 3 vols. (Stanford, Calif.: Stanford University Press, 1961).

Burdzhalov, E. N. *Russia's Second Revolution: The February 1917 Uprising in Petrograd*, trans. Donald J. Raleigh (Bloomington: Indiana University Press, 1987).

Carr, E. H. *A History of Soviet Russia: The Bolshevik Revolution 1917–1923*, 3 vols. (London: Macmillan, 1953; Pelican Books, 1966).

Chamberlin, William Henry. *The Russian Revolution* 2 vols. (New York: Grosset & Dunlap, 1965 [1935]).

Corney, Frederick C. *Telling October: Memory and the Making of the Bolshevik Revolution* (Ithaca: Cornell University Press, 2004).

Donald, Moira. 'Bolshevik Activity among Working Women of Petrograd in 1917', *International Review of Social History* 27 (1982): 129–60.

Ferro, Marc. *The Russian Revolution of February 1917* (London: Routledge and Kegan Paul, 1972).

—— *October 1917: A Social History of the October Revolution* (London: Routledge and Kegan Paul, 1980).

Figes, Orlando. *Peasant Russia, Civil War: The Volga Countryside in Revolution 1917–21* (Oxford: Clarendon Press, 1989).

—— *A People's Tragedy: The Russian Revolution, 1891–1924* (London: Jonathan Cape, 1996; New York: Viking, 1997).

Figes, Orlando, and Boris Kolonitskii. *Interpreting the Russian Revolution: The Language and Symbols of 1917* (New Haven: Yale University Press, 1999).

Fitzpatrick, Sheila. *The Russian Revolution*, 2nd edn (Oxford: Oxford University Press, 1994).

Frankel, E. R. et al. (eds.) *Revolution in Russia: Reassessments of 1917* (Cambridge: Cambridge University Press, 1992).

Friedgut, T. H. *Iuzovka and Revolution,* Vol. II: *Politics and Revolution in Russia's Donbass, 1869–1924* (Princeton: Princeton University Press, 1994).

Galili, Ziva. *The Menshevik Leaders in the Russian Revolution: Social Realities and Political Strategies* (Princeton: Princeton University Press, 1989).

Getzler, Israel. *Kronstadt, 1917–1921: The Fate of a Soviet Democracy* (Cambridge: Cambridge University Press, 1983).

Geyer, Dietrich. *The Russian Revolution* (New York: St. Martin's Press, 1987).

Gill, Graeme J. *Peasants and Government in the Russian Revolution* (London: Macmillan, 1979).

Gimpel'son, E. G. *Formirovanie sovetskoi politicheskoi sistemy, 1917–1923 gg.* (Moscow: Nauka, 1995).

Hasegawa, Tsuyoshi. *The February Revolution: Petrograd, 1917* (Seattle: University of Washington Press, 1981).

Iarov, Sergei. *Konformizm v sovetskoi Rossii: Petrograd, 1917–1920-kh godov* (St. Petersburg: Evropeiskii dom, 2006).

Kaiser, D. H. (ed.). *The Workers' Revolution in Russia, 1917* (Cambridge: Cambridge University Press, 1987).

Kanishchev, V. V. *Russkii bunt, bessmyslennyi i besposhchadnyi. Pogromnoe dvizhenie v gorodakh Rossii, 1917–1918* (Tambov: Tambovskii gosudarstvennyi universitet, 1995).

Keep, J. L. H. *The Russian Revolution: A Study in Mass Mobilization* (New York: Norton, 1976).

Kolonitskii, B. I. 'Antibourgeois Propaganda and Anti-*Burzhui* Consciousness in 1917', *Russian Review* 53, 2 (1994): 183–96.

—— *Simvoly vlasti i bor'ba za vlast'* (St. Petersburg: Dmitrii Bulanin, 2001).

McDaniel, Tim. *Autocracy, Capitalism, and Revolution in Russia* (Berkeley: University of California Press, 1988).

Pipes, Richard. *The Russian Revolution* (New York: Vintage, 1990).

Protasov, L. G. *Vserossiiskoe uchreditel'noe sobranie: istoriia rozhdeniia i gibeli* (Moscow: Rosspen, 1997).

Rabinowitch, Alexander. *Prelude to Revolution: The Petrograd Bolsheviks and the July 1917 Uprising* (Bloomington: Indiana University Press, 1968).

Rabinowitch, Alexander. *The Bolsheviks Come to Power: The Revolution of 1917 in Petrograd* (New York: Norton, 1976).

Rabinowitch, Alexander. The Bolsheviks in Power: The First Year of Soviet Rule in Petrograd (Bloomington.: Indiana University Press, 2007).

Radkey, Oliver. *Russia Goes to the Polls: The Elections to the All-Russian Constituent Assembly, 1917* (Revised edition. Ithaca: Cornell University Press, 1990).

Radkey, Oliver. *The Agrarian Foes of Bolshevism* (New York: Columbia University Press, 1958).

Raleigh, Donald. *Revolution on the Volga: 1917 in Saratov* (Ithaca: Cornell, 1986).

Rosenberg, Willam G. *Liberals in the Russian Revolution: The Constitutional Democratic Party, 1917–21* (Princeton: Princeton University Press, 1974).

Shliapnikov, A. G. *Kanun semnadtsatogo goda. Semnadtsatyi god*, 3 vols. (Moscow: Izdatel'stvo politicheskoi literatury, 1992–94).

Smith, S. A. *Red Petrograd: Revolution in the Factories, 1917–18* (Cambridge: Cambridge University Press, 1983).

Smith, Steven. 'The "Social" and the "Political" in the Russian Revolution.' *The Historical Journal* 38, 3 (1995): 733–43.

Suny, Ronald Grigor. *The Baku Commune, 1917–1918: Class and Nationality in the Russian Revolution* (Princeton: Princeton University Press, 1972).

—— 'Toward a Social History of the October Revolution', *American Historical Review* 88, 1 (1983): 31–52.

—— 'Revision and Retreat in the Historiography of 1917: Social History and its Critics', *Russian Review* 53, 2 (1994): 165–82.

Wildman, A. K. *The End of the Russian Imperial Army: The Old Army and the Soldiers' Revolt (March–April 1917); The End of the Russian Imperial Army: The Road to Soviet Power and Peace* (Princeton: Princeton University Press, 1980, 1987).

The Russian Civil War

Adelman, Jonathan R. 'The Development of the Soviet Party Apparat in the Civil War: Center, Localities, and Nationality Areas', *Russian History* 9, pt. 1 (1982): 86–110.

Bordiugov, Gennadii A. 'Chrezvychainye mery i "Chrezvychaishchina" v Sovetskoi respublike i drugikh gosudarstvennykh obrazovaniiakh na territorii Rossii v 1918–20 gg.', *Cahiers du Monde russe et sovi' etique* 38, 1–2 (1997): 29–44.

Brovkin, Vladimir N. *Behind the Front Lines of the Civil War: Political Parties and Social Movements in Russia, 1918–1922* (Princeton: Princeton University Press, 1994).

Budnitskii, Oleg Vital'evich. *Rossiiskie evrei mezhdu krasnymi i belymi, 1917–1920* (Moscow: ROSSPEN, 2005). [English translation by Penn Press ca. 2011]

Buldakov, V. P. *Krasnaia smuta: Priroda i posledstviia revoliutsionnogo nasiliia* (Moscow: Rosspen, 1997).

David-Fox, Michael. *Revolution of the Mind: Higher Learning among the Bolsheviks, 1918–1929* (Ithaca, N.Y.: Cornell University Press, 1997).

Fitzpatrick, Sheila. 'The Civil War as a Formative Experience', in Abbott Gleason, Peter Kenez and Richard Stites (eds). *Bolshevik Culture: Experiment and Order in the Russian Revolution* (Bloomington: Indiana University Press, 1985), pp. 57–76.

Getzler, Israel. *Kronstadt, 1917–1921: The Fall of a Soviet Democracy* (Cambridge: Cambridge University Press, 1983).

Gimpel'son, E. G. *Formirovanie Sovetskoi politicheskoi sistemy 1917–1923 gg.* (Moscow: Nauka, 1995).

Hafner, Lutz. *Die Partei der Linken. Sozialrevolutionäre in der russischen Revolution von 1917/18* (Cologne: Beiträge zur Geschichte Osteuropas, 1994).

Holquist, Peter. 'Violent Russia, Deadly Marxism: Russia in the Epoch of Violence', *Kritika: Explorations in Russian and Eurasian History* 4, 3 (Summer 2003): 627–52.

Kenez, Peter. *Civil War in South Russia, 1918: The First Year of the Volunteer Army* (Berkeley: University of California Press, 1971).

—— *Civil War in South Russia, 1919–1920: The Defeat of the Whites* (Berkeley: University of California Press, 1977).

Koenker, D. P., and William G. Rosenberg. *Strikes and Revolution in Russia, 1917* (Princeton: Princeton University Press, 1989).

Koenker, Diane P., William G. Rosenberg, and Ronald G. Suny (eds). *Party, State, and Society in the Russian Civil War: Explorations in Social History* (Bloomington: Indiana University Press, 1989).

Leonov, S. V. *Rozhdenie sovetskoi imperii: Gosudarstvo i ideologiia, 1917–1922 gg.* (Moscow: Dialog MGU, 1997).

Lih, Lars T. *Bread and Authority in Russia, 1914–1921* (Berkeley and Los Angeles: University of California Press, 1990).

Lincoln, Bruce W. *Red Victory* (New York: Simon and Schuster, 1989).

Litvin, A. L. 'Krasnyi i belyi terror v Rossii, 1917–22', *Otechestvennaia istoriia*, 6 (1993): 46–62.

Malle, Silvana. *The Economic Organisation of War Communism, 1918–1921* (Cambridge: Cambridge University Press, 1985).

Mawdsley, Evan. *The Russian Civil War* (Boston: Allen and Unwin, 1987).

McAuley, Mary. *Bread and Justice: State and Society in Petrograd, 1917–1922* (Oxford: Oxford University Press, 1991).

Narskii, Igor'. *Zhizn' v katastrofe: Budni naseleniia Urala v 1917–1922 gg.* (Moscow: Rosspen, 2001).

Patenaude, Bertrand M. *The Big Show in Bololand: The American Relief Expedition to Soviet Russia in the Famine of 1921* (Stanford, Calif.: Stanford University Press, 2002).

Pavliuchenkov, S. A. *Voennyi kommunizm v Rossii: Vlast' i massy* (Moscow: RKT–Istoriia, 1997).

Pereira, Norman G. O. *White Siberia: The Politics of Civil War* (Montreal and Kingston: McGill-Queen's University Press, 1996).

Pipes, Richard. *Russia under the Bolshevik Regime* (New York: Vintage, 1993).

Radkey, Oliver. *The Unknown Civil War in Soviet Russia: A Study of the Green Movement in the Tambov Region, 1920–1921* (Stanford, Calif.: Hoover Institution Press, 1976).

Raleigh, Donald J. *Experiencing Russia's Civil War: Politics, Society, and Revolutionary Culture in Saratov, 1917–1922* (Princeton: Princeton University Press, 2002).

Sakwa, Richard. *Soviet Communists in Power: A Study of Moscow during the Civil War, 1918–21* (Basingstoke: Macmillan, 1988).

Sapir, Jacques. 'La Guerre civile et l'économie de guerre: Origines du système soviétique', *Cahiers du Monde russe et soviétique* 38, 1–2 (1997): 9–28.

Schapiro, Leonard. *The Origin of the Communist Autocracy: Political Opposition in the Soviet State. First Phase, 1917–1922* [2nd edition] (Cambridge, Mass.: Harvard University Press, 1977).

Scheibert, Peter. *Lenin an der Macht: das russische Volk in der Revolution, 1918–1922* (Weinheim: Acta Humaniora, 1984).

Smele, Jonathan. *Civil War in Siberia: The Anti-Bolshevik Government of Admiral Kolchak, 1918–1920* (New York: Cambridge University Press, 1996).

Swain, Geoffrey. *The Origins of the Russian Civil War* (London and New York: Longman, 1996).

Von Geldern, James R. *Bolshevik Festivals, 1917–1920* (Berkeley and Los Angeles: University of California Press, 1993).

Von Hagen, Mark, *Soldiers in the Proletarian Dictatorship: The Red Army and the Soviet Socialist State, 1917–1930* (Ithaca, N.Y.: Cornell University Press, 1990).

The Soviet Union in the interwar period

Alexopoulos, Golfo. *Stalin's Outcasts: Aliens, Citizens, and the Soviet State, 1926–1936* (Ithaca, N.Y., and London: Cornell University Press, 2003).

Andrle, Vladimir. 'Demons and Devil's Advocates: Problems in Historical Writing on the Stalin Era', in Nick Lampert and Gabor Rittersporn (eds), *Stalinism: Its Nature and Aftermath: Essays in Honour of Moshe Lewin* (Armonk: M. E. Sharpe, 1992): 25–47

Atkinson, Dorothy. *The End of the Russian Land Commune, 1905–1930* (Stanford, Calif.: Stanford University Press, 1983).

Baberowski, Jörg. *Der rote Terror: die Geschichte des Stalinismus* (Munich: Deutsche Verlags-Anstalt, 2003)

Ball, Alan M. *And Now My Soul Is Hardened: Abandoned Children in Soviet Russia, 1918–1930* (Berkeley: University of California Press, 1994).

Ball, Alan M. *Russia's Last Capitalists: The Nepmen, 1921–1929* (Berkeley: University of California Press, 1987).

Binner, Rolf, and Marc Junge. 'Wie der Terror "Gross" wurde: Massenmord und Lagerhaft nach Befehl 00447', *Cahiers du monde russe* 42, 2–4 (2001).

Binner, Rolf, and Marc Junge. *Kak terror stal Bol'shim: Sekretnyi prikaz no. 00447 i. tekhnologiia ego ispolneniia* (Moscow: AIRO-XX, 2003).

Blum, Alain, and Martine Mespoulet. *L'anarchie bureaucratique: pouvoir et statistique sous Staline* (Paris: Découverte, 2003).

Carr, E. H., and R. W. Davies. *Foundations of a Planned Economy1926–1929*, 3 vols (London: Macmillan, 1969–78).

Chase, William. *Workers, Society, and the Soviet State: Labor and Life in Moscow, 1918–1929* (Urbana: University of Illinois Press, 1987).

Chinsky, Pavel. *Micro-histoire de la grande terreur: la fabrique de culpabilité à l'ère stalinienne* (Paris: Denoël, 2005).

Cohen, Stephen. *Bukharin and the Bolshevik Revolution: A Political Biography, 1888–1938* (Oxford: Oxford University Press, 1980).

Conquest, Robert. *The Harvest of Sorrow: Soviet Collectivization and the Terror-Famine* (London: Hutchinson, 1986).

Daniels, Robert Vincent. *The Conscience of the Revolution: Communist Opposition in Soviet Russia* (Cambridge, Mass.: Harvard University Press, 1960).

Danilov, V. P. *Rural Russia under the New Regime*, trans. Orlando Figes (London: Hutchinson, 1988).

Davies, R. W. *The Socialist Offensive: The Collectivization of Soviet Agriculture, 1929–1930* (Cambridge, Mass.: Harvard University Press, 1980).

—— *The Soviet Economy in Turmoil, 1929–1930* (Cambridge, Mass.: Harvard University Press, 1989).

Davies, R. W., and Mark Harrison. 'The Soviet Military-Economic Effort under the Second Five-Year Plan (1933–37)', *Europe–Asia Studies* 49, 3 (1997): 369–406.

Davies, Sarah. '"Us against Them": Social Identity in Soviet Russia, 1934–41', *Russian Review* 56, 1 (January 1997): 70–89.

—— *Popular Opinion in Stalin's Russia: Terror, Propaganda and Dissent, 1934–1941* (Cambridge: Cambridge University Press, 1997).

Dekel-Chen, Jonathan. *Farming the Red Land: Jewish Agricultural Colonization and Local Soviet Power, 1924–1941* (New Haven: Yale University Press, 2005).

Dunham, Vera S. *In Stalin's Time: Middle Class Values in Soviet Fiction* (Durham, N.C.: Duke University Press, 1990).

Edele, Mark. 'Soviet Society, Social Structure, and Everyday Life: Major Frameworks Reconsidered', *Kritika: Explorations in Russian and Eurasian History* 8, 2 (2007): 349–73.

Erickson, John. *The Soviet High Command: A Military-Political History, 1918–1941* (London: Macmillan, 1962).

Erlich, Alexander. *The Soviet Industrialization Debate, 1924–1928* (Cambridge, Mass.: Harvard University Press, 1960).

Fainsod, Merle. *Smolensk under Soviet Rule* (New York: Vintage, 1958).

Figes, Orlando. *The Whisperers: Private Life in Stalin's Russia* (New York: Metropolitan Books, 2007).

—— 'Private Life in Stalin's Russia: Family Narratives, Memory and Oral History.' *History Workshop Journal* 65, 1 (Spring 2008).

Filtzer, Donald. *Soviet Workers and Stalinist Industrialization: The Formation of Modern Soviet Production Relations, 1928–1941* (Armonk, N.Y.: M.E. Sharpe, 1986).

Fitzpatrick, Sheila (ed.). *Cultural Revolution in Russia, 1928–1931* (Bloomington: Indiana University Press, 1978).

Fitzpatrick, Sheila. 'Stalin and the Making of a New Elite, 1928–39', *Slavic Review* 38, 3 (1979): 377–402.

—— *Education and Social Mobility in the Soviet Union, 1921–1934* (Cambridge: Cambridge University Press, 1979).

—— *Stalin's Peasants: Resistance and Survival in the Russian Village after Collectivization* (New York and Oxford: Oxford University Press, 1994).

—— *Everyday Stalinism: Ordinary Life in Extraordinary Times: Soviet Russia in the 1930s* (New York and Oxford: Oxford University Press, 1999).

—— *Stalinism: New Directions* (London and New York: Routledge, 2000).

—— *Tear off the Masks! Identity and Imposture in Twentieth-Century Russia* (Princeton: Princeton University Press, 2005).

Fitzpatrick, Sheila, and Robert Gellately (eds). *Accusatory Practices: Denunciations in Modern European History, 1789–1989* (Chicago and London: University of Chicago Press, 1997).

Getty, J. Arch. *Origins of the Great Purges: The Soviet Communist Party Reconsidered, 1933–1938* (Cambridge: Cambridge University Press, 1985).

—— *The Road to Terror: Stalin and the Self-Destruction of the Bolsheviks* (New Haven: Yale University Press, 1999).

Getty, J. Arch, and Roberta T. Manning (eds). *Stalinist Terror: New Perspectives* (Cambridge: Cambridge University Press, 1993).

Geyer, Michael, and Sheila Fitzpatrick (eds). *Beyond Totalitarianism: Stalinism and Nazism Compared* (New York: Cambridge University Press, 2009).

Goldman, Wendy Z. *Women, the State and Revolution: Soviet Family Policy and Social Life, 1917–1936* (Cambridge: Cambridge University Press, 1993).

—— *Women at the Gates: Gender and Industry in Stalin's Russia* (Cambridge: Cambridge University Press, 2002).

Gor'kov, Iurii. *Gosudarstvennyi Komitet Oborony postanovliaet. 1941–1945. Tsifry i dokumenty* (Moscow: Olma Press, 2002).

Gouldner, Alvin. 'Stalinism: A Study of Internal Colonialism', *Telos* 34 (1977–78): 5–48.

Graziosi, Andrea. 'Collectivization, Peasant Revolts, and Government Policies through the Reports of the Ukrainian GPU', *Cahiers du Monde russe et soviétique* 35, 3 (1994): 437–631.

Gregory, Paul. *Terror by Quota* (New Haven: Yale University Press, 2009)

Hagenloh, Paul. *Stalin's Police: Public Order and Mass Repression in the USSR, 1926–1941* (Baltimore: Johns Hopkins University Press/Woodrow Wilson Center, 2009).

Halfin, Igal. 'The Demonization of the Opposition: Stalinist Memory and the "Communist Archive" at Leningrad Communist University', *Kritika* 2, 1 (Winter 2001), 45–80.

Harris, James. *The Great Urals: Regionalism and the Evolution of the Soviet System* (Ithaca: Cornell University Press, 1999).

Harrison, Mark (ed.). *Guns and Rubles: The Defense Industry in the Stalinist State* (New Haven: Yale University Press, 2008).

Haslam, Jonathan. 'Political Opposition to Stalin and the Origins of the Terror in Russia, 1932–36', *Historical Journal* 29, 2 (1986): 395–418.

Heinzen, James. *Inventing a Soviet Countryside: State Power and the Transformation of Rural Russia, 1917–1929* (Pittsburgh: University of Pittsburgh Press, 2004).

Hoffmann, David. *Peasant Metropolis: Social Identities in Moscow, 1929–1941* (Ithaca, N.Y.: Cornell University Press, 1994).

—— *Stalinist Values: The Cultural Norms of Soviet Modernity, 1917–1941* (Ithaca, N.Y.: Cornell University Press, 2003).

Husband, William. *'Godless Communists': Atheism and Society in Soviet Russia, 1917–1932* (DeKalb: Northern Illinois University Press, 2000).

Kenez, Peter. *The Birth of the Propaganda State: Soviet Methods of Mass Mobilization, 1917–1929* (Cambridge: Cambridge University Press, 1985).

Khlevniuk, Oleg. 'The Objectives of the Great Terror, 1937–38', in Julian Cooper, Maureen Perrie and E. A. Rees (eds), *Soviet History, 1917–5 3: Essays in Honour of R. W. Davies* (London and Basingstoke: St. Martin's Press, 1995), pp. 158–76.

—— *Politbiuro. Mekhanizmy politicheskoi vlasti v 1930-e gody* (Moscow: Rosspen, 1996).

Khlevniuk, Oleg et al. (eds). *Stalinskoe Politburo v 30-e gody* (Moscow: AIRO-XX, 1995).

Kostyrchenko, G. V. *Tainaia politika Stalina: Vlast' i antisemitizm* (Moscow: Mezhdunarodnye otnosheniia, 2001).

Kotkin, Stephen. *Magnetic Mountain: Stalinism as a Civilization* (Berkeley: University of California Press, 1995). Response: Igal Halfin and Jochen Hellbeck. 'Rethinking the Stalinist Subject: Stephen Kotkin's "Magnetic Mountain" and the State of Soviet Historical Studies', *Jahrbücher für Geschichte Osteuropas* 44 (1996): 456–63.

—— 'Modern Times: The Soviet Union and the Interwar Conjuncture', *Kritika* 2, 1 (Winter 2001).

Kozlov, V. A., and S. M. Zav'ialov (eds). *Neizvestnaia Rossiia. XX vek*, vols i–iii (Moscow: Istoricheskoe nasledie, 1992, 1993).

Kuromiya, Hiroaki. *Stalin's Industrial Revolution 1928–1932* (Cambridge: Cambridge University Press, 1988).

Lebina, N. B. *Povsednevnaia zhizn' sovetskogo goroda, 1920–1930-e gody*. (St. Petersburg: Letnii sad, 1999).

Lenoe, Matthew. *Closer to the Masses: Stalinist Culture, Social Revolution, and Soviet Newspapers* (Cambridge: Harvard University Press, 2004).

Lewin, Moshe. *Russian Peasants and Soviet Power: A Study of Collectivization* (Evanston, Ill.: Northwestern University Press, 1968).

—— *The Making of the Soviet System: Essays in the Social History of Interwar Russia* (New York: Pantheon Books, 1985).

McCauley, Martin (ed.). *Stalin and Stalinism* (London: Longman Press, 1995).

Medvedev, Roy. *Let History Judge: The Origins and Consequences of Stalinism*, revised edn (New York: Oxford University Press, 1989).

Merl, Stephan. *Bauern unter Stalin: die Formierung des sowjetischen Kolchossystems, 1930–1941* (Berlin: Duncker and Humblot, 1990).

Miller, Frank J. *Folklore for Stalin: Russian Folklore and Pseudofolklore in the Stalin Era* (Armonk, NY: M.E. Sharpe, 1990).

Montefiore, Simon Sebag. *Stalin: The Court of the Red Tsar* (London: Weidenfeld and Nicolson, 2003).

Nove, Alec. *Was Stalin Really Necessary? Some Problems of Soviet Political Economy* (London: George Allen and Unwin, 1964).

Osokina, Elena. *Our Daily Bread: Socialist Distribution and the Art of Survival in Stalin's Russia 1927–1941* (Armonk, N.Y.: M.E. Sharpe, 2001).

Paperno, Irina. 'Dreams of Terror: Dreams from Stalinist Russia as a Historical Source.' *Kritika: Explorations in Russian and Eurasian History* 7, 4 (Fall 2006), 793–824.

Pechenkin, A. A. 'Gosudarstvennyi komitet oborony v 1941 godu', *Otechestvennaia istoriia* 4–5 (1994): 126–41.

Pethybridge, Roger. *One Step Backwards, Two Steps Forward: Soviet Society and Politics in the New Economic Policy* (Oxford: Oxford University Press, 1990).

Rabinowitch, Alexander, and Richard Stites (eds). *Russia in the Era of NEP: Explorations in Soviet Society and Culture* (Bloomington: Indiana University Press, 1991).

Raleigh, Donald (ed.). *Provincial Landscapes: Local Dimensions of Soviet Power, 1917–1953* (Pittsburgh: University of Pittsburgh Press, 2001), pp. 194–216.

Reese, Roger. *Stalin's Reluctant Soldiers: A Social History of the Red Army, 1925–1941* (Lawrence: University Press of Kansas, 1996.)

Reiman, Michel. *The Birth of Stalinism: The USSR on the Eve of the 'Second Revolution'*, trans. George Saunders (Bloomington: Indiana University Press, 1987).

Rigby, T. H. *Essays in Historical Interpretation* (New York: Norton, 1977), pp. 53–76.

Rousso, Henry (ed.). *Stalinism and Nazism: History and Memory Compared* (Lincoln and London: University of Nebraska Press, 1999).

Rubenstein, Joshua, and Vladimir Naumov (eds). *Stalin's Secret Pogrom: The Postwar Inquisition of the Jewish Anti-Fascist Committee*, trans. Laura Esther Wolfson (New Haven: Yale University Press, 2002).

Schlögel, Karl. *Terror und Traum: Moskau, 1937* (Munich: Hanser, 2008).

Shearer, David R. *Industry, State, and Society in Stalin's Russia, 1926–1934* (Ithaca, N.Y.: Cornell University Press, 1996).

—— *Policing Stalin's Socialism: Repression and Social Order in the Soviet Union, 1924–1953* (New Haven: Yale University Press, 2009)

Siegelbaum, Lewis H. *Stakhanovism and the Politics of Productivity in the USSR 1935–1941* (Cambridge: Cambridge University Press, 1988).

—— *Soviet State and Society Between Revolutions, 1918–1929* (Cambridge: Cambridge University Press, 1992).

Smith, Jeremy. *The Bolsheviks and the National Question, 1917–23* (New York: St. Martin's Press, 1999).

Solomon, Peter H., Jr. *Soviet Criminal Justice under Stalin* (Cambridge: Cambridge University Press, 1996).

Stites, Richard. *Revolutionary Dreams: Utopian Vision and Experimental Life in the Russian Revolution* (Oxford: Oxford University Press, 1989).

Studer, Brigitte, and Heiko Haumann (eds). *Stalinistische Subjekte. Individuum und System in der Sowjetunion und der Komintern 1929–1953* (Zürich: Chronos, 2006).

Thurston, Robert W. *Life and Terror in Stalin's Russia, 1934–1941* (New Haven and London: Yale University Press, 1996).

Timasheff, Nicholas S. *The Great Retreat: The Growth and Decline of Communism in Russia* (New York: E.P. Dutton and Co., 1946).

Tucker, Robert C. (ed.). *Stalinism: Essays in Historical Interpretation* (New York: Norton, 1977).

Tucker, Robert C. *The Soviet Political Mind* (New York: Norton, 1971).

Tumarkin, Nina. *Lenin Lives! The Lenin Cult in Soviet Russia* (Cambridge, Mass.: Harvard University Press, 1983).

Viola, Lynne. *The Best Sons of the Fatherland: Workers in the Vanguard of Soviet Collectivization* (New York: Oxford University Press, 1987).

—— *Peasant Rebels under Stalin: Collectivization and the Culture of Peasant Resistance* (New York: Oxford University Press, 1996).

—— *Contending with Stalinism: Soviet Power and Popular Resistance in the 1930s* (Ithaca, N.Y., and London: Cornell University Press, 2002).

Ward, Chris. *Stalin's Russia* (London: Arnold, 1993).

Wehner, Markus, *Bauernpolitik im proletarischen Staat: Die Bauernfrage als zentrales Problem der sowjetischen Innenpolitik 1921–1928* (Cologne: Boehlau Verlag, 1998).

Werth, Nicolas. *La Terreur et le désarroi. Staline et son système* (Paris: Perrin, 2007).

Youngblood, Denise. *Movies for the Masses: Popular Cinema and Soviet Society in the 1920s* (Cambridge: Cambridge University Press, 1992).

The Second World War

Andreyev, Catherine. *Vlasov and the Russian Liberation Movement: Soviet Reality and Emigré Theories* (Cambridge: Cambridge University Press, 1987).

Barber, John (ed.). *Zhizn' i smert' v blokadnom Leningrade. Istoriko-meditsinskii aspekt* (St. Petersburg: Dmitrii Bulanin, 2001).

Barber, John, and Mark Harrison. *The Soviet Home Front 1941–1945: A Social and Economic History of the USSR in World War II* (London: Longman, 1991).

Beevor, Antony. *Stalingrad* (London: Viking, 1998).

—— *Berlin: The Downfall, 1945* (London: Viking, 2002).

Bialer, Seweryn. *Stalin and his Generals: Soviet Military Memoirs of World War II* (New York: Pegasus, 1969).

Burds, Jeffrey. 'The Soviet War against "Fifth Columnists": The Case of Chechnya, 1942–44', *Journal of Contemporary History* 42, 2 (April 2007).

Dallin, Alexander. *German Rule in Russia, 1941–1945: A Study of Occupation Policies* (New York: St. Martin's Press, 1957; revised edn Boulder, Colo.: Westview Press, 1981).

Dobroszyski, Lucjan, and Jeffrey Gurock (eds). *The Holocaust in the Soviet Union* (M.E. Sharpe, 1993).

Ellman, Michael, and Sergei Maksudov. 'Soviet Deaths in the Great PatrioticWar', *Europe–Asia Studies* 46, 4 (1994): 671–80.

Erickson, John. *Stalin's War with Germany*, 2 vols (London: Weidenfeld and Nicolson, 1975–83).

—— 'Red Army Battlefield Performance, 1941–45: The System and the Soldier', in Paul Addison and Angus Calder (eds), *Time to Kill: The Soldier's Experience of War in the West, 1939–1945* (London: Pimlico, 1997), pp. 233–48.

Erickson, John, and David Dilks (eds). *Barbarossa: The Axis and the Allies* (Edinburgh: Edinburgh University Press, 1994).

Feferman, Kiril. 'Soviet Investigation of Nazi Crimes in the USSR: Documenting the Holocaust', *Journal of Genocide Research* 5, 4 (December 2003).

Gitelman, Zvi (ed.). *Bitter Legacy: Confronting the Holocaust in the USSR* (Bloomington: Indiana University Press, 1997).

Glantz, David M. *Accounting for War: Soviet Production, Employment, and the Defence Burden, 1940–1945* (Cambridge: Cambridge University Press, 1996).

—— *Stumbling Colossus: The Red Army on the Eve of World War* (Lawrence: University Press of Kansas, 1998).

—— 'The Economics of World War II: An Overview', in Mark Harrison (ed.), *The Economics of World War II: Six Great Powers in International Comparison* (Cambridge: Cambridge University Press, 1998), pp. 1–42.

—— 'Wartime Mobilisation: A German Comparison', in John Barber and Mark Harrison (eds), *The Soviet Defence Industry Complex from Stalin to Khrushchev* (London: Macmillan, 2000), pp. 99–117.

—— 'Counting Soviet Deaths in the Great Patriotic War: Comment', *Europe–Asia Studies* 55, 6 (2003): 939–44.

—— *Colossus Reborn: The Red Army at War, 1941–1943* (Lawrence: University Press of Kansas, 2005).

Glantz, David M., and House, Jonathan. *When Titans Clashed: How the Red Army Stopped Hitler* (Lawrence: University Press of Kansas, 1995).

Gross, Jan. *Revolution from Abroad: The Soviet Conquest of Poland's Western Ukraine and Western Belorussia* (Princeton: Princeton University Press, 2002).

Harrison, Mark. *Soviet Planning in Peace and War, 1938–1945* (Cambridge: Cambridge University Press, 1985).

Krivosheev, G. F. *Grif sekretnosti sniat. Poteri vooruzhennykh sil SSSR v voinakh, boevykh deistviiakh i voennykh konfliktakh. Statisticheskoe issledovanie* (Moscow: Voennoe izdatel'stvo, 1993).

Krivosheev, G. F. et al. *Rossiia i SSSR v voinakh XX veka. Statisticheskoe issledovanie* (Moscow: OLMAPRESS, 2003).

Kumanev, G. A. *Ryadom so Stalinym. Otkrovennye svidetel'stva. Vstrechi, besedy, interv'iu, dokumenty* (Moscow: Bylina, 1999).

Levin, Dov. *The Lesser of Two Evils: East European Jewry Under Soviet Rule, 1939–1941*, trans. Naftali Greenwood (Philadelphia: JPS, 1995).

Lieberman, Sanford R. 'Crisis Management in the USSR: Wartime System of Administration and Control', in Susan J. Linz (ed.), *The Impact of World War II on the Soviet Union* (Totowa, N.J.: Rowman and Allanheld, 1985).

Linz, Susan J. (ed.). *The Impact of World War II on the Soviet Union* (Totowa, N.J.: Rowman and Allanheld, 1985).

Mawdsley, Evan. 'Crossing the Rubicon: Soviet Plans for Offensive War in 1940–41', *International History Review* 25, 4 (2003): 818–65.

McCagg, William O. *Stalin Embattled, 1943–1948* (Detroit: Wayne State University Press, 1978).

Menning, Bruce W. 'A Decade Half-Full: Post-Cold War Studies in Russian and Soviet Military History', *Kritika* 2, 2 (Spring 2001): 341–62.

Merridale, Catherine. *Ivan's War: Life and Death in the Red Army, 1939–1945* (New York: Metropolitan Books, 2006).

Mertsalov, A. N., and L. A. Mertsalov. *Stalinizm i voina* (Moscow: Terra-Knizhnyi klub, 1998).

Moine, Nathalie. 'La commission d'enquête soviétique sur les crimes de guerre nazis: entre reconquête du territoire, écriture du récit de la guerre et usages justiciers.' *Mouvement social* 222 (2008): 81–109.

Moskoff, William. *The Bread of Affliction: The Food Supply in the USSR during World War II* (Cambridge: Cambridge University Press, 1990).

Murphy, David. *What Stalin Knew: The Enigma of Barbarossa* (New Haven: Yale University Press, 2005).

Pleshakov, Constantine. *Stalin's Folly: The Tragic First Ten Days of WW II on the Eastern Front* (New York: Houghton Mifflin, 2005).

Redlich, Shimon. *War, Holocaust, and Stalinism* (London: Harwood Academic Publishers, 1995).

Reese, Roger R. *The Soviet Military Experience* (London: Routledge, 2000).

Rieber, Alfred J. 'Civil Wars in the Soviet Union', *Kritika: Explorations in Russian and Eurasian History* 4, 1 (2003): 129–62.

Roberts, Geoffrey. *Victory at Stalingrad: The Battle that Changed History* (London: Longman, 2000).

Salisbury, Harrison. *The 900 Days: the Siege of Leningrad* (London: Pan, 1969).

Samuelson, Lennart. *Plans for Stalin's War Machine: Tukhachevskii and Military-Economic Planning, 1925–41* (London and Basingstoke: Macmillan, 2000).

Sapir, Jacques. 'The Economics of War in the Soviet Union during World War II', in Ian Kershaw and Moshe Lewin (eds), *Stalinism and Nazism: Dictatorships in Comparison* (Cambridge: Cambridge University Press, 1997), pp. 208–36.

Simonov, Konstantin. *Glazami cheloveka moego pokoleniia. Razmyshleniia o I.V. Staline* (Moscow: Novosti, 1989).

Siniavskaia, Elena. *Frontovoe pokolenie: Istoriko-psikhologicheskoe issledovanie* (Moscow: IRI-RAN, 1995).

Sorokina, M. A. 'People and Procedures: Toward a History of the Investigation of Nazi Crimes in the USSR', *Kritika: Explorations in Russian and Eurasian History* 6, 4 (2005): 797–831.

Suvorov (Rezun), Viktor. *Ice-Breaker: Who Started the Second World War?* (London: Hamish Hamilton, 1990).

Swain, Geoffrey. *Between Stalin and Hitler: Class War and Race War on the Dvina, 1940–1946* (London and New York: Routledge-Curzon, 2004).

Torchinov, V. A., and A. M. Leontiuk. *Vokrug Stalina. Istoriko-biograficheskii spravochnik* (St. Petersburg: Filologicheskii fakul'tet Sankt-Peterburgskogo gosudarstvennogo universiteta, 2000).

Watson, Derek. 'Molotov, the Making of the Grand Alliance and the Second Front, 1939–42', *Europe–Asia Studies* 54, 1 (2002): 51–85.

Weeks, Albert L. *Stalin's Other War: Soviet Grand Strategy,1939–1941* (Lanham, Md.: Rowman and Littlefield, 2002).

Weiner, Amir. 'Saving Private Ivan: From What, Why, and How?' *Kritika* 1, 2 (Spring 2000), 305–36.

Weiner, Amir. 'The Making of a Dominant Myth: The Second World War and the Construction of Political Identities Within the Soviet Polity', *Russian Review* 55, 4 (October 1996): 638–60.

—— *Making Sense of War: The Second World War and the Fate of the Bolshevik Revolution* (Princeton: Princeton University Press, 2001).

Werth, Alexander. *Russia at War, 1941–1945* (London: Barrie and Rockcliffe, 1964).

The late Stalin era and the early Cold War, 1945–53

Behrends, Jan C. 'Vom Panslavismus zum "Friedenskampf": Außenpolitik, Herrschaftslegitimation und Massenmobilisierung im sowjetischen Nachkriegsimperium (1944–53)', *Jahrbücher für Geschichte Osteuropas* 56, 1 (2008): 27–53.

Brandenberger, David. 'Stalin, the Leningrad Affair, and the Limits of Postwar Soviet Russocentrism.' *Russian Review* 63, 2 (April 2004): 241–55.

Conner, Walter D. *Socialism's Dilemmas: State and Society in the Soviet Bloc* (New York: Columbia University Press, 1988).

Filtzer, Donald A. *Soviet Workers and Late Stalinism: Labour and the Restoration of the Stalinist System after World War II* (New York: Cambridge University Press, 2002).

Fürst, Juliane. 'Prisoners of the Soviet Self? Political Youth Opposition in Late Stalinism', *Europe–Asia Studies* 54, 3 (2002): 353–75. Response by Hiroaki Kuromiya, with follow-up by Juliane Fürst, *Europe–Asia Studies* 55, 5 (2003): 789–802.

—— 'In Search of Soviet Salvation: Young People Write to the Stalinist Authorities', *Contemporary European History* 15, 3 (August 2006): 327–45.

—— (ed.). *Late Stalinist Russia: Society between Reconstruction and Reinvention* (London: Routledge, 2006).

Gorlitski, Yoram and Oleg Khlevniuk. *Cold Peace: Stalin and the Soviet Ruling Circle, 1945–1953* (New York: Oxford University Press, 2004).

Khlevniuk, Oleg. 'Stalin i organy gosudarstvennoi bezopasnosti v poslevoennyi period', *Cahiers du monde russe* 42, 2–4 (April–December 2001), 535–48.

Madieveski, Samson. '1953: La Déportation des Juifs Soviétiques était-elle programmée?', *Cahiers du Monde russe et soviétique* 41, 4 (2000): 561–68.

Pryzhkov, A. B. 'Sovetskoe poslevoennoe obshchestvo i predposylki khrushchevskikh reform', *Voprosy istorii* 2 (2002): 33–43.

Zezina, Maria. 'Crisis in the Union of Soviet Writers in the Early 1950s', *Europe–Asia Studies* 46, 4 (1994): 649–61.

Zima, Veniamin. *Golod v SSSR 1946–1947: proiskhozhdenie i posledstviia* (Moscow: IRI-RAN, 1996).

Zubkova, Elena. *Obshchestvo i reformy 1945–1964* (Moscow: Rossiia molodaia, 1993).

—— *Russia after the War: Hopes, Illusions, and Disappointments, 1945–1957* (Armonk, N.Y.: M.E. Sharpe, 1998).

—— *Poslevoennoe sovetskoe obshchestvo: Politika and povsednevnost', 1945–1953* (Moscow: ROSSPEN, 2000).

The Soviet Union after Stalin

Aksiutin, Iurii. *Khrushchevskaia 'ottepel' i obshchestvennye nastroeniia v SSSR v 1953–1964 gg*, (Moscow: ROSSPEN, 2004).

Alexseyeva, Lyudmilla. *Soviet Dissent: Contemporary Movements for National, Religious, and Human Rights* (Middletown, Conn.: Wesleyan University Press, 1985).

Alexseyeva, Lyudmilla, and Paul Goldberg. *The Thaw Generation: Coming of Age in the Post-Stalin Era* (Pittsburgh: Pittsburgh University Press, 1993).

Arbatov, Georgi. *The System: An Insider's Life in Soviet Politics* (New York: Times Books, 1992).

Artizov, Andrei et al. *Reabilitatsiia: Kak eto bylo: Dokumenty Prezidiuma TSK KPSS i drugie materialy: mart 1953–fevral' 1956* (Moscow: Demokratiia, 2000-).

Bacon, Edwin, and Mark Sandle (eds). *Brezhnev Reconsidered* (London: Palgrave, 2002).

Baron, Samuel H. *Bloody Saturday in the Soviet Union: Novocherkassk, 1962* (Stanford, Calif.: Stanford University Press, 2001).

Bezborodov, A. B. *Fenomen Akademicheskogo Dissidentstva v SSSR* (Moscow: Rossiiskii gos. gumanitarnyi universitet, 1998).

Bialer, Seweryn. *Stalin's Successors: Leadership, Stability, and Change in the Soviet Union* (Cambridge and New York: Cambridge University Press, 1980).

Bittner, Stephen V. *The Many Lives of Khrushchev's Thaw: Experience and Memory in Moscow's Arbat* (Ithaca, N.Y.: Cornell University Press, 2008).

Blium, Arlen. *Kak eto delalos' v Leningrade: Tsenzura v gody ottepeli, zastoia i perestroika, 1953–1991* (Sankt-Peterburg: Akademicheskii proekt, 2005).

Boobbyer, Philip. 'Religious Experiences of the Soviet Dissidents', *Religion, State & Society* 27, 3–4, (1999): 373–90.

—— *Conscience, Dissent, and Reform in Soviet Russia* (London and New York: Routledge, 2005).

Breslauer, George. 'On the Adaptability of Soviet Welfare-State Authoritarianism', in Erik P. Hoffmann and Robbin F. Laird (eds), *The Soviet Polity in the Modern World* (New York: Aldine, 1984): 219–45.

Breslauer, George. *Khrushchev and Brezhnev as Leaders: Building Authority in Soviet Politics* (London and Boston: Allen and Unwin, 1982).

Brown, Archie, and Michael Kaser (eds). *The Soviet Union since the Fall of Khrushchev* (New York: The Free Press, 1975).

Brudny, Yitzhak M. *Reinventing Russia: Russian Nationalism and the Collapse of the Soviet State, 1953–1991* (Cambridge, Mass.: Harvard University Press, 1998).

Bruskilovskaia, L. B. *Kul'tura Povsednevnosti v Epokhu 'Ottepeli': Metamorfozy Stilia* (Moscow: URAO, 2001).

Bushnell, John. 'Urban Leisure Culture in Post-Stalin Russia: Stability as a Social Problem?', in Terry L. Thompson and Richard Sheldon (eds), *Soviet Society and Culture: Essays in Honor of Vera S. Dunham* (Boulder, Colo.: Westview Press, 1988).

—— *Moscow Graffiti: Language and Subculture* (Boston: Unwin Hyman, 1990).

Chernaiev, A. S. *Moia zhizn' i moe vremia* (Moscow: Mezhdunarodnye otnosheniia, 1995).

Climenti, Marco. *Storia del Dissenso Sovietico, 1953–1991* (Rome: Odradek, 2007).

Cohen, Stephen F., Alexander Rabinowitch, and Robert Sharlet (eds). *The Soviet Union since Stalin* (Bloomington: Indiana University Press, 1980).

Colton, Timothy, and Thane Gustafson (eds). *Soldiers and the Soviet State: Civil–Military Relations from Brezhnev to Gorbachev* (Princeton: Princeton University Press, 1990).

Cook, Linda J. *The Soviet Social Contract and Why it Failed: Welfare Policy and Workers' Politics from Brezhnev to Yeltsin* (Cambridge, Mass.: Harvard University Press, 1993).

—— 'Wie freie Menschen: Ursprung und Wurzeln des Dissens in der Sowjetunion', in Wolfgang Eichwede (ed.), *Samizdat. Alternative Kultur in Zentral-und Osteuropa: die 60er bis 80er Jahre* (Bremen, Edition Temmen: 2000): 38–50.

Dobrynin, Anatoly. *In Confidence: Moscow's Ambassador to America's Six Cold War Presidents (1962–1986)* (New York: Random House, 1995).

Dobson, Miriam. *Khrushchev's Cold Summer: Gulag Returnees, Crime, and the Fate of Reform after Stalin* (Ithaca, N.Y.: Cornell University Press, 2009).

Edele, Mark. *Soviet Veterans of World War II: A Popular Movement in an Authoritarian Society, 1941–1991* (Oxford: Oxford University Press, 2009)

Evangelista, Matthew. *Unarmed Forces: The Transnational Movement to End the Cold War* (Ithaca, N.Y.: Cornell University Press, 2002).

Field, Deborah. '"Irreconcilable Differences": Divorce and Conceptions of Private Life in the Khrushchev Era', *Russian Review* 57, 4 (October 1998): 599–613.

Filippov, Oleg. *Khronika chastnoi zhizni, 1957–1969* (Tomsk-Moscow: Volodei, 2004).

Filtzer, Donald. *Soviet Workers and De-Stalinization: The Consolidation of the Modern System of Soviet Production Relations* (Cambridge: Cambridge University Press, 1992).

Frankel, Edith Rogovin. *Novy Mir: A Case Study in the Politics of Literature* (New York: Cambridge University Press, 1981).

Glazov, Yuri. *The Russian Mind Since Stalin's Death* (Dordrecht: D. Reidel, 1985).

Grinevskii, Oleg. *Tysiacha i odin den' Nikity Sergeevicha* (Moscow: Vagrius, 1998).

Grossman, Gregory. 'The "Second Economy" of the USSR', *Problems of Communism* 26 (September–October 1977): 25–40.

Groys, Boris. 'The Other Gaze: Russian Unofficial Art's View of the Soviet World', in Aleés Erjavec (ed.), *Postmodernism and the Postsocialist Condition: Politicized Art under Late Socialism* (2003).

Gustafson, Thane. *Crisis amidst Plenty: The Politics of Soviet Energy under Brezhnev and Gorbachev* (Princeton: Princeton University Press, 1989).

Hanson, Stephen E. *Time and Revolution: Marxism and the Design of Soviet Institutions* (Chapel Hill: University of North Carolina Press, 1997).

Hessler, Julie. 'Death of an African Student in Moscow: Race, Politics, and the Cold War', *Cahiers du monde russe et soviétique* 47, 1–2 (2007): 33–63.

Hopkins, Mark. *Mass Media in the Soviet Union* (New York: Pegasus, 1970).

Hough, Jerry F. *The Soviet Prefects: The Local Party Organs in Industrial Decision Making* (Cambridge, Mass.: Harvard University Press, 1969).

—— *The Soviet Union and Social Science Theory* (Cambridge, Mass.: Harvard University Press, 1977).

Hough, Jerry F., and Fainsod, Merle. *How the Soviet Union is Governed* (Cambridge, Mass.: Harvard University Press, 1979).

Inkeles, Alex, and Raymond Bauer. *The Soviet Citizen: Daily Life in a Totalitarian Society* (Cambridge: Harvard University Press, 1959).

Jelen, Christian, and Thierry Wolton. *L'occident des dissidents* (Paris: Stock, 1979).

Johnson, Priscilla, and Leopold Labedz (eds). *Khrushchev and the Arts: The Politics of Soviet Culture, 1962–1964* (Cambridge, Mass.: MIT Press, 1965).

Jones, Polly (ed.). *The Dilemmas of De-Stalinization: Negotiating Cultural and Social Change in the Khrushchev Era* (London and New York: Routledge, 2006).

Junge, Marc [Mark Iunge]. *Strakh pered proshlym: reabilitatsiia N. I. Bukharina ot Khrushcheva do Gorbacheva* (Moscow, AIRO-XX, 2003).

Keep, John. *Last of the Empires: A History of the Soviet Union, 1945–1991* (New York: Oxford, 1995).

Khrushchev, N. S. *Vospominaniia – vremia, liudi, vlast'*, 4 vols (Moscow: Moskovskie novosti, 1999).

Khrushchev, Sergei N. *Khrushchev on Khrushchev: An Inside Account of the Man and his Era*, trans. and ed. William Taubman (Boston: Little, Brown, 1990).

Kozlov, V. A. *Mass Uprisings in the USSR: Protest and Rebellion in the Post-Stalin Years* (New York: M.E. Sharpe, 2002).

Lapidus, Gail. 'Ethnonationalism and Political Stability: The Soviet Case', *World Politics* 36, 4 (July 1984): 555–80.

Lewin, Moshe. *Stalinism and the Seeds of Soviet Reform: The Debates of the 1960s* (Armonk, N.Y.: M.E. Sharpe, 1991).

MacFadyen, David. *Red Stars: Personality and the Soviet Popular Song, 1955–1991* (Montreal and Kingston, Ont., 2001).

Mawdsley, Evan, and Stephen White. *The Soviet Elite from Lenin to Gorbachev: The Central Committee and its Members, 1917–1991* (Oxford and New York: Oxford University Press, 2000).

McCauley, Martin (ed.). *Khrushchev and Khrushchevism* (Bloomington: Indiana University Press, 1987).

Millar, James R. 'The Little Deal: Brezhnev's Contribution to Acquisitive Socialism', *Slavic Review* 44, 4 (Winter 1985): 694–706

Millar, James (ed.). *Politics, Work, and Daily Life in the USSR: A Survey of Former Soviet Citizens* (Cambridge: Cambridge University Press, 1987), pp. 241–75.

Mitrokhin, Nikolai. *Russkaia partiia: dvizhenie russkikh natsionalistov v SSSR 1953–1985* (Moscow: NLO, 2003).

Nathans, Benjamin. 'Soviet Rights-Talk in the Post-Stalin Era', in Stefan-Ludwig Hoffmann (ed.), *Human Rights in the Twentieth Century: A Critical History* (Cambridge: Cambridge University Press, 2010): 166–90.

Pikhoia, R. G. *Sovetskii Soiuz: Istoriia vlasti, 1945–1991* (Moscow: Izd-vo RAGS, 1998) [revised and enlarged edn Novosibirsk: Sibirskii khronograf, 2000].

Pockney, B. P. *Soviet Statistics since 1950* (New York: St. Martin's Press, 1991).

Pyzhikov, Aleksandr. *Khruschevskaia ottepel', 1953–1964* (Moscow: Olma-Press, 2002).

Reddaway, Peter. 'Policy on Dissent Since Khrushchev', in Archie Brown, Peter Reddaway, and T. H. Rigby (eds), *Authority, Power, and Policy in the USSR: Essays Dedicated to Leonard Shapiro* (London, 1980).

Remington, Thomas F. 'Soviet Public Opinion and the Effectiveness of Party Ideological Work', *Carl Beck Papers in Russian and East European Studies* 204 (Pittsburgh: University of Pittsburgh Press, 1983).

Rogov, Kirill Iur'evich (ed.). *Semidesiatye kak predmet istorii russkoi kul'tury* (Moscow/Venice: Rossiia/Russia, 1998).

Rozhdestvennyi, S. D. [Veniamin Ioffe]. 'Materialy k istorii samodeiatel'nykh politicheskikh ob'edinenii v SSSR posle 1945 goda', *Pamiat'* 5 (1981): 226–83.

Sakharov, Andrei. *Memoirs*, trans. Richard Lourie (New York: Alfred A. Knopf, 1990).

Schlögel, Karl. *Der renitente Held: Arbeiterprotest in der Sowjetunion, 1953–1983* (Hamburg: Junius, 1984).

Shatz, Marshall. *Soviet Dissent in Historical Perspective* (Cambridge: Cambridge University Press, 1980).

Shlapentokh, Vladimir. *Public and Private Life of the Soviet People: Changing Values in Post-Stalin Russia* (New York, 1989).

Spechler, Dina. *Permitted Dissent in the USSR: Novy Mir and the Soviet Regime* (New York: Praeger, 1982).

Stephan, Anke. *Von der Küche auf den Roten Platz: Lebenswege sowjetischer Dissidentinnen* (Zürich: Pano Verlag, 2005)

Tokes, Rudolph (ed.). *Dissent in the USSR: Politics, Ideology, and People* (Baltimore, MD: Johns Hopkins University Press, 1975).

Tumarkin, Nina. *The Living and the Dead: The Rise and Fall of the Cult of World War II in Russia* (New York: Basic Books, 1994).

Vail', Petr, and Aleksandr Genis. *60-e. Mir sovetskogo cheloveka* (Moscow: NLO, 2001).

Vaissie, Cecile. *Pour Votre Liberte et Pour la Notre: Le Combat des Dissidents de Russie* (Paris: Laffont, 1999).

Voronkov, Viktor and Jan Wielgoh. 'Soviet Russia', in Detlef Pollack and Jan Wielgohs (eds), *Dissent and Opposition in Communist Eastern Europe: Origins of Civil society and Democratic Transition* (2004), pp. 95–118.

Weiner, Amir. 'Déjà Vu All Over Again: Prague Spring, Romanian Summer, and Soviet Autumn on Russia's Western Frontier', *Journal of Contemporary European History* 15, 2 (June 2006): 159–94.

—— 'The Empires Pay a Visit: Gulag Returnees, East European Rebellions, and Soviet Frontier Politics', *The Journal of Modern History*, 78, 2 (2006): 333–76.

Weiner, Doug. *Little Corners of Freedom: Russian Nature Protection from Stalin to Gorbachev* (Berkeley: University of California Press, 1999).

Willerton, John P. *Patronage and Politics in the USSR* (Cambridge and New York: Cambridge University Press, 1992).

Williams, Kieran. 'New Sources on Soviet Decision Making During the 1968 Czechoslovak Crisis'. *Europe–Asia Studies* 48, 3 (May 1996): 457–70.

Wolfe, Thomas. *Soviet Journalism: The Press and the Socialist Person after Stalin* (Bloomington: Indiana University Press, 2005).

Yakovlev, Aleksandr I., *Omut pamiati* (Moscow: Vagrius, 2000).

Yanov, Alexander. *The Russian New Right: Right-Wing Ideologies in the Contemporary USSR* (Berkeley: Institute of International Studies, University of California, 1978).

—— *The Drama of the Soviet 1960s: A Lost Reform* (Berkeley: Institute of International Studies, University of California, 1984).

Yurchak, Alexei. *Everything Was Forever, Until It Was No More: The Last Soviet Generation* (Princeton: Princeton University Press, 2006).

Zaslavsky, Victor. *The Neo-Stalinist State: Class, Ethnicity and Consensus in Soviet Society* (Armonk, N.Y.: M.E. Sharpe, 1982).

Zezina, M. *Sovetskaia khudozhestvennaia intelligentsiia i vlast' v 1950-e i 1960-e gody* (Moscow: Dialog-MGU, 1999).

Zubkova, Elena. *Obshchestvo i reformy: 1945–1964* (Moscow: Rossiia molodaia, 1993).

The Soviet Union under Gorbachev

Acton, Edward. 'Revolutionaries and Dissidents: The Role of the Russian Intellectual in the Downfall of Tsarism and Communism', in Jeremy Jennings and Anthony Kemp-Welch (eds), *Intellectuals in Politics: From the Dreyfus Affair to Salman Rushdie* (New York, 1997), pp. 149–68 {photocopy}

Afanas'ev, Iu. N. (ed.). *Inogo ne dano* (Moscow: Progress, 1988).

Aganbegyan, Abel. *Moving the Mountain: Inside the Perestroika Revolution*, trans. Helen Szamuely (London: Bantam Press, 1989).

Bahry, Donna. 'Society Transformed? Rethinking the Social Roots of Perestroika', *Slavic Review* 52, 3 (Autumn 1993): 512–54

Bakatin, Vadim. *Doroga v proshedshem vremeni* (Moscow: Dom, 1999).

Beissinger, Mark R. *Nationalist Mobilization and the Collapse of the Soviet State* (Cambridge: Cambridge University Press, 2002).

Beschloss, Michael R., and Talbott, Strobe. *At the Highest Levels: The Inside Story of the End of the Cold War* (London: Little, Brown, 1993).

Boldin, V. I. *Krushenie p'edestala. Shtrikhi k portretu M. S. Gorbacheva* (Moscow: Respublika, 1995).

Bovin, Aleksandr. *XX vek kak zhizn': vospominaniia* (Moscow: Zakharov, 2003).

Boym, Svetlana. *Common Places: Mythologies of Everyday Life in Russia* (Cambridge: Harvard University Press, 1994).

Braithwaite, Rodric. *Across the Moscow River: The World Turned Upside Down* (New Haven and London: Yale University Press, 2002).

Breslauer, George W. *Gorbachev and Yeltsin as Leaders* (New York and Cambridge: Cambridge University Press, 2002).

Brown, Archie. *Seven Years that Changed the World: Perestroika in Perspective* (New York: Oxford University Press, 2007)

Brown, Archie (ed.). *The Demise of Marxism–Leninism in Russia* (London and New York: Palgrave Macmillan, 2004).

Brown, Archie, and Lilia Shevtsova (eds). *Gorbachev, Yeltsin, and Putin: Political Leadership in Russia's Transition* (Washington: Carnegie Endowment for International Peace, 2001).

Brumberg, Abraham (ed.). *Chronicle of a Revolution: A Western–Soviet Inquiry into Perestroika* (New York: Pantheon, 1990).

Brutents, K. N. *Tridsat' let na staroi ploshchadi* (Moscow: Mezhdunarodnye otnosheniia, 1998).

Bunce, Valerie. *Subversive Institutions: The Design and the Destruction of Socialism and the State* (Cambridge: Cambridge University Press, 1999).

Chernyaev, Anatoly. *My Six Years with Gorbachev*, trans. and ed. Robert English and Elizabeth Tucker, Foreword by Jack F. Matlock, Jr. (University Park, Pa.: Pennsylvania State University Press, 2000).

Cohen, Stephen F. 'Was the Soviet System Reformable?', *Slavic Review* 63, 3 (Autumn 2004): 459–88.

Cohen, Stephen F., and Katrina van den Heuvel. *Voices of Glasnost: Interviewswith Gorbachev's Reformers* (New York: Norton, 1989).

Dallin, Alexander, and Gail W. Lapidus (eds). *The Soviet System: From Crisis to Collapse*, revised edn (Boulder, Colo.:Westview Press, 1995).

Duhamel, Luc. 'The Last Campaign against Corruption in Soviet Moscow', *Europe–Asia Studies* 56, 2 (March 2004): 187–212.

Dunlop, John D. *The Rise of Russia and the Fall of the Soviet Union* (Princeton: Princeton University Press, 1993).

Ellman, Michael, and Vladimir Kontorovich (eds). *The Destruction of the Soviet Economic System: An Insiders' History* (Armonk, N.Y.: M.E. Sharpe, 1998).

English, Robert D. *Russia and the Idea of the West: Gorbachev, Intellectuals, and the End of the Cold War* (New York: Columbia University Press, 2000).

Filtzer, Donald. *Soviet Workers and the Collapse of Perestroika* (Cambridge: Cambridge University Press, 1994).

Goldman, Marshall. *Lost Opportunity: What Has Made Economic Reform in Russia so Difficult?* (New York: W.W. Norton, 1996).

Grachev, Andrei. *Final Days: The Inside Story of the Collapse of the Soviet Union*, trans. Margo Milne with Foreword by Archie Brown (Boulder, Colo.: Westview Press, 1995).

Hermann, Richard K., and Richard Ned Lebow (eds). *Ending the Cold War: Interpretations, Causation, and the Study of International Relations* (New York: Palgrave Macmillan, 2004).

Hewett, Ed A. *Reforming the Soviet Economy* (Washington: Brookings Institution Press, 1988).

Hough, Jerry F. *Democratization and Revolution in Russia, 1985–1991* (Washington: Brookings Institution Press, 1997).

Kotkin, Stephen. *Armageddon Averted: The Soviet Collapse 1970–2000* (Oxford and New York: Oxford University Press, 2001).

Kramer, Mark. 'The Collapse of East European Communism and the Repercussions within the Soviet Union (Part 1)', *Journal of Cold War Studies* 5, 4 (Fall 2003): 178–256.

Kriuchkov, Vladimir. *Lichnoe delo*, 2 vols (Moscow: Olimp, 1996).

Lewin, Moshe. *The Gorbachev Phenomenon: A Historical Interpretation* [2nd expanded edn] (Berkeley: University of California Press, 1991).

Ligachev, Yegor. *Inside Gorbachev's Kremlin*, trans. Catherine A. Fitzpatrick, Michele A. Berdy and Dobrochna Dyrcz-Freeman, with Introduction by Stephen F. Cohen (New York: Pantheon, 1993).

Lukin, Alexander. *The Political Culture of the Russian 'Democrats'* (Oxford: Oxford University Press, 2000).

Matlock, Jack F. Jr. *Autopsy for an Empire: The American Ambassador's Account of the Collapse of the Soviet Union* (New York: Random House, 1995).

Mau, Vladimir. 'Perestroika: Theoretical and Political Problems of Economic Reform in the USSR', *Europe–Asia Studies* 47, 3 (1995): 387–411.

McFaul, Michael. *Russia's Unfinished Revolution: Political Change from Gorbachev to Putin* (Ithaca, N.Y.: Cornell University Press, 2001).

Ries, Nancy. *Russian Talk: Culture and Conversation During Perestroika* (Ithaca, N.Y.: Cornell University Press, 1997).

Rowley, David. 'Interpretations of the End of the Soviet Union: Three Paradigms', *Kritika: Explorations in Russian and Eurasian History* 2, 2 (2001): 395–426.

Solnick, Steven. *Stealing the State: Control and Collapse in Soviet Institutions* (Cambridge, Mass.: Harvard University Press, 1998).

Zubok, Vladislav. 'Gorbachev and the End of the Cold War: Perspectives on History and Personality', *Cold War History*, 2 (January 2002): 61–100.

Index

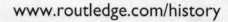